YOUR

YORKSHIRE TERRIER PUPPY

MONTH BY MONTH

LIZ PALIKA, DEB ELDREDGE, DVM, and
PRESTON and **MARYLOU GROVES**

ALPHA

A member of Penguin Group (USA) Inc.

ALPHA BOOKS

Published by Penguin Group (USA) Inc.

Penguin Group (USA) Inc., 375 Hudson Street, New York, New York 10014, USA • Penguin Group (Canada), 90 Eglinton Avenue East, Suite 700, Toronto, Ontario M4P 2Y3, Canada (a division of Pearson Penguin Canada Inc.) • Penguin Books Ltd., 80 Strand, London WC2R 0RL, England • Penguin Ireland, 25 St. Stephen's Green, Dublin 2, Ireland (a division of Penguin Books Ltd.) • Penguin Group (Australia), 250 Camberwell Road, Camberwell, Victoria 3124, Australia (a division of Pearson Australia Group Pty. Ltd.) • Penguin Books India Pvt. Ltd., 11 Community Centre, Panchsheel Park, New Delhi—110 017, India • Penguin Group (NZ), 67 Apollo Drive, Rosedale, North Shore, Auckland 1311, New Zealand (a division of Pearson New Zealand Ltd.) • Penguin Books (South Africa) (Pty.) Ltd., 24 Sturdee Avenue, Rosebank, Johannesburg 2196, South Africa • Penguin Books Ltd., Registered Offices: 80 Strand, London WC2R 0RL, England

International Standard Book Number: 978-1-61564-223-6
Library of Congress Catalog Card Number: 2012944460

15   14   13   8   7   6   5   4   3   2

Interpretation of the printing code: The rightmost number of the first series of numbers is the year of the book's printing; the rightmost number of the second series of numbers is the number of the book's printing. For example, a printing code of 13-1 shows that the first printing occurred in 2013.

Printed in the United States of America

Note: This publication contains the opinions and ideas of its authors. It is intended to provide helpful and informative material on the subject matter covered. It is sold with the understanding that the authors and publisher are not engaged in rendering professional services in the book. If the reader requires personal assistance or advice, a competent professional should be consulted.

The authors and publisher specifically disclaim any responsibility for any liability, loss, or risk, personal or otherwise, which is incurred as a consequence, directly or indirectly, of the use and application of any of the contents of this book.

Most Alpha books are available at special quantity discounts for bulk purchases for sales promotions, premiums, fund-raising, or educational use. Special books, or book excerpts, can also be created to fit specific needs. For details, write: Special Markets, Alpha Books, 375 Hudson Street, New York, NY 10014.

Publisher: *Mike Sanders*

Executive Managing Editor: *Billy Fields*

Senior Development Editor: *Christy Wagner*

Senior Production Editor: *Janette Lynn*

Copy Editor: *Jan Zoya*

Cover and Book Designer: *Kurt Owens*

Indexer: *Brad Herriman*

Layout: *Ayanna Lacey*

Proofreader: *Jeanne Clark*

Contents at a Glance

Appendixes

Contents

Months 6: The Zoomies Begin — 121

Months 8: Creating a Good Canine Citizen 175

Months 9: Your Adorable Athlete 197

Months 11: Adolescence Wanes   247

Introduction

Yorkshire Terriers, or Yorkies as they're commonly known, are tiny but feisty little dogs. Although often seen in public dressed in clothes, with ribbons in their topknots, and lovingly carried in their owners' arms, these are real dogs.

Yorkies love nothing more than chasing lizards in the woodpile. They like to shake the stuffing out of a toy as they "kill" it. Yet this breed is also an affectionate one, happy to snuggle with you in front of the fireplace on a cold winter evening.

A newborn Yorkie is a tiny thing that will fit in the palm of your hand. Yet in the next 12 months, he'll grow into a small but sturdy little Terrier who will excel in obedience competitions, agility, or tracking; work as an excellent therapy dog; or love you dearly as a family pet.

In the following chapters, we share with you the journey a Yorkshire Terrier puppy takes from birth to one year of age. Many changes take place in those 12 months.

We talk about what happens when your puppy is still at the breeder's home and offer tips on choosing the puppy who's right for you. We discuss how old the puppy should be when you bring her home and what may happen if she's too young.

Then, month by month, we explain all the various things that happen with your puppy, including physical development, health, nutrition, social skills, behavior, training, and much more. All these can be complicated subjects individually, but when your puppy is growing and changing so rapidly, it's easy to get overwhelmed.

The Extras

Throughout this book you'll find sidebars that provide extra bits of information. Here's what to look for:

> ### DOG TALK

These are definitions of some terms you might not understand.

> ### TIPS AND TAILS

These hints can help you deal with specific puppy-raising situations.

> **HAPPY PUPPY**

These notes help you make your Yorkshire Terrier puppy a happy dog.

Trademarks

All terms mentioned in this book that are known to be or are suspected of being trademarks or service marks have been appropriately capitalized. Alpha Books and Penguin Group (USA) Inc. cannot attest to the accuracy of this information. Use of a term in this book should not be regarded as affecting the validity of any trademark or service mark.

Siblings

Welcome to the first 2 months of your Yorkshire Terrier's life! It might not seem like the things that happen during the first 2 months should be important—after all, she isn't a part of your family yet. But anything that happens with your puppy now affects her life with you later. These first 2 months or so begin building the foundation of your Yorkie puppy's life with you.

Experts feel that who a dog is at adulthood is the result of 40 percent nature and 60 percent nurture. The nature includes the dog's breed, genetics, and individual inheritance from her parents and ancestors. The nurture consists of her experiences after birth, including the care she receives from her mother, her littermates, and her breeder, as well as her health, nutrition, and veterinary care. The relationship she has with her owners is also an important part of her development and personality.

Physical Development

Amazing changes occur during the first 2 months of your puppy's life. At birth, puppies tend to weigh about 1 percent of the mother dog's prepregnancy weight if she has 4 puppies. Most Yorkie puppies are about 4 inches long and tend to weigh from 3.5 to 5.5 ounces.

From Birth Through Day 14

Newborn Yorkshire Terriers don't look much like Yorkies. Their coat is short, they are black with tan points, and their tiny ears are folded. They are blind and deaf, and they don't have any teeth yet. Your newborn puppy can lift her head, but she's very shaky and wobbly.

During this *neonatal period,* the puppy cannot eliminate on her own and needs her mother's help. The mother dog will lick the puppy's belly and genitalia to stimulate urination and defecation.

When picked up, the puppy will curve into a comma shape; this is normal during the neonatal stage. The only senses she's using now are smell, taste, and her ability to feel her mother's and littermates' body warmth.

At this age, your Yorkshire Terrier puppy needs a warm environment because she can only maintain her body temperature about 10 degrees above that of her surroundings for a very short time. So if the mother dog leaves the puppies to eat or relieve herself, and the room where the puppies are is cool—even the lower 70s—your puppy will quickly get chilled.

Being too cold is one of the greatest dangers to newborn puppies, especially puppies as small as your Yorkie puppy. The room where the puppies are, or the *whelping box* area, needs to be kept quite warm. The breeder should use a heating pad or a heat lamp to keep the area accessible to the puppies between 85°F and 90°F. She will check the temperature around the puppies often, verify it with a thermometer, and adjust it as necessary.

> ### DOG TALK
>
> The **neonatal period** is the first 2 weeks of a puppy's life. A **whelping box** is a low-sided enclosure to keep the mother dog and her puppies enclosed and warm.

The puppies' tails are docked (or surgically shortened) before they are 3 days old. Although this is illegal in many countries, it is still done in the United States. For more information on the tail and docking, see Month 9.

To move, while burrowing under her littermates for warmth or to find her mother's nipple to nurse, your puppy will use swimming motions with her legs. Most of her strength right now is in her front legs. By the time she's 5 to 7 days old, she can lift herself up on her front legs. Her back legs are still too weak to support herself, though.

During this stage, 90 percent of your puppy's time is spent sleeping. As she's sleeping, she may twitch, kick, and appear as if she's dreaming. This sleep pattern is called *activated sleep.* This movement helps your puppy strengthen her muscles while sleeping. When she's developed enough to stand, all the exercise that occurred while she was sleeping will help ensure her muscles are strong enough so she can stand.

During **activated sleep,** your puppy kicks, twitches, stretches, and makes other movements while she sleeps. This is normal for newborns and helps them develop muscle tone.

Between 1½ and 2 weeks old, your Yorkie puppy's eyes and ears open. Her eyes will be blue, and it will take her a couple days to be able to focus her eyes and see clearly, although many puppies will track movements almost right away. Loud noises may startle her as she gets used to listening.

Days 15 Through 28

At 15 days, your puppy will weigh between 10 and 14 ounces. She should be gaining weight daily, even if just a little. By her twenty-eighth day, she should be anywhere from 15 to 28 ounces.

Your puppy is learning to recognize her mother and littermates as she uses her eyes. She also begins to make noises other than grunts, especially as she hears her littermates make noises, too. The puppies will whine, yelp, and squeak.

At 2 to 2½ weeks old, your puppy is beginning to eliminate on her own, and when she can take a few wobbly steps, she'll try to walk away from her littermates to eliminate. This is the first demonstration of that instinct to keep her sleeping area clean.

Yorkie puppies need to be kept warm, and it's easy to do this if they're kept in a small, warm area. However, the puppies also need enough room so they can move away from their littermates to relieve themselves. It takes a little bit of work to satisfy both needs, but your breeder should know how to set up the necessary space for the puppies.

Toward the end of this period, your puppy will be sleeping less and becoming more active. She's walking better now, and although she's still not very coordinated, she isn't falling down nearly as much as she was just days ago.

By about 4 weeks, your puppy will have a full set of very sharp, needlelike baby teeth. Often the mother dog will begin weaning the puppies at this point because those baby teeth will begin to hurt her as the puppies nurse.

Days 29 Through 42

Your Yorkie is becoming more interested in exploring things around her by now. Her senses are becoming more important to her, especially as she uses them more. She's also moving her head more as she learns to focus her senses.

Your puppy is walking, and she may even attempt some small jumps or pounces. Newborn puppies cry only when cold, hungry, or distressed, but now your puppy is discovering her voice and may bark a little. She may also whine, cry, or howl.

By 5 weeks of age, the mother dog is still watchful of her puppies but has begun to distance herself from them. Although she's probably still nursing at least a few times a day, she's not spending all of her time with the puppies as she did when they were younger.

When the puppies are between 5 and 6 weeks old, the breeder can gradually reduce the temperature in the whelping box area. The puppies will still be getting warmth from each other, their mother, and any blankets in their area. They're also better able to maintain their own body temperature now.

Days 43 Through 60

Your puppy's ears begin to stand up anytime between 6 and 8 weeks of age. If the ears don't stand on their own, you can help them.

You will need three small pieces of first-aid adhesive tape. With your fingers, stand one ear upright and gently fold the sides of the ear forward to form a pyramid shape. Using a small piece of tape, gently tape the ear into this position. Repeat for the other ear. With the third piece of tape, fasten the two ears together above your puppy's head so each ear helps support the other.

If the ears get wet, remove the tape, dry the ears, and tape them again. Otherwise, remove the tape every 3 or 4 days to clean the ears. Continue to retape the ears until they stand well on their own.

Your puppy is becoming more active and is playing more with her littermates. The puppies' coordination is much better, and they're not tripping over their own paws nearly as much as they have in the past few weeks.

By the end of this period, your Yorkie puppy will weigh between 22 and 35 ounces. She's still tiny but when you hold her, she feels solid. If you take your puppy's weight at 8 weeks and triple it, you can get a reasonable idea of what your puppy will weigh as an adult. So for example, if your puppy weighs 32 ounces right now (2 pounds), she'll weigh about 6 pounds when she's grown up.

Health

A newborn Yorkshire Terrier's body temperature is cooler than an adult dog's. It's about 94°F to 97°F, rather than the adult's 101°F to 102°F. The normal heartbeat for a neonatal puppy is about 200 beats per minute—twice what an adult's pulse would be when calm.

By about 4 weeks—from 22 days to 28 days—the heart rate will slow to about 170 beats per minute. The puppy's temperature will be about 100°F. This has not yet reached the adult temperature of 101°F to 102°F or adult pulse of 90 to 160. However, as she grows, her vital signs will change.

The Mother Dog's Care

Besides giving birth, nursing the puppies, and helping them eliminate, mother Yorkshire Terriers are also very protective of their puppies. Breeders shouldn't invite people over to see the newborn puppies at this age because the mother is apt to growl, bark, and even lunge at strangers who want to see her puppies. She should be allowed privacy to care for her babies.

Yorkshire Terrier *dams* are quite emotional. Each mother has a different attitude and temperament, which is also influenced by the relationship she and the breeder have. More than one pregnant Yorkshire Terrier has scoffed at the whelping box and given birth in the owner's bedroom or on the owner's bed because she wanted to be as close as possible to her owner.

> ### DOG TALK
>
> **Dam** is the term used to refer to the mother dog. The father is called the *sire*.

Breeder Vigilance

Although the mother dog provides most of the puppies' care, she cannot raise a litter all by herself. The breeder is an important part of this, too. The breeder watches so that when problems occur, she can handle them quickly before harm comes to either the puppies or the mother dog. The breeder also observes the mother dog to be sure she's allowing the puppies to nurse until full.

The breeder …

🐾 Ensures the mother dog isn't losing too much weight as she nurses the puppies.

- 🐾 Watches that the mother dog is producing enough milk so that the puppies get enough milk.
- 🐾 Keeps an eye on the mother dog's breasts to be sure she doesn't develop *mastitis*.
- 🐾 Watches for a puppy who isn't thriving as well as the others.
- 🐾 Ensures that the largest puppy isn't preventing smaller puppies from eating.

> ### DOG TALK
>
> **Mastitis** is an infection or abscess of one or more of the mother dog's mammary glands. This is usually caused by bacteria from a scratch or wound in the skin of a nipple. Keeping the puppies' nails trimmed and smooth is one way to help prevent mastitis.

Most of the time solutions are easy. The breeder can feed the mother dog more or add some protein and fat to her diet. The smallest puppy may need some supplemental feedings. But the fact remains, these solutions are easy when problems are seen as they occur, and the breeder's vigilance can then affect a change.

Raising a Singleton

The average litter size for Yorkshire Terriers is between two to four puppies. However, a litter can be only one puppy, or sometimes, unfortunately, only one puppy survives. A singleton puppy can be a challenge.

The singleton puppy has access to all the mother's milk and may overeat. She may then develop soft stools or even diarrhea, which can lead to dehydration. To prevent this, the breeder might have to step in and interrupt her nursing or shorten the time she's allowed to nurse.

The opposite can happen, too, though. One puppy may not be enough to stimulate the mother's milk production. If this happens, the puppy might not get enough milk and will need supplemental feeding.

Touch

The biggest loss a singleton puppy has is the lack of littermates. Puppies in a litter touch each other all the time, crawling on and over each other, snuggling together for warmth, and, later, playing together.

Touch is important for the survival of puppies, just as it is for human infants. When your puppy is very young, during her first couple weeks, this lack of touch can cause her not to thrive. It's important then that the mother dog be encouraged to spend a lot of time with the puppy. If she's not willing to do that or if the puppy is restless or unhappy, the breeder will hold the puppy.

The breeder often holds the puppy up against her skin, perhaps under a shirt, while she's doing normal things. The puppy is then moved, feels movement, and is warmed by the contact with the breeder's skin.

Behavioral Problems

The lack of littermates can and often does cause behavioral problems for a singleton puppy. The interactions between the puppies in the litter are the first education for the puppies, and without those lessons, the singleton puppy is at a disadvantage.

Littermates bite each other and teach each other bite inhibition, or how hard to bite and when to stop. Although the mother Yorkie can also teach this lesson, she's going to be far more tolerant to her single puppy than the littermates would be. Therefore, unless the mother dog is a very good teacher, your singleton puppy isn't going to learn to control her mouth and teeth. This could affect her relationship with you and your family later.

Littermates also jostle each other, push and shove when trying to get a nipple to feed from, and cause other minor frustrations for each other. A singleton puppy has all the nipples for herself and can feed when and where she wants, with no other littermates to shove her around. Although this peaceful scenario sounds wonderful, it's not. The puppy won't learn any coping skills, and it's important for puppies to learn how to overcome small frustrations.

Littermates also teach social skills. Together, they learn how to play, when the play is too rough, and how to give or get forgiveness for rough play. Again, these are important lessons for the future.

Puppies also learn verbal language and body language from each other. Although baby puppies are round, unsteady, and clumsy, they begin using body language very early. They also begin whining, barking, and growling quite young. Although much of this is instinctive, your puppy needs to practice on someone and her littermates are perfect for this. Without littermates, the puppy's skills won't be nearly as good as they could have been.

The breeder can help the puppy overcome some of these hurdles. Taking the puppy off her mother's nipple once in a while can duplicate what a littermate might have done, for example. This doesn't have to happen at every feeding, but the breeder will probably do it at least once a day.

The breeder will probably rub the puppy while she's sleeping, too, as if a litter-mate was crawling over her. A stuffed toy, such as a teddy bear with the button eyes removed (because those could be a hazard), can provide distraction, something to cuddle with, and an object to climb over.

Foster Mom and Littermates

The ideal solution for a singleton puppy is being placed with a mother dog with pup-pies who can foster your puppy. The nursing mom and puppies wouldn't need to be the same breed, but somewhere near the same size or just a little bigger would be preferable. If the mom and puppies are a much larger breed, the fostering wouldn't work. Not only would the Yorkie puppy have trouble nursing, but chances are she could be inadvertently hurt because she's so much smaller.

A foster mom can nurse your puppy as well as clean her and provide the affection mother dogs have for their puppies. Her puppies could become your puppy's siblings, providing the same benefits your puppy's natural siblings would provide.

Nutrition

Newborn Yorkshire Terrier puppies are born with a strong suckling reflex; if you put a finger in the puppy's mouth, she'll immediately begin to suck on it. Her mouth also feels warm and wet. If her mouth is dry, she's dehydrated and needs immediate veteri-nary help.

At this point in life, nursing provides not only the important first milk, *colostrum*, but also the energy for life. A newborn has no subcutaneous fat, and without those fat reserves to provide energy, it all must come from the mother's milk.

> **DOG TALK**
>
> **Colostrum,** often defined as "the first milk," contains vitamins, minerals, protein, antibodies, and other immune substances a newborn puppy needs.

If the puppy isn't nursing well, or the mother dog isn't producing enough milk, the breeder will supplement the puppy's nutrition with bottle feedings.

Young puppies can be prone to dehydration. The puppy's immature kidneys excrete large amounts of urine, and nursing often is needed to maintain fluid levels in the body. A puppy who doesn't nurse often enough risks becoming dehydrated.

When gently pinched and released, a well-hydrated puppy's skin immediately returns to shape. If the skin remains pinched in a fold, the puppy is dehydrated.

Mother's Milk

Canine milk is comprised of about 10 percent fat, 9 percent protein, and 4 percent sugar with about 150 calories per gram. During the first day and a half after the puppies are born, the mother dog also produces colostrum. This important first milk helps nourish the puppies as well as provide protection from infectious diseases. It contains maternal antibodies, too, which kickstart the puppy's immune system.

The mother dog needs excellent nutrition herself to produce milk and continue to produce it for a growing litter. As a general rule, she should have three times the calories now that she ate prior to her pregnancy. Her diet needs to be high in protein and fat especially.

A mother Yorkies has a small stomach, so the breeder supplies the mother the extra food she needs now by feeding her normal food and adding extra small meals throughout the day. The breeder might also add calories by adding high-calorie but healthy additions to her meals.

Yorkshire Terrier puppies nurse between six and eight times a day when first born. The puppies compete for the nipples, with the largest puppy usually taking the nipple she wants. However, a determined smaller puppy can also be successful. The breeder watches the smallest puppy in the litter to be sure she gets a chance to nurse, too.

The puppies continue to gain weight steadily each day. Ideally, the puppies should be weighed at birth and then daily as they grow to be sure they're gaining weight.

Supplementation

Mother Yorkies produce a lot of milk for their litters, and as long as all the puppies are steadily gaining weight and none are crying and restless, everything is probably fine. However, sometimes puppies need help. The breeder will watch for the following:

🐾 At any given time after feeding, if a puppy is restless and crying, she may not have gotten enough to eat.

🐾 A small puppy in the litter who cannot compete with larger siblings may need supplemental feeding to catch up.

🐾 A puppy who loses weight after birth and after 36 hours is not regaining that lost weight needs supplemental feeding.

🐾 If the mother isn't producing enough milk, or if the mother isn't producing any milk, supplemental (or replacement) feeding is necessary.

If supplemental feeding is needed, the breeder won't give straight cow's milk to the puppies. It will cause diarrhea, which could kill the puppies. Cow's milk is less calorie-dense than dog's milk, and it derives more calories from lactose than from protein or fat. Goat's milk is marginally better than cow's milk but should be used alone only in an emergency.

The best solution for supplementing or replacing the mother dog's milk is a commercial formula made specifically for puppies. These are usually available as liquids (canned) or as powder that needs to be mixed prior to feeding. The breeder will feed each puppy using a small bottle with a nipple. She'll hold the puppy upright (head up) or on her belly, as she would be with her mother. The puppy should not be held on her back (as with a human infant); she could choke in that position.

A 1-week-old Yorkie puppy who weighs between 4 and 6 ounces needs to eat six times a day and consume between 20 and 24 calories. A 2-week-old needs to eat four times a day, while a 4-week-old can get by on three meals. The calories need to increase while the number of feedings decreases. A 1-month-old Yorkie who weighs about 1 pound needs about 90 calories per day.

Weaning

Your puppy's baby teeth began coming in between the third and fourth week of life, and most are entirely through the gums by 4 weeks. Although the mother dog continues nursing the litter for another week or so, she's going to start cutting them back—*weaning* them—at about 4 weeks.

> **DOG TALK**
>
> **Weaning** is the process of changing the puppy from nursing on her mother to eating puppy food. Ideally, this happens gradually over a few days to a week or so.

Many breeders offer some formula made specifically for nursing puppies close to day 21 in preparation for weaning. Many puppies, however, have no idea this offering is food if it's offered in a saucer or bowl, and they make a mess crawling through it. At some point, some of the food will end up in the puppies' mouths, and they will discover it tastes good.

Puppies should nurse until the mother dog has had enough, or until the puppies are 5 or 6 weeks old. However, if the litter is large or if the mother dog's condition deteriorates—she is thin and her coat is dry and thin, for example—the breeder will wean the puppies. Sometimes a mother dog gives her all to her puppies and her health shouldn't be allowed to suffer.

To help the mother dog wean her puppies, the breeder removes her from her puppies about 2 hours before each scheduled meal. This way, the puppies will be hungry at feeding time. The food should either be a quality food specifically for weaning puppies or a home-cooked recipe approved for puppies.

Meat-based foods are preferable and more attractive to the puppies, but some breeders use a dampened dry kibble food. Dry kibble shouldn't be used at this age because the puppies may choke on a kibble. Many breeders recommend a gruel the puppies can lap up. Puppies initially play in the food rather than eat it. But at some point, they all remember they're hungry and discover this new stuff tastes good.

The breeder puts the mother dog back in with her puppies after they've eaten. She'll probably finish up any leftover food from the saucers, from the floor, and from the puppies.

The breeder should allow the puppies to continue to nurse during the introduction to food. This ensures that the puppies are well nourished during the transition and can help prevent diarrhea due to a too-rapid introduction to a new food.

> **TIPS AND TAILS**

A puppy who has eaten too much food will have soft stools. A puppy who hasn't eaten enough will be restless and whining.

Gradually, over several days or even a week, the puppies will nurse less and less. Eventually, the mother dog will stop allowing the puppies to nurse or will only allow them to nurse for a few seconds. At this point, the breeder returns the mother dog's feeding to her prepregnancy amounts and schedule.

Grooming

For the first month, the mother Yorkie takes care of almost all of the puppies' grooming needs. She washes them after birth—a part of the bonding process between the mother dog and her babies. She also washes their faces after nursing and licks their bellies and genitalia to stimulate elimination.

The breeder will trim the tiny puppies' sharp toenails within the first few days so they don't scratch and irritate the mother dog's belly as the puppies nurse. She'll use a set of small canine nail clippers.

If the puppies do scratch the mother dog's belly, the breeder will wash the scratches regularly to prevent infection. After washing, she'll ensure all the soap is rinsed off so the puppies don't ingest soap residue.

Once the puppies start the weaning process, the mother dog will be less interested in keeping the puppies clean and the breeder will need to step in to get this done. She'll wash their faces after each meal, as well as their feet and anything else that gets covered in food. Sometimes the entire puppy ends up in the food bowl, but that's okay. These grooming sessions introduce the puppy to body care and handling.

Social Skills

Your Yorkie's mother and her littermates provide a great introduction to life with other dogs. Wise breeders can also begin working on social handling techniques that will benefit the puppy as she grows up.

> ### TIPS AND TAILS

> In their Bio Sensor dog-training programs, the U.S. Army exposes puppies to several exercises early in life. Dogs exposed to these exercises, which cause neurological stimuli, are found to be more able to handle stress, both in daily living and also in new situations later in life. Their physical functions improve as well, including cardiac function, adrenal function, physical tolerance to stress, and immune system strength. Although a program for military working dogs has little to do with Yorkshire Terriers, many breeders of dogs of all sizes, shapes, and working abilities have utilized this program. The benefits apply to all dogs, not just working dogs.

Beginning on the third or fourth day after the puppies are born and continuing through the third week, the breeder puts each puppy through some daily exercises. These include …

🐾 Holding the puppy upright, with her head up and tail down, securely in both hands for 3 to 5 seconds.

🐾 Holding the puppy securely and reversing the direction, so the head is down and the tail up, for 3 to 5 seconds.

- Holding the puppy securely on her back with her feet upward for 3 to 5 seconds.

- Using a cotton swab, tickling the puppy between the toes of one paw (any paw) for 3 to 5 seconds.

- Placing the puppy paws down on a cool, damp towel and allowing her to stand or explore for 3 to 5 seconds.

In addition to these exercises, the breeder also handles the puppies each day. This can include petting, cuddling, and, as the puppies get older, playing with them.

Behavior

Between days 22 and 28, your puppy will notice dogs other than her mother and littermates. If the breeder has another safe, friendly, healthy adult dog in the house, she'll allow him to interact with the puppies if the mother dog will allow it.

Initially, the dog can just lie down and let the puppies crawl on or investigate him. He may wash their faces and bottoms or bring them toys. All these interactions are great; it begins the puppies' socialization to other dogs.

At this age, your puppy is also able to bond with people. A wise breeder has various members of her family hold your puppy, pet her gently, and let her get used to people other than just the breeder. This helps prepare the puppy for bonding with you and your family later.

At this time, the breeder also supplies some things for the puppy to play with and explore. A cardboard box, an empty round oatmeal container, a feather, and other safe items that have a different sound, texture, or smell are great for young Yorkie puppies to check out.

> ### HAPPY PUPPY

When a puppy is introduced to a variety of sights, sounds, smells, and surfaces during early puppyhood, she learns to explore the unknown and investigate new things. Most importantly, she learns to cope with change. This serves her well in adulthood.

The Importance of Mom's Teaching

The mother Yorkie's importance extends far beyond simply giving birth to the puppies and nursing them. Her attitude also affects the puppies.

A first-time mother Yorkie who is uneasy with her new job can make her babies uneasy, too. They may fuss more than normal, may not gain weight as they should, and may not sleep as deeply as they need. A fearful mother Yorkie can make her babies fearful, too, as can an overly aggressive mother. Ideally, only female Yorkshire Terriers with calm, stable, happy temperaments are used for breeding.

The breeder can also affect both the mother dog's state of emotions and her litter's. The breeder needs to be calm and relaxed around the mother dog, both during the birth of her litter and afterward. A calm, relaxed, happy breeder is more apt to have a calm, relaxed, happy Yorkshire Terrier mother dog.

As the puppies in her litter begin to play and wrestle with each other—and with her—the mother Yorkie will also become an active teacher. If a puppy pounces on her and bites her too hard, she'll probably growl at the puppy. As the puppy gets older, her correction will increase until the puppy understands she needs to control the strength of her bite. This lesson, called *bite inhibition,* is very important to her life with people.

> ### DOG TALK
>
> **Bite inhibition** is a lesson a puppy learns from her mother and littermates on how to control her bite, biting hard enough to communicate but not so hard as to injure.

An inexperienced breeder often interferes with the mother dog's lessons, feeling she's being mean to her puppies. A breeders stops these lessons, she's doing the puppies a disservice because the mother Yorkie is teaching her puppies to accept rules for social behavior. The mother's body language (postures and facial expressions), her growl, and her actions all teach her puppies valuable lessons.

Littermates Teach, Too

The puppies begin to play with each other and play fight at about 2½ weeks old. They are adorable when they do this; they're clumsy and uncoordinated and fall down constantly yet they make tiny growls, roll with each other, and try to pounce. But as they play, their muscles gain strength as their actions teach each other important lessons.

When the puppies play, they interact with each other, teaching each other how to play and how hard to bite. When one puppy is too rough, her littermates tell her, via cries and other reactions, that she's not playing nicely. If she continues to play too roughly, a puppy may even be temporarily shunned by other littermates. This doesn't last very long, and soon the pups are all romping and rolling together again.

Month 2 >	Month 3	> Month 4
	Socialization at home with new owner and other pets	
	Fear imprint period	
	Begin house and crate training	
	Rapid growth	
	1st DHPP vaccines	

This month (weeks 9 through 12) brings big changes to your Yorkshire Terrier puppy's life. Toward the end of this month, he will leave his mother and littermates and join your household as your newest family member. Although this is very exciting, it can also be a little scary—both for you and your puppy.

It can be worrisome for you because this tiny life is now completely dependent on you. The change can be frightening for your puppy because everything is new, and his mother and brothers and sisters are no longer by his side. That's okay—you'll both get through it.

Before your puppy comes home, though, you have a lot to do. You need to go shopping, puppy-proof your house and yard, and plan on how you'll incorporate this new little life into your family.

Preparing for Your Puppy

Your puppy is going to need some things. Don't plan on bringing your puppy home and then going shopping; it's better to have everything on hand first.

Food: Find out what food the breeder is feeding the puppies so you can purchase the same brand. If you plan on eventually feeding a different food, that's fine. You can make changes later. Right now, though, keep your puppy on the food he's used to so he won't have an upset stomach.

Food and water bowls: The best food bowl for your puppy right now is a shallow cereal bowl and a saucer. If the bowl is too tall, your puppy will have to reach into it, and that could put pressure on his neck as he tries to eat. The water bowl can be a little taller because you're going to keep that full anyway.

Crate: You will need at least one crate for your puppy to sleep in at night, but you might also want a second one for the car. A solid-sided plastic crate is best during early puppyhood.

Collar: Your puppy needs a soft nylon or cotton collar so he can begin wearing identification right away. It's best to have an adjustable collar that you can make larger as he grows.

Leash: A 4-foot lightweight leash can help keep him safe. Don't get a retractable leash; they're not safe for your Yorkie (see Month 4).

Identification: Have an identification tag made with your cell phone number on it, even before you bring home your puppy. Then you can fasten it to his new collar so he is immediately identified in case of an emergency. Don't worry if you don't have his name figured out yet; you can make a new tag later.

Cleaning supplies: Your puppy will be tiny when you bring him home, but he'll still have some accidents, so you need to be prepared with some cleaning supplies. White vinegar is a good nontoxic cleaner you can use to clean up dirt as well as housetraining accidents. If you use a commercial cleaner, read the labels to be sure it's safe to use around a tiny puppy.

Toys: Choose a few small soft toys for your puppy to play with. Be sure they contain no small parts he could chew off and swallow.

Grooming supplies: You need a few supplies to begin with, including a pin brush, a wide-toothed comb, a pair of grooming scissors, a pair of scissor-type nail trimmers for small dogs, and some shampoo that's safe for puppies. You can add more grooming supplies later when your puppy's adult coat starts to grow in.

Plastic bags: You'll need some plastic bags for picking up after your puppy. You can recycle grocery store plastic bags or pick up a couple rolls of biodegradable bags. Just invert a bag over your hand, pick up your puppy's feces, turn the bag back over, tie it off, and dispose of it in the trash. It makes the chore easy.

Exercise pen: Your puppy can't have free run of the house for quite a while. Later in the book, we discuss why his freedom needs to be restricted, but for now, when you go shopping, pick up an exercise pen. These freestanding small fence panels create a safe place for your puppy, just like a playpen does for a baby.

When your puppy joins your household, you may find you need some additional supplies, but these will get you started. You can pick up anything else as you need it.

Puppy-Proofing Your House

Before your puppy comes home, you need to be sure the house is safe for him. That means looking at the house from his point of view, not yours. Lie on your stomach on the floor, lift your head, and look around your house. That's how your puppy views his surroundings. As you look around, remember he's a tiny puppy who can fit into very small places.

To protect your valuables (and even your not-so-valuables), and to keep your puppy safe, you must puppy-proof your house. Just because he's tiny, don't assume that things on end tables, coffee tables, or even low shelves are safe. He's going to be growing fast and becoming more athletic. It won't be long before he's jumping and climbing.

In the kitchen, for example, install childproof latches on the lower cupboards that contain potentially harmful products. In addition, put the following away in a safe place he can't get to:

- 🐾 Floor-cleaning and waxing-products
- 🐾 Insect and rodent traps, sprays, and other controls
- 🐾 Kitchen and oven cleaners
- 🐾 Candy and chocolate
- 🐾 Grease and spices
- 🐾 Knives and other sharp implements

In the bathroom, put safely away all these products:

- 🐾 Medicines, vitamins, and minerals
- 🐾 Makeup, nail polish, nail-polish remover, and lotions

🐾 Hair products, including hair coloring, sprays, and gels

🐾 Shower, bathroom, toilet, and floor cleaners

🐾 Bath products, including bubble bath, shower gels, and soaps

🐾 Personal hygiene products

In the living areas, put away, put out of reach, or tuck safely away these items:

🐾 Cell phones, electronic devices, remote controls, batteries, and chargers

🐾 Pens, pencils, felt-tip markers, crayons, and craft supplies

🐾 Electrical cords

Houseplants are attractive to puppies. The dirt smells good, especially if the plant has been potted using compost, blood meal, or manure. But many houseplants are dangerous to pets. Check out Appendix C for a list of dangerous ones.

> ### HAPPY PUPPY
>
> Your Yorkshire Terrier puppy doesn't have to have free run of the house to be happy. As long as he gets plenty of time with you, you can restrict his freedom and he'll still be a happy puppy. Preventing him from getting into trouble helps keep him healthy and safe.

Some things you may not even realize are dangerous could be. Your recliner, with the foot rest up, makes an inviting cave for a little Yorkie. But when you lower the foot rest, it could crush a tiny puppy. A rocking chair could come down on a tiny leg and break it. Just be aware of potential dangers, and especially keep an eye on your Yorkie puppy all the time he's not in his crate or playpen.

If you do a good job of puppy-proofing your house, you not only help keep your puppy safe but you also minimize any damage your puppy might do to your property. Replacing cell phones, remote controls, wiring, or, worse yet, the rungs on your dining room chairs can get expensive.

If your puppy has chewed on something and perhaps swallowed pieces, and you're concerned it might be harmful, call your veterinarian right away. If she's not available, call the emergency veterinary clinic.

Puppy-Proofing Your Yard

Although your Yorkshire Terrier puppy will prefer to spend all his time with you, he'll still need to go out in the yard to relieve himself and to play. It's important that your yard is safe and secure.

> **TIPS AND TAILS**
>
> Your Yorkie should spend little, if any, time outside unsupervised. Birds of prey, coyotes, and other predators could easily steal away a Yorkie, especially a puppy.

The fence around your yard needs to be secure and solid. If there are any gaps in the fence, broken boards, or gaps under it, your puppy may work at those until he can squeeze through.

Ideally, he shouldn't be able to see through the fence. Keep in mind that, as they get older, Yorkshire Terriers are watchful and protective. If he can see through the fence, he'll bark at anything or anyone he can see. That can quickly turn into a problem behavior.

Also in your yard:

- Put away gloves, trowels, and other gardening tools.
- Be sure all fertilizers, insecticides, and other chemicals are out of reach. Be careful using any chemicals around your puppy; be sure they're safe to use.
- Put away any kids' toys.
- For the time being, put away lawn chairs, cushions, umbrellas, and garden décor.
- Protect any cables, cords, and hoses.
- Be sure the puppy can't get to the hot-tub cover or electrical cord.

Encourage all family members to get in the habit of putting away anything they use in the backyard when they've finished their chore or activity. If things are put away, your Yorkie puppy can't chew on them.

Check the plants in the backyard to be sure none are poisonous. (See Appendix C for a list of potentially poisonous plants.) In addition, think about putting temporary fencing around your favorite plants, potted plants, flower gardens, and vegetable gardens. It's going to be a couple years before your puppy understands what he can play with and what he needs to ignore.

If you have a pool, either in-ground or above, think about how you will protect your Yorkie puppy from accidentally getting in the pool. A tiny puppy who falls in will quickly become exhausted trying to climb out and may drown. The best solution is secure fencing around the pool, with a locking gate.

Finding Professionals to Help You

You will need a few pet professionals to help you with your Yorkshire Terrier, both now when he's a puppy and throughout his life. Although you can certainly change professionals if you find yourself unhappy with someone, it's nice to have some people lined up before you bring home your new puppy. Then, if you need help, you have someone to call.

Veterinarian: The first and most important professional you need in your corner is a veterinarian. You're going to want to have your puppy checked over by a veterinarian soon after bringing him home to be sure he's healthy and to get started on his vaccinations.

> **TIPS AND TAILS**
>
> The veterinarian you choose should be knowledgeable of the particular health problems Yorkshire Terriers may face. Don't hesitate to ask prospective veterinarians whether they're familiar with the breed.

Choosing a veterinarian doesn't have to be difficult, but you should do more than simply pick the closest clinic to you. Ask dog-owning neighbors where they take their dogs and if they're happy with the vet and her staff. Are the prices reasonable? Cost isn't everything—the quality of care is—but you should also be able to afford that care.

Find out whether the veterinarian is available after hours or in case of an emergency. If she's not, what emergency clinic(s) does she work with? What are her payment policies? What pet insurance companies does she accept? What credit cards does she take? Find out all this information; it's important.

Trainer: Yorkies are tiny dogs with a working-dog heritage—mousers and ratters—but today, they're primarily pets. However, that doesn't mean Yorkies shouldn't be trained. The happiest Yorkshire Terriers are those whose owners understand that these dogs need both physical and mental challenges. Training is a huge part of this.

As with veterinarians, ask dog-owning friends and neighbors who they recommend. Local veterinarians can also refer you to local reputable trainers. If a couple different trainers' names keep coming up, call those trainers and talk to them. What kind of training do they offer? Do they have puppy classes as well as obedience classes? How about private training in case a behavioral problem pops up later?

Ask about training methods, too. Every trainer has his or her own style of teaching people and training dogs, but if you aren't comfortable with that style, it won't work for you. Go watch the trainer's class, too, to see whether you'll be able to work with that trainer.

Ask how the trainer works to keep small dogs safe. Most trainers hold classes of various-size dogs, and that's fine as long as tiny dogs are protected from rowdy larger ones. Of course, that also means the trainer should be aware of little dogs who try to egg on the big ones!

Groomer: Many Yorkie owners do a lot of their dog's grooming at home, and that's how it should be. A Yorkie's coat requires a lot of care. But a professional groomer is going to be a huge help when it comes time for a thorough bath and a haircut.

As with other professionals, ask friends and neighbors for referrals. You can also ask your veterinarian who she recommends. When you talk to a local groomer, as with the veterinarian, ask whether she's comfortable with Yorkshire Terriers. Visit the grooming shop. Is it clean? Do the dogs look comfortable?

Pet sitting and boarding: Many dog owners enjoy vacations more when they can take their dog with them. Unfortunately, there will be times when your Yorkshire Terrier won't be able to go with you. In that case, you're going to either have someone come to the house to take care of him, or he'll need to go to a boarding kennel.

As with other professionals, you can get referrals from other dog owners, but ask your veterinarian for a referral, too. Search for local pet-sitting organizations. Then, long before you ever leave on vacation, ask the pet-sitter to come over and meet your Yorkshire Terrier. You want to be sure your Yorkie thinks of the pet-sitter as a friend.

> ## TIPS AND TAILS

Appendix E contains a list of resources, including professional organizations for veterinarians, trainers, pet professionals, and pet-sitters. These resources can help you find professionals in your area.

Choosing Your Puppy

Choosing the right Yorkshire Terrier puppy for you and your family is both the hardest and yet the easiest thing you'll have to do. The decision is hard because how can you tell what that adorable little puppy is going to grow up to be like? What's the difference between two puppies in the same litter? Yet at the same time, it's easy because all the puppies are so wonderful.

Choosing the right puppy is important. This Yorkshire Terrier is going to be your companion for his lifetime—the next 14 to 16 years—so you need to choose wisely.

Where to Find a Puppy

The best source of a healthy Yorkshire Terrier puppy is from a reputable breeder. A reputable breeder is someone who knows her breed inside and out:

- ❧ She keeps up on the latest information concerning health, genetics, diseases, testing, and more.

- ❧ She shows her Yorkshire Terriers in dog shows, obedience trials, agility, or rally competitions.

- ❧ She chooses the best dogs possible to breed and tests those dogs for health concerns prior to breeding.

- ❧ She will answer any questions you have about her dogs.

- ❧ She will ask you just as many questions to see whether you would be an appropriate owner for one of her puppies.

- ❧ She sells her puppies with a contract and will take back any of her puppies, no matter what age, if at any time they cannot remain in their home.

- ❧ A reputable breeder will be available to answer questions for the life of your dog.

> **TIPS AND TAILS**
>
> Yorkshire Terriers being considered for breeding should have their patellas checked and registered with the Orthopedic Foundation for Animals (OFA). They should also be checked for Legg-Calve-Perthes disease, autoimmune thyroiditis, and hip dysplasia, all three of which are also registered with the OFA. Eye disorders, including progressive retinal atrophy, should be evaluated with the Canine Eye Registry Foundation (CERF).

You can also sometimes find Yorkshire Terrier puppies at your local shelter or through a Yorkshire Terrier rescue group. These can often be wonderful puppies, and by adopting one, you're potentially saving the puppy's life. Just understand that this puppy is an unknown; you don't know the parents—whether they were healthy and had good temperaments—or how the puppies were raised.

Don't buy a Yorkshire Terrier from a child with a box of puppies outside the grocery store or from a flea market or pet store. Don't buy a Yorkie from a website or through eBay. Not only are these puppies unknowns and bred by someone who obviously didn't have the puppies' best interest at heart, but by buying a puppy from these people, you give them incentive to continue irresponsible breeding.

You can find a reputable breeder by going to the website of the Yorkshire Terrier Dog Club of America or Canada (see Appendix E), or do an internet search for a local Yorkshire Terrier club. Talk to your veterinarian, too; she may have a client who's a reputable breeder. If you see a healthy, well-mannered Yorkshire Terrier while out on a walk, ask the owners where they got their dog and whether they would recommend that breeder.

Each Puppy Is an Individual

When you find a breeder, you'll talk to her, answer her questions, and then be put on a waiting list for a puppy. Often you'll have to wait for a litter to be born and raised by the mom and breeder. The breeder may invite you to see the puppies at some point, and this will give you a chance to meet the mother dog and her puppies.

The breeder will probably ask you to bring the entire family, including any children in the family. Just be aware this is a chance for her to meet you all and judge whether you would be the right family for her puppy.

> **TIPS AND TAILS**
>
> Most breeders won't sell a puppy to a family with very young children. Until the kids are old enough and responsible enough to be gentle with a Yorkie, the Yorkie is in too much danger. Young kids can be too rough, even unintentionally.

As a general rule, Yorkies share some characteristics:

- 😺 They need a lot of grooming.
- 😺 They tend to be barkers.
- 😺 They have a high energy level; they are not couch potatoes.

🐾   They are very playful.

🐾   They are bright, curious, and aware.

🐾   They are watchful but are also friendly.

🐾   They are affectionate but not clingy.

🐾   They are fairly good with gentle, respectful older children.

🐾   They don't need a lot of exercise.

🐾   They don't need a lot of space.

🐾   They aren't always friendly with other pets and can have a high prey drive.

🐾   They're not always easy to train and can be independent.

🐾   They can be a challenge to housetrain.

🐾   They're not always the best choice for someone who has never owned a dog before.

Now, these statements are from information provided by Yorkie owners, dog trainers, and veterinarians. This information is also an average, which means some Yorkies are better or worse than these statements. As with all dogs, there are individuals within the breed. But these characteristics are more true than not.

As you consider all the aspects of this breed, talk to the breeder. Let her know your thoughts, concerns, and plans for the future. Would you like to train and compete in rally or obedience? (See Month 12 for more information.) Would you like to do volunteer therapy dog work? Is this puppy to be a pet?

The breeder has been watching these puppies for the last several weeks and knows them best. She knows which puppy is more affectionate and which is bolder. She can guide you to the puppy who would be best for you.

Many breeders also do puppy testing that can pinpoint personality traits. These are usually done between 6 and 7 weeks of age, so if your breeder does these tests, it will happen before you meet the puppies. But you can ask your breeder if she does them, and if so, can she explain the results.

If you meet the mother dog, meet the puppies, and fall in love with one of those puppies, be sure you can provide what this puppy needs and can live with the consequences of owning a puppy. Remember, this is a 14- to 16-year commitment.

What Age Is Best?

Never bring home a Yorkie puppy before he's 12 weeks old. This is so important that The Yorkshire Terrier Club of America Code of Conduct requires breeders keep the puppies until at least 12 weeks of age so the puppy can spend time with his mother, littermates, and other Yorkies.

Not only can the puppy get a better start on life by remaining with the breeder a little longer (especially in regard to the potential problem with hypoglycemia—more on this coming up), but the mother Yorkie teaches her puppies to accept discipline and that the world does not revolve around them. Your puppy's littermates teach him how to be a puppy and how to interact with other puppies. He learns how to play and how hard (or easy) to bite while playing with other puppies.

These are important lessons that carry through to his relationships with people, and if he leaves for his new home too early, he'll miss out on them. Dog trainers and behaviorists routinely try to help puppies who have not had these lessons, and it's impossible to re-create those lessons later.

The traditional age to bring a puppy home has been 8 weeks of age. Although this age is better than 6 or 7 weeks, 8 weeks can also pose a challenge because many puppies hit a *fear period* at that age. Anything that frightens the puppy during this time—such as a car ride or a trip to the veterinarian's clinic—can become an ongoing, lifelong fear.

> **DOG TALK**

Fear periods are stages in the puppy's life when he becomes worried or afraid for no apparent reason other than his age.

The period between 8 and 12 weeks is also the beginning of the prime age for socialization. Because your Yorkie puppy will be staying with the breeder for this time period, the breeder will need to begin those important socialization lessons. But that's okay; wise breeders know this and will do what the puppies need because they, too, want the puppies to succeed in their new lives. When you bring home your puppy, you'll continue those lessons.

Physical Development

When your puppy comes home toward the end of this month, you'll find that his motor skills are getting better. In fact, if you saw him at the breeder's a few weeks ago, you'll probably notice a big change. He's still clumsy but not as much as he was. He's running, is learning how to clamber over small obstacles in his path, and may even try climbing.

His senses are better now, too. He's able to track movements visually and is swiveling his ears to follow sounds. His nose is also becoming more important to him, and he's teaching himself how to sort through scents.

The trademarks of Yorkshire Terriers at this age are needle-sharp puppy teeth, that wonderful milky puppy breath, and those big dark eyes. Protect yourself from those teeth by handing your puppy a toy whenever he wants to chew on you. Enjoy the puppy breath because that disappears far too quickly. And don't let those eyes mesmerize you ... too much.

> **TIPS AND TAILS**
>
> As soon as you choose your puppy at the breeder's home, put a buckle collar on him with a tag engraved with your cell-phone number. Don't wait until you get home or until you choose the puppy's name; instead, put this on right away just in case of an accident.

Health

The vast majority of Yorkshire Terrier puppies at this age are healthy, active little puppies. They're absolutely adorable, with those big dark eyes.

But you need to look past those adorable eyes, stop hugging your puppy for a few seconds, and get started on ensuring that your Yorkshire Terrier will remain healthy.

The Breeder's Health Records

When you signed the contract with the breeder buying your Yorkshire Terrier puppy, she should have given you a copy of your puppy's health record, too. Look through the paperwork she gave you for this, and if you can't find it, call the breeder and ask for a copy.

This paperwork is important because your veterinarian needs to see what the breeder has already done for your puppy. This prevents duplication or lets her know what needs to be done next.

Breeders normally treat the puppies for roundworms, which are common in puppies, at least once. Your puppy probably also got at least one distemper vaccination, usually at 7 or 8 weeks of age. Anything given earlier is usually ineffective because the puppy usually has antibodies from his mother until he's at least 6 weeks old.

But don't guess about what the breeder might have done; get copies of the puppy's records. This prevents mistakes, and you don't want to make any mistakes when it comes to your puppy's health.

The First Vet Visit

Your new puppy should go see the veterinarian very soon after coming home. Many breeders require this within 48 hours, and most include this stipulation in their sales contract. There are several reasons why this is important and why your breeder may require it.

This first visit with your veterinarian can establish that your puppy is healthy. Your veterinarian will examine your puppy to look for signs of disease or *congenital health defects.*

> **DOG TALK**
>
> A **congenital health defect** is one that exists at birth. It can be genetic or can be acquired before or during birth.

If it turns out your puppy is not healthy, you have the right (if you so desire) to return the puppy to the breeder. If you do this within the first day or so, it won't be so heartbreaking. If you decide to keep the puppy, the breeder should either refund your purchase price, give you a partial refund, or work with you to pay the veterinary costs.

Bring a small sample of your puppy's feces to the first visit. The vet will check this for signs of internal parasites.

During the first visit, your veterinarian will give your puppy a thorough exam:

Eyes: Your Yorkie puppy's eyes should be clear and clean of matter. The vet will also check your puppy's eyelids to be sure the eyelashes aren't turned inward and rubbing against the eyes. Other problems with the eyes can sometimes indicate the presence of diseases elsewhere in the body.

Ears: Your Yorkshire Terrier puppy's ears should be clean, dry, and pink. Redness, discharge, and matter caked to the inside of the ear are symptoms of a problem. The vet will also check to be sure the ears don't contain any foreign matter.

Mouth: Your veterinarian will take a look at your puppy's teeth to be sure they look good, none are missing, and there are no problems with them. She'll also look at his gums, tongue, inside of his mouth, and his throat. A normal, healthy puppy will have a pink tongue, gums, and inside of the mouth. Black spots are fine, but other colors can point toward health problems.

Glands: The veterinarian will also palpate lymph glands on your puppy's neck and at various other locations on the body. An enlarged gland may indicate an infection in the body.

Heart: She will listen to your puppy's heart for any congenital heart defects.

Lungs: She will also listen to his lungs to be sure your puppy is breathing well and his lungs are clear.

Abdomen: By gently feeling your puppy's abdomen, the veterinarian can be sure everything feels as it should. While doing this, she will watch your puppy to see if he flinches when anything is touched. The flinching could be a sign that something hurts.

The veterinarian will also watch your puppy walk, watching for a normal gait or any limping or soreness. She'll check over your puppy's entire body, including his paws and toenails, his skin and coat, and under his tail. She'll point out any problems, or potential problems, but hopefully give your Yorkshire Terrier a clean bill of health.

Liver Shunts

There is one health threat you must know about. Yorkies are, unfortunately, 36 times more apt to develop a liver shunt than all other dog breeds. A liver shunt can cause significant problems for your puppy. Although your veterinarian can do a bile acid test to determine whether your puppy is affected, you should also understand what's happening so you can call your veterinarian should you suspect a problem.

When your puppy was developing in his mother's womb, his liver wasn't functioning because his mother's was working for him. At birth or very shortly thereafter, the blood vessel that was funneling the fetal puppy's blood past his nonfunctioning liver closes. When this blood vessel closes, the puppy's liver is then able to filter the blood.

If the blood vessel remains open, the liver is not removing toxins from the bloodstream or performing any of the other necessary tasks that keep the puppy healthy. The blood vessel diversion can be inside the liver (intrahepatic) or outside (extrahepatic).

A puppy with a liver shunt is usually smaller than normal and may have poor muscle development. He may suffer from seizures, may stare into space, and could be unresponsive. If you feel your puppy isn't developing well or even if you just feel something isn't right, call your veterinarian. If the bile acid test reveals your puppy has this disorder, your vet will discuss your options. They could range from diet management to surgery, but surgery usually produces the best results.

Vaccinations and Vaccination Schedule

When a dog is exposed to or gets sick with an infectious disease, his immune system creates *antibodies* against that disease. This is called an active immunity and prevents the dog from getting sick from this particular disease again in the future.

An **antibody** is a substance made from protein and produced by the immune system. It protects against disease.

Your puppy's immune system continues to make these antibodies long after the source of the infection is gone. And if your puppy is exposed to the same disease again later, his body will produce even more antibodies. This protection generally lasts for the dog's lifetime.

Vaccinations allow for a controlled exposure to an infectious disease so your puppy's body can produce those antibodies. Modified live virus (MLV) vaccines contain live viruses that live in the animal. These viruses have been modified so the puppy should not get sick from the virus. The immune system tends to react quickly to these vaccines, producing antibodies right away.

Killed virus vaccinations contain killed viruses so they cannot make the puppy sick. However, although the body does make antibodies in response to killed vaccines, it does so at a slower rate than to a modified live vaccine.

Puppies (and later, adult dogs) are given a variety of vaccinations on a regular basis. Some of these are considered essential—these are called core vaccines—while others are given based on the dog's geographical location, whether the dog travels or not, and other dog-specific aspects. These are called noncore vaccines.

A third category of vaccines is available for specific circumstances. These circumstances might include outbreaks of certain diseases in your area or special dangers. Your veterinarian will recommend these vaccines if needed.

The diseases and vaccinations normally considered core, or essential, include the following:

Distemper: Canine distemper is a virus similar to the human measles virus. It can affect many of the dog's organs, including the skin, eyes, and intestinal and respiratory tracts. The virus can be transmitted through urine, feces, and saliva. The first symptoms are usually a nasal and eye discharge. This is a potentially fatal disease, and those dogs who do survive often have lasting neurological damage.

Hepatitis: Canine hepatitis is a virus found worldwide. It's spread through nasal discharge as well as urine, usually through direct contact. The virus begins with a sore throat, and the dog will not want to swallow, drink, or eat. It spreads rapidly to other organs and develops quickly. Dogs can die within hours of the first symptoms.

Parvovirus: This virus, often referred to simply as parvo, has killed thousands of dogs, usually puppies. Because the virus continues to mutate and change, it's still a deadly threat. This virus is often called the most deadly, dangerous, and fatal disease known to dogs. Vomiting, diarrhea, dehydration, and death are common. Sudden death may also occur from heart damage caused by this disease.

Rabies: This virus is almost always fatal once the disease has been contracted. It is transmitted through contact with an infected animal, usually a bat, raccoon, or skunk. The first symptom is usually drooling because of problems swallowing, followed by staggering, seizures, and changes from normal behavior. Rabies vaccinations are required by law.

Most veterinarians recommend all puppies and dogs be vaccinated with these vaccines. These diseases are serious, potentially fatal, and difficult to treat.

> ### TIPS AND TAILS
>
> Wait in your veterinarian's office for a half an hour after your pet receives a vaccination. If your Yorkie is going to have a reaction to the vaccination, it will usually begin in that time period.

The diseases and vaccines that are considered noncore—or not essential—include the following:

Leptospirosis: This is a bacteria rather than a virus. It affects the kidneys and is passed from the kidneys to the urine. It's transmitted to other dogs when they sniff the contaminated urine. This disease also attacks the liver. Lepto, as it's called, can be spread to other animals, including people. Symptoms include a fever, nausea, and dehydration, and the bacteria can be fatal. Reactions to this vaccine are not uncommon.

Parainfluenza: This virus is one of several viruses called canine cough or kennel cough. It's easily spread when an infected dog coughs, which also happens to be one of the first and primary symptoms. It may turn into pneumonia, but it's generally just a cough that goes away in a week or two.

Bordetella bronchiseptica: Bordetella is a bacteria that causes coughing and other respiratory problems. This, too, is one of the diseases classified under the canine cough or kennel cough umbrella. It's very contagious and can easily spread from one dog to another through coughing. It's rarely dangerous to healthy dogs, but puppies can get quite sick.

Lyme disease: This disease is caused by a bacteria spread by infected ticks. Originally identified in Connecticut, it's now found in all 48 contiguous states. A fever is the first symptom, followed by muscle soreness, weakness, and joint pain. Severe, permanent joint and kidney damage are possible.

Discuss these vaccinations with your veterinarian. She may recommend one or more of them depending on where you live and your dog's activities.

New vaccines are continually being developed and introduced. Most have some specific applications. These include the following:

Rattlesnake venom: If you live in an area where rattlesnakes are common and your dog likes to chase reptiles, this vaccine could gain you some time to get your puppy to help after a snake bite.

Porphyromonas: This is a vaccination against the bacteria that causes periodontitis (gum disease).

These vaccines are usually only recommended in specific situations. Talk to your veterinarian about whether they're necessary for your Yorkie.

Vaccinations for dogs are important because they save lives. In fact, many of the diseases that killed thousands of lives—such as canine distemper—are extremely uncommon now because of vaccinations. However, vaccines are not innocuous and can cause problems. They should be given wisely and with caution.

Most veterinarians recommend that puppies get their first vaccinations between 6 and 8 weeks of age. As mentioned, if the mother's antibodies are still effective in the puppy's body, that first vaccination may not be effective. That's why most puppies get a *series* of vaccines early in life. The shots are usually given 3 or 4 weeks apart. You and your veterinarian can talk about the best vaccination schedule for your Yorkie puppy.

Internal Parasites

The thought that parasites can be living inside your Yorkshire Terrier puppy is disgusting. Unfortunately, parasites are common, and that's why your veterinarian asked you to bring a sample of your puppy's feces to the first exam.

Roundworms: It's fairly common for puppies to have roundworms. In fact, most breeders treat the whole litter for roundworms as a matter of course. These parasites are generally limited to puppies, but adult dogs—as well as people—can become infested with this *zoonotic disease,* too. Roundworms live in the intestinal tract but can migrate to the lungs, the trachea, and even the eyes. Roundworm eggs are passed out of the puppy's (or other animal's) body via the feces. Keeping the yard clean and disposing of feces promptly is the best way to prevent an infestation.

A **zoonotic disease** is transmissible from one species to another, for example, from dogs to humans.

Hookworms: Like roundworms, hookworms can infest both dogs and people, too. This worm also lives in the intestinal tract, where it grabs on to the tissues of the intestinal tract and bites, causing the puppy to lose some blood. Unfortunately, the worm does this several times a day, causing blood loss each time. A puppy with a severe infestation can quickly become anemic. As with roundworms, cleanliness is the key to preventing infestations.

Whipworms: These hardy, long-lived worms live in the lower part of the intestinal tract, where they can survive for years, causing diarrhea, nausea, and intestinal cramping. The eggs are passed out via the feces and can live in the environment for as long as 5 years. These worms are also more than willing to live in human hosts as well as canine ones. Picking up feces regularly is important.

Tapeworms: Puppies pick up tapeworms through an intermediate host, the flea. When the flea bites the puppy, the puppy chews at that spot and ingests the flea. The flea carries tapeworm eggs that then hatch in the puppy's intestinal tract. Dogs can also get these parasites by eating mice or voles. Tapeworms can cause diarrhea and soft stools. Controlling fleas is the key to preventing tapeworm infestations.

A Yorkshire Terrier puppy with a heavy infestation may have a poor coat, unhealthy skin, and soft stools. He will also have a round, full belly. A puppy with a few parasites may not yet be showing signs, so the easiest way to test for internal intestinal parasites is to take a small, fresh piece of stool to your veterinarian and have it checked under a microscope. If any signs of parasites, such as a piece of a worm or parasite eggs, are present the vet can identify them and start your Yorkie puppy on a course of treatment.

Nutrition

Tiny puppies use a lot of energy while playing, and because they're so small, they don't have the energy reserves to maintain both their energy needs and body functions. Therefore, you need to feed your Yorkie puppy four or five small meals each day, or preferably every 3 or 4 hours throughout the day and evening. If you need to leave him alone for several hours, leave some food out for him.

If your Yorkie expends too much energy, either playing or because of stress, he could suffer from low blood sugar, or hypoglycemia. If your puppy appears weak, sleepy, or uncoordinated, give him a nutritional supplement such as Nutri-Cal or give him a teaspoon of corn syrup or pancake syrup. Then call your veterinarian because this is an extremely serious condition. But be sure to raise his blood sugar *first* and then call your veterinarian. (See also Month 6.)

Food from the Breeder

Be sure to bring home some of the dog food the breeder has been feeding your puppy. Your puppy's first few days home are stressful enough; he doesn't need to change foods now, too.

If you plan on continuing to feed your puppy that food, that's fine. You can buy more in the next few days when you run out. However, if you'd like to change foods, don't do it immediately. Feed your Yorkie puppy the food he's accustomed to for a couple weeks and only then begin adding small amounts of the new food to a slightly decreased amount of the old food. Over a couple weeks, slowly increase the amounts of new food while you decrease the old food.

If at any time your puppy has diarrhea, stop adding the new food for a few days. When his stools have firmed up again, you can resume adding the new food, but do it even more slowly. Many Yorkshire Terriers have a sensitive digestive system and they don't tolerate change well. Make changes slowly.

Feeding Practices

Feeding your Yorkshire Terrier puppy involves more than filling a bowl with dry kibble and placing it on the floor so he can nibble all day long. Although *free feeding* your puppy is easy, it's not the best way to feed him.

> **DOG TALK**
>
> **Free feeding** is the practice of giving your puppy food and allowing him to eat all day long at his leisure.

Your Yorkshire Terrier puppy needs scheduled meals. This helps the housetraining process immensely because he'll have to relieve himself after each meal. If he nibbles all day long, it's much more difficult to tell when he needs to go outside.

Plus, if your puppy doesn't feel well, one of the first questions your veterinarian will ask is, "How is his appetite?" If you're free feeding him, you won't be able to answer that question.

The only time free feeding is acceptable is if you're going to be gone for several hours. If this will cause your puppy to go too long between meals, you can leave out some food for him to nibble on as he needs it.

Feed your puppy either in his crate or in his exercise pen. He shouldn't have to worry about getting jostled or stepped on while he's eating. Don't let the other dogs, the family cat, or the kids mess with him while he's eating either.

> **HAPPY PUPPY**

If you have several dogs, be sure each has his or her own bowl, and don't let the older dogs steal the puppy's food. Feeding time should be stress free.

Water

Your puppy's body is about 75 percent water, and losing as little as 15 percent of that can result in dehydration and even death. Your puppy needs a ready source of clean, fresh water.

He may need more than one water bowl depending on how he's kept. He may need one in an out-of-the-way spot in the kitchen, one in his exercise pen, and one outside.

During hot weather, a larger water bowl may be advisable—and don't be surprised if your Yorkie climbs into it! To your little Yorkie puppy, a water bowl can also be used as a swimming pool.

> **TIPS AND TAILS**

Keep your Yorkie's water fresh, and clean the bowl daily because bacteria can build up from bits of food and saliva dropped into the water.

If you're worried your puppy isn't drinking enough, especially in hot weather, offer him some ice cubes. You can also make some ice cubes out of diluted, low-sodium chicken broth. Just give him these outside so they don't stain your carpet.

Grooming

Grooming is going to be a life-long process for your Yorkshire Terrier, so it's important to teach him this can be a pleasurable experience as soon as possible. You also want him to know that even if it's not so much fun—such as trimming his toenails or cleaning under his tail—he needs to trust you as you groom him.

The easiest way to do this is by touching him kindly and gently all over his body. You want to teach your puppy that your hands are never rough or hurtful.

Start by sitting on the sofa and encouraging your puppy to join you. Bring him up on your lap, and encourage him to lie down. Don't pin him down; this is not a wrestling match.

Begin by petting him, and when he's comfortable, gently rub your hands over him. Do this slowly so you relax him. Let your fingers get to know the feel of his body so if he has a lump, cut, imbedded tick, or any other problem, your fingers will find it even if you can't see it through his coat.

Touch him all over, from his nose to the tip of his tail. Feel between each toe, and touch each toenail. Run your hands up each leg, and check out his private parts. Feel around his head, neck, and chest.

Do this for a few days before introducing a pin brush. After giving your puppy a massage, gently begin brushing him. Move the brush in the direction the hair grows. Don't be concerned so much about being thorough right now; instead, show your puppy that this brushing is simply an extension of that wonderful feeling he gets when you massage him.

Take your time introducing the massage and brushing. After all, you want him to relax and enjoy this. If he does, grooming chores in the future will be much easier.

Social Skills

Your Yorkshire Terrier puppy is going to be living in a world with more people than dogs, and he needs to know how to behave in this world. He learned canine social skills from his mother and littermates, and although those are important, he now needs to learn more about living with people.

Socialization Basics

People were a part of your puppy's life from the very beginning because his breeder began handling him even before his eyes opened. He was picked up, held, moved, stroked, and cuddled. Before your puppy left the breeder's place to come home with you, the breeder most likely continued this *socialization* by bringing in a few other people so the puppy met more than just the breeder and her family.

Socialization is the process of introducing your puppy to the world around him, including different sights, sounds, smells, and surfaces as well as other people and animals.

The breeder also accustomed the puppies to the sounds and smells of living with people. Your puppy heard the sounds of the vacuum cleaner and garbage disposal as well as the clanging of pots and pans. He smelled dinner cooking and the flowers in a vase on the table. The breeder gave your Yorkie puppy a good head-start with socialization, but now you need to continue it. Give your puppy a few days to settle into your home and then pick back up with the socialization.

If your veterinarian says your puppy hasn't had all his vaccinations yet and shouldn't meet other dogs right now, you can still socialize your puppy to the world around him without risking his health. Simply avoid other dogs, and don't allow your puppy to sniff where other dogs have relieved themselves.

Introduce your tiny puppy to a few neighbors or extended family first. Take him with you as you walk down the driveway or go to the mailbox. Let one person at a time pet your Yorkie puppy while you hold him in your arms. If your puppy is calm, hand him to the other person and let her pet your puppy.

You can take your puppy to outdoor shopping centers, to the local elementary school when the kids are on their way to school, and to the local garden center. There are lots of places where your puppy can see, hear, and smell new things and people and not be at risk for catching a contagious disease.

The idea of socialization is to teach your Yorkshire Terrier that the world is a great place. It's not scary, not threatening, and not something to worry about. To convey this message, make introductions fun and happy and accompanied by lots of verbal praise in a happy tone of voice as well as a few tasty treats.

For example, show your Yorkshire Terrier puppy a closed umbrella. Move it around and encourage him to step up to it and sniff it. Ask him, "What is it?" in a happy tone of voice. Pop a treat in his mouth when he does explore it. Then open the umbrella. If your puppy jumps back, simply ask him again, "What is it?" Turn the umbrella upside down on the ground, and drop a few treats on it. Point at them and encourage your puppy to come up to the umbrella and get the treats. Praise him when he does.

Use this jolly routine for anything new, especially anything your puppy is worried about. You can even ask your neighbor on the motorcycle or the garbage-truck driver to stop, talk nicely to your puppy, and offer him a treat. The mail carrier and delivery truck driver can also help with socialization.

Your Puppy and Children

Kids and puppies seem to be made for each other. They both love to run, play, and make noise. However, your Yorkshire Terrier puppy is very tiny and fragile right now. A child who is too rough or careless could hurt your puppy badly, even unintentionally. For this reason, many breeders won't sell a Yorkie puppy to a family with young children.

If you do have kids, it's important that both your puppy and the children in his life know how to interact with each other so no one gets hurt. Don't forget that this applies to *all* children in his life—not just your children but also your kids' friends, grandchildren, neighbor kids, and even children you meet while on walks.

Don't let very young children play with the puppy at all. One yank on your Yorkie's hair, ear, or tail, and your Yorkie could retaliate by biting. Just don't let it happen.

Interactions between dogs and kids should be calm and gentle. No wrestling, no tug of war, and no play fighting. Instead, the kids can give the puppy a massage or tummy rub. They can play hide and seek: Let the kids hide and then let your Yorkie puppy find them. The kids can throw the ball for the puppy to fetch.

Teach the children that hugging the puppy too tightly can hurt him. Dressing him up in doll's clothes can scare him and make him angry. Always supervise interactions between your puppy and kids. Then if either gets overexcited, you can remedy the situation before anyone gets hurt.

Remember, your puppy has a mouthful of needle-sharp puppy teeth right now, so it's important that he understand he's not allowed to use his teeth when playing with people and most importantly with kids. To prevent the puppy from biting on the kids or grabbing their clothes, have the kids hand the puppy a dog toy when he gets bitey. Teach the puppy, "Get a toy! Good to have a toy!" If he has a toy in his mouth, he can't use his mouth inappropriately.

> ## TIPS AND TAILS
>
> Never leave your Yorkshire Terrier alone with children. Puppies and kids can be great friends, but it has to happen with adult supervision.

Puppyhood is a great time to teach good habits. Establish some rules for interactions between the puppy and the kids in his life and enforce those rules.

Behavior

Your puppy's mind is developing just as much as his body is right now. He's learning all the time, and this is important for you to remember because everything you do with him is teaching him something.

If he cries and you coming running, he's going to remember that. He may begin crying just to get your attention, and that could easily become a very bad habit. He may also learn that when he sits nicely in front of you and looks at you with those big dark brown eyes, you'll talk nicely to him and give him a treat. Now that's a good habit to get started!

Just keep in mind he's constantly learning. Think about what the two of you are doing together and what you want him to continue doing as he grows up.

Sleeping Routines

Although your puppy isn't sleeping as much now as he did just a few weeks ago, he's still going to have to sleep a lot. He'll sleep, relieve himself, eat, relieve himself, play, and sleep some more.

In the "Training" section later in this chapter, we talk about crate training. The crate should be your puppy's sleeping place, and in that section, we discuss why this is important and how to introduce your puppy to his crate. Just keep in mind that when your puppy is ready for a nap or when he's going to bed for the night, he needs to be in his crate.

> ### HAPPY PUPPY
>
> Puppies, like young children, can become overexcited and overstimulated and get grumpy as a result. When you see your puppy reaching this point, put him in his crate for a nap. He'll be much happier when he wakes up.

How much your puppy sleeps is hard to determine. If he's going through a growth stage, he may sleep more than he will in between those growth spurts. Let him sleep as much as he needs to right now.

As far as nighttime sleeping is concerned, your puppy will probably wake up at least once a night, maybe even twice, and need to go outside to relieve himself. When you take him outside, don't interact with him, and certainly don't play with him. Just take him outside, let him relieve himself, quietly praise him, and bring him back inside to his crate. If you keep things calm and quiet, he should go back to sleep fairly quickly.

Curiosity

Your Yorkshire Terrier has an unlimited curiosity about everything around him. Things like the furniture, the kids' toys, your books, the plants out in the yard, and even the lizards in the pile of rocks are all new and exciting to him.

Unfortunately, this curiosity can get him into trouble. Your puppy doesn't know what's safe to play with and what isn't. Nor does he understand that something he chews up may be expensive to replace. This is why puppy-proofing your house and yard is so important. (You did that already, right?)

Your supervision is also important. When your puppy wants to gnaw on the TV remote control, you can interrupt him with a sharp, "No, that's not yours." Then, lead him to one of his toys and tell him, "Here, get your toy! Good to have a toy!" Praise him with a happy tone of voice to turn his curiosity into a teaching moment.

He's Biting!

Your Yorkie puppy is tiny, but he has a good set of very sharp puppy teeth and right now he's not afraid to use them. Unfortunately, that means he may chew up things, as we've discussed. He also may grab people with his mouth, which is why his play with children needs to be supervised.

We've mentioned one technique of distracting him from biting: by giving him a toy instead. When he has a toy in his mouth, he can't bite or grab clothes. So when he gets excited, with you or with the kids, hand him a small soft toy and tell him, "Get a toy. Good to have a toy! Yeah!" Make a big fuss over him when he holds the toy in his mouth.

When you see him pick up a toy on his own, praise him even more. "Good to have a toy! Look at you! What a special puppy you are!" Your praise should make him prance and dance.

If your puppy doesn't have a toy and grabs clothes or skin with his teeth, first yell, "Ouch!" in a high-pitched voice, as if you were one of his littermates who was hurt by his teeth. Make direct eye contact with him as you say this, as his mother would have done when he misbehaved.

If his biting stops at that moment, walk him to his toys and praise him for picking one up and playing with it. If he continues and appears overexcited, take him to his crate for a timeout until he calms down.

Training

Training your Yorkshire Terrier is going to be an ongoing process over his lifetime. If you thought only puppies need training, you're wrong.

A bored Yorkshire Terrier of any age is going to get into trouble. Training, whether it's obedience, trick training, or performance sports, will keep your dog's mind challenged and busy, and he'll be less likely to get into trouble.

Training Techniques

There are as many different training techniques, methods, and styles as there are dogs, owners, and dog trainers. Although the proponents of each technique tend to think theirs is the best, or easiest, or kindest, as long as the technique is easy to use and humane for the dog, no one technique is really any better than another.

The training technique we use in this book is a lure-and-reward technique. It's easy for dog owners to understand and use, and it's just as easy for the dogs to learn. This technique is also kind and humane for the dog.

Here are the basic training steps of this technique:

❧ Show your Yorkie puppy what you want him to do.

❧ Praise and reward him for doing it.

❧ Should he do something you don't want him to do, interrupt him.

❧ Then show him what you want him to do, and praise and reward him.

It sounds easy, right? It is. Let's look at how it works in a little more detail. Say, for example, your Yorkshire Terrier puppy is jumping up on your legs, scratching you with his sharp toenails:

❧ Have your puppy on leash, and hold the leash in your left hand. Have a pocketful of treats and one treat in your right hand.

❧ Let your puppy sniff the treat and then tell him, "Sweetie, sit," while moving the treat over his head toward his tail just slightly. As his head goes up and back, his hips will go down.

❧ When his hips touch the ground, tell him, "Good boy to sit! Wonderful!" and give him the treat.

❧ Now, use the hand holding the leash to also hold his collar. Use your right hand to pet your puppy while he's sitting. As you pet him, praise him, "Good boy, yes, you are."

🐾 When he's calm, tell him, "Sweetie, okay!" and release his collar so he
can get up and move around.

Your puppy jumps on you for attention, but if he gets attention while he's sitting,
he no longer needs to jump up. So be sure he gets all his petting while he's sitting
nicely.

However, if he jumps up before you can have him sit, tell him, "No jump," as you
take his collar and help him sit. Then praise him for sitting.

Rather than just telling your puppy what not to do, you're teaching him what to
do instead. This makes training much easier—and a whole lot more fun for you and
your puppy.

Crate Training Your Puppy

The crate is your Yorkshire Terrier puppy's bed. It can confine him at night when
everyone is sleeping, but can also keep him safe for short periods of time during the
day. The crate is not a cupboard where you can store your puppy all the time—that's
abusing the crate. Instead, by using the crate, your puppy learns to control his bladder
and bowels. Remember, puppies have an instinct to keep their bed clean.

> **TIPS AND TAILS**
>
> Crates work well for puppy training because puppies like confined dark
> places to hide and sleep. The crate becomes your puppy's safe and secure
> den.

Several different types of crates are available, as we touched on earlier. The hard
plastic crate that comes apart so the top can be inverted and stored in the bottom half
is the most common type. It's bulky, but it's easy to clean and easy for your Yorkie to
get used to. A wire crate that looks more like a cage is also easy to use. It's often heavy,
although it is collapsible and stores flat.

Soft-sided nylon crates and carry bags are great for small dogs, but don't use one
while your Yorkie is very small. They could collapse and potentially hurt your puppy,
and they don't offer any protection from outside dangers. Plus, more than one small
terrier has learned how to claw his way out of soft-sided crates. Later, when your
Yorkie is older, well trained, and physically a little sturdier, you can use a soft-sided
crate or carrier if you prefer.

Whether you choose a plastic crate or a metal one is totally up to you. Take a
look at the variety of crates at your local pet-supply store before buying one. Think

about your ability to move it, store it, and use it, and choose a crate that will give your Yorkshire Terrier room to stand up, turn around, and lie down when he's full size.

You want the crate to be a good thing. Ideally, when you say, "Sweetie, go to bed!" your Yorkie puppy will run to his crate and dash in with his tail wagging wildly. If your puppy hates his crate and makes you push him inside, there's a problem.

To get your puppy used to his crate …

- ❧ Set up the crate in a room where people in the house hang out. Lots of foot traffic is good. This isn't going to be a permanent location for the crate; it's just here now for introductions.

- ❧ Prop the crate door open so it won't close accidentally. Have a good handful of treats. Let your puppy smell the treats, and toss one toward the crate but not into it. Let your puppy go eat it and praise him as he does: "Good boy!"

- ❧ Do that a couple more times and then toss a treat into the crate. When your puppy steps into the crate for the treat, praise him with the command you're going to use, such as, "Good to go to bed! Yeah!"

- ❧ Repeat a few more times and then stop. Do this each time you walk by the crate throughout the day.

At mealtime, put your puppy's food bowl inside the crate, pushing it to the back. Let him go in, and close the door behind him. Let your puppy eat in peace, and don't open the door immediately after he's finished. Let him figure out the door is closed. Then, if he's calm and quiet, open the door and praise him.

If he barks, paws at the door, or throws a temper tantrum, don't let him out. In fact, walk away and go to another room. When he calms down, come back and let him out.

Begin putting him in the crate and closing the door for a few minutes—2 or 3— every now and then throughout the day. Always give him a treat when he's inside, and never let him out if he's throwing a fit.

Some Yorkshire Terrier puppies can learn this lesson all in one day. If your breeder introduced the crate to the puppy when she still had him, he'll switch over to the crate at your house with no problem.

When your puppy is used to the crate, put it in the place you'd like it to remain. In your bedroom is great because he can sleep in your room, hearing you, smelling you, and being close even though you're asleep. If you're short of room, you might be able to move your bedside table out and put the crate there.

Don't isolate your puppy. If you put him in the laundry room or garage, he'll be very unhappy and might develop behavioral problems such as barking and howling. Your Yorkshire Terrier puppy needs to be near you.

> **HAPPY PUPPY**

> When your puppy is comfortable with the crate, it will become his bed at night and his refuge when he's tired or stressed. Leave the door to the crate open during the day, and let him run in and out as he wishes. At times, you might find him curled up in it sound asleep with the door wide open, and that's wonderful.

One of the biggest benefits of using the crate—besides teaching housetraining skills—is preventing bad behavior from occurring, so you don't want to stop using the crate until your Yorkie is mentally grown up and well trained. For a Yorkshire Terrier, this can be 18 to 24 months old. Even then, many owners leave the crate out as the dog's bed and just take the door off so the dog can come and go as he pleases.

Prioritizing Housetraining

Housetraining is a basic skill necessary for every dog who lives inside; after all, mistakes can ruin carpet and make life miserable. Plus, a Yorkshire Terrier is so small and their accidents so tiny, a bad habit can be developed before you realize it. Tiny dogs actually can be worse than big dogs when it comes to housetraining, even though big dogs make bigger messes. Big dog accidents are more obvious, and owners tend to catch them more quickly.

Housetraining consists of teaching your Yorkie puppy where he needs to relieve himself. You may have a certain section of the backyard where you want him to go as well as on a part of your sidewalk where it would be convenient and easy to clean up. You may also want to teach him to relieve himself in a specific spot inside, such as a doggy litter box or on potty pads.

The second part of housetraining is teaching your puppy to try to relieve himself when you ask him to. This is just as important as teaching him where to go. For example, if you teach your dog to relieve himself in one corner of the backyard and on the vacant lot in your neighborhood, you also need to be able to ask him to go on command in other places. If you're traveling, his familiar places won't be there and he'll need to go someplace new.

First, decide where you want your Yorkshire Terrier puppy to relieve himself. There doesn't have to be anything special about this spot; it just needs to be a place where your puppy has easy access and where you are willing to clean up after him.

To teach him to use this spot—outside or in a litter box or on potty pads inside—walk him on leash to that place. That means when your puppy needs to go, such as waking up first thing in the morning, put a leash on him and walk him to the door as you ask him, "Do you have to go?" Then have him go outside with you to the spot or walk him to the litter box or potty pads. When he relieves herself, praise him enthusiastically, "Good boy to go!"

> ### HAPPY PUPPY
>
> A large cat litter box works for most Yorkie puppies. You can use either potty pads or a commercial litter made for dogs in it. Do not use clumping cat litters because these can cause an intestinal obstruction if your puppy ingests them.

Don't send your puppy outside all by himself. If you do, you can't teach him where to go, and you can't praise him for doing it. In addition, you really won't know if he's gone or not. He may show up at the door asking to come in and have an accident on the carpet inside the door.

By taking him outside or to his litter box or potty pads, you can teach him where to go, teach him a command that means "Try to go now," and reward him for doing it. All of this helps create a reliably housetrained dog.

Don't Delay

Begin your housetraining efforts right away. The sooner you begin the housetraining process, the sooner you can build new habits.

If you delay housetraining—perhaps using the excuse that you want your new puppy to settle into the house first—chances are your puppy will learn habits you'll regret later, such as relieving himself on the carpet, for example. Getting your puppy started on a new schedule for eating, sleeping, and going outside as soon as possible are the keys to housetraining success.

Dealing with Housetraining Accidents

Accidents do happen, even when you're vigilant. A puppy can be playing one second and squatting the next. However, accidents usually occur when the owner gets distracted or gets busy with something other than the puppy.

When an accident does happen, how you react is important. After all, the puppy does have to urinate and defecate. If you convey to the puppy that urinating and/or defecating is wrong, your puppy will try to hide it. He may no longer relieve himself in front of you, even outside. You may find puddles or piles behind the drapes or the sofa.

So if you catch your puppy in the act, use your voice to interrupt him, "No, not here!" Then take him outside. Tell him to go now using your normal, soft voice, and praise him if he has anything left or tries to comply. Then bring him inside and put him in his crate while you clean up his mess.

Do not yell at your Yorkie puppy for this accident. Instead, promise yourself you'll do better next time. You'll be sure he gets outside quicker, you'll stick to his schedule, or you'll supervise him better.

If you find an accident after the fact—after the puppy has finished and moved away—do not punish him at all. Don't drag him to it and yell at him, and definitely don't stick his nose in it. He has to go; it's a natural biological action. If you need to yell, yell at yourself for allowing it to happen.

You and Your Puppy

Your new Yorkshire Terrier puppy is so small, yet when he first joins your household, he will be a major disruption. Plus, most new puppy owners try so hard to do everything right that the stress levels in the home can rise significantly.

But you know what? Everything is going to be fine. You have all the help you need right here. So relax and enjoy your puppy.

What to Expect

If at all possible, bring your new puppy home on a Friday if you have Saturday and Sunday off from work. This way he can get to know you and the household a little bit before he's left all alone when the work and school week begins again on Monday. If you stay at home or work from home, this obviously isn't nearly as important.

When you first bring home your puppy, take him from the car to the place where you want him to relieve himself. Let him wander around, sniff, and decide where he wants to go. Have everyone leave him alone right now; after all, if he doesn't relieve himself here, he will when he gets inside the house. Let him have some quiet time right now, and praise him when he relieves himself.

When you do go inside, it's time to meet the family. Have everyone sit on the floor, and let your puppy go from person to person. No one should hold or restrain him; just let him get to know everyone on his own terms.

Limit this visiting to people who live in the house, though. Neighbors and other family members can meet him in a few days. Of course you want to show off this adorable bit of a puppy, but don't do it now. That will be too overwhelming and frightening for your new Yorkie puppy right now. In fact, if neighbors try to greet you and your puppy as you drive up, politely tell them, "Not now, thanks! We'll introduce him in a few days."

> ### HAPPY PUPPY
>
> Keep these first interactions calm and quiet. No wrestling with the puppy or play fighting right now. Instead, show him this new home is safe and not at all threatening.

After the first introductions, family members need to go back to a normal routine as much as possible. This helps your puppy learn the household routine and how life proceeds. He'll also need to spend some time alone now and then throughout the day, so be sure you've showed him where his crate is. When you can't supervise your puppy, put him in his crate with a chew toy.

Over the next few days, don't be surprised if your puppy cries. This is an entirely new situation for him, with people he doesn't know, and in a strange place. He may be lonely for his littermates, he may not know where to find food or water, and he may even be a little frightened.

Be careful not to develop the habit of running to your puppy each and every time he cries. If he needs to go outside, take him outside. But if he's been outside and still cries, offer him a toy or something to chew on and then leave him alone again. Only when he's quiet should you go give him some attention. Reward the behaviors or actions you want him to continue to do in the future.

The first few days will be tough for you and your puppy. He'll probably wake you up a few times during the night, he may have some housetraining accidents, he may cry and whine, and he may play fight with those sharp puppy teeth. Just react calmly to all these situations. Your confidence will help your Yorkie puppy be calm, too.

Being a Parent

This Yorkshire Terrier may well become a great friend later, but right now he needs a parent's leadership and guidance. You need to establish some ground rules for your relationship. The most important rule right now is to be sure he's not treating you like one of his littermates.

He can sit on your lap, snuggle next to you on the sofa, or fall asleep in your arms. However, don't let him jump all over you; climb on top of you; or chew on your pant legs, feet, or hands. That's being rude, and if he was that rough with his mother, his mother would growl at him.

So play with your puppy, but if he gets too excited, stop the play time. Take him to his crate or exercise pen, and give him a timeout for a few minutes.

Try to think of yourself as a parent rather than a playmate, and you'll be fine. Just don't get frustrated when your puppy doesn't understand right away. After all, you don't look anything like his mother!

Setting Up a Schedule

Your Yorkie has a teeny tiny bladder and needs considerable help, including a schedule, to become housetrained. A schedule for his life, which includes eating as well as housetraining, also provides him with a sense of security. If you normally aren't an organized person or don't live with any kind of a schedule, try to change that for at least the first year of your Yorkie's life.

Housetraining is much easier when the puppy has a schedule for eating, napping, and going outside to relieve himself. He's also going to need to go outside after play sessions, and in these early months, about every 2 hours when he's awake. A schedule helps his internal clock become accustomed to things happening regularly.

Schedules also promote security and trust. When your puppy realizes that certain things happen in an orderly manner at planned times, he'll feel more comfortable.

With some organization, or at least a plan, you can also be sure things are done when they need to be done and you're not procrastinating. The breeder began socialization, for example, and you need to continue it. If you don't do it in these early weeks, you can miss that window of time when socialization is so important.

Here are some other points to put on your schedule:

- ❧ Your puppy needs four or five meals a day right now. A tiny meal every 3 or 4 hours during the day and evening would work well.
- ❧ He needs to go outside to relieve himself after waking up, after eating, after playing, and about every 2 hours when awake.
- ❧ He needs at least a couple play sessions with you each day as well as time to begin his training.
- ❧ Set aside time to begin introducing him to brushing, nail clipping, and other grooming chores.
- ❧ Make time for socialization.
- ❧ Your puppy needs to sleep often now and at regular times. A schedule promotes healthy sleep habits that help your puppy grow and develop as he should.

You'll probably add to this list as time goes on. For example, your Yorkie will also need to make a couple trips to the veterinarian over the next several weeks. So create a plan, and check it often.

Learning to Shuffle

A tiny puppy presents an unusual problem: If you step on him or kick him, he could be horribly hurt or even killed. Yorkshire Terrier puppies of this age are very small and fragile.

To make matters worse, you may find that your puppy likes to stay close to your feet. He may weave in and out around your feet, bounce on top of them, and grab your pant legs. This makes it tough to avoid him when you're walking.

Most Yorkie puppy owners learn to do a shuffle step when their puppy mobs their feet. By shuffling, you won't accidentally kick or step on him, and your shuffle can teach him to move out of the way.

TIPS AND TAILS

Don't pick up your Yorkie to get him out of the way. He needs to develop skills to avoid your feet, and if you pick him up, that won't happen. So shuffle and teach him, "Sweetie, move. Good!" This helps him avoid accidental injuries.

Four on the Floor

| Socialization at home with new owner and other pets |
| Teething begins—heavy chewing period |
| Enroll in puppy class |
| Rapid growth |
| 2nd DHPP vaccines |
| Switch to a food for all life stage |

Your Yorkshire Terrier puppy's fourth month is a fun one! Her personality is becoming more apparent, and her attachment to you is strong. She's also more curious about the world around her, and she's playing more.

Socialization is vital this month, as is training. Both come in to play when you're teaching her to walk on her own four paws. (No, you shouldn't carry her around *all* the time.)

Physical Development

By the end of this month, your puppy will begin teething. She'll lose her puppy teeth, and over the next couple months, her large adult terrier teeth will grow in.

Your puppy's motor skills are better now, too. Although she was never as uncoordinated as a larger puppy might be, your Yorkie is still gaining coordination this month.

Beginning this month, you'll see some changes in your puppy's coat as her baby coat slowly transitions to her adult coat. The length of the coat will change as well as the texture and color. These changes are gradual, however. Your Yorkie won't have her full-length adult coat until she's about 3 years old.

Surviving Teething

It might seem like your puppy just got her puppy teeth, and that's true; it's only been a few months. However, at some point during your puppy's fourth month, she'll begin losing her puppy teeth and her adult teeth will start to come in. The actual time of teething varies with each individual puppy. Some start earlier in the month while others may not begin until later. Don't worry, though; there's no right or wrong time for this to happen.

The start of teething doesn't announce itself. Many owners find out their puppy is teething when they're walking around the house in bare feet and step on a needle-sharp puppy tooth. These little daggers are as sharp as a thorn and hurt when you step on them. Or you may discover your puppy is teething when you see drops of blood on a toy or a chew bone.

> **HAPPY PUPPY**

> To ease the pain of teething, make some special ice cubes for your Yorkie puppy. Dilute some chicken broth with water, and freeze it in ice-cube trays. Give your puppy an ice cube to chew on as a cooling treat. Put a towel under her so the broth doesn't stain your carpet.

The first teeth your puppy will lose are her tiny incisors at the front of her mouth. Don't expect to find these, though, because they're so tiny. In fact, many puppies actually swallow these when they fall out.

The big canine teeth usually grow in next. Once in a while, the canines will grow in next to the puppy canines. If the puppy tooth is loose, it will eventually come out on its own. However, if the puppy canine still feels well anchored, it might need to be pulled. This doesn't need an emergency trip to the veterinarian's clinic, but definitely ask your vet about it the next time you go in.

Later in the fourth month or early in the fifth, your puppy's premolars—the teeth just past the canines—will come in. The last teeth to come in are the big molars, and sometimes these don't grow in until the puppy's seventh month. When all your Yorkie's adult teeth are grown in, she'll have 42 teeth.

During teething, your puppy's gums will be swollen. She might want to chew anything and everything she can fit in her mouth. You may find that she's chewing on the strangest things—not just your shoes, but also rocks or sticks. Prevention is best at this time. Keep as many things put away as possible and don't allow your puppy to have too much freedom right now. (We share more tips on dealing with teething and chewing later in this chapter.)

She might be fussy, fidgety, and grumpy now, too. She may run a slight fever at times and may even be a little nauseated. Because she doesn't feel well, she might be alternately clingy and standoffish. Don't worry. These are all normal during this stage, and it will all pass as her adult teeth come in.

Keep an eye on your Yorkie's teeth as they're growing in. Watch for baby teeth that haven't fallen out or for any adult teeth that don't look right. If you have any questions or see what might be a problem, call your veterinarian.

She Can't Fly (Although She Thinks She Can)

Yorkshire Terrier puppies gain coordination rapidly. They aren't nearly as clumsy and silly as many larger-breed puppies are. However, this coordination can also lead to problems because many Yorkie puppies are far too brave for their own good.

Because of her small size, your Yorkie puppy can be fragile, and if she leaps from a high bed or the back of the sofa, she can hurt herself—even break a leg. This can be painful and frightening for your puppy, and you could be looking at expensive vet bills. Plus, she could develop arthritis in the injured leg in the future.

It's important to help your puppy keep herself safe. Don't let her have free run of the house. Restricting her freedom is important for housetraining and preventing her from getting into trouble, and by keeping her close and supervised, you can prevent her from acting like a superhero trying to fly.

> ### TIPS AND TAILS
>
> When you're not busy and can keep a close eye on your puppy, let her have more freedom in the house, but let her drag a lightweight leash. That way, if she starts to do something she shouldn't do, you can stop her. This gives you a chance to both keep her safe and teach her what's allowed and what isn't.

Teach your puppy how to maneuver around the house safely on her own four paws. Walk her on leash up and down the stairs. Have her walk slowly with you; don't let her dash ahead; and keep her from walking under, around, or in between your feet. Praise her for walking slowly and nicely behind you or beside you on the stairs.

When she's snuggling with you on the furniture, prevent her from dashing off the chair or sofa in one big leap. Instead, use your hands and help her slide off the sofa. Hold her and show her to get down by sliding down—as if on a kid's slide—and then praise her. You'll have to repeat this over and over until it becomes a habit, but the repetition is worth it if it helps keep her safe.

Health

At this age, your Yorkie has been in to see the veterinarian and had her first thorough examination. She's also well on her way to completing her puppy vaccinations. Ideally, she's not having any problems and appears healthy.

Things can happen, though. Your Yorkie might eat something she shouldn't, or she may show signs of a health concern. It's important to be able to recognize a problem early, before it turns into an emergency.

Keep in mind your veterinarian is your partner in your puppy's continued good health. If you have any questions, call your vet. If it's after hours, leave a message, or if your vet answers emails, drop him a message that way.

Recognizing Symptoms of a Problem

Although your Yorkie can't speak to tell you when she doesn't feel well, her body language and actions communicate well. But that means you need to watch her to learn what her normal behaviors and actions are so you can recognize when something is different.

For example, if she's normally active and full of fun first thing in the morning, and you know this, you'll know something is wrong if, one morning, she doesn't want to play and only wants to be picked up and held. Some Yorkies are quite subtle, and the changes in behavior might not be so obvious. Just get in the habit of watching your puppy so you can see any changes.

Eating habits: It's a good idea to pay attention to any change in your puppy's eating habits. Although her appetite will often vary depending on how fast she's growing on any given day or week, if your puppy refuses to eat for more than half a day, offer her a special treat such as cheese, a hard-boiled egg, or some Nutri-Cal. If she doesn't eat all day, call your veterinarian.

Vomiting: Vomiting once isn't necessarily a problem. Your puppy might have eaten too fast, or perhaps she drank too much water too quickly. But if she can't keep down any food, call your veterinarian. If you notice anything different in the vomit, such as pieces of foreign objects—things that might have been chewed and eaten— save those and call your veterinarian.

Urine and feces: Watch your Yorkshire Terrier puppy's urinary and bowel habits. Long-time dog owners like to joke that no one in the world pays as much attention to feces as dog owners. And with good reason: Many health problems show up first as changes in the digestive system. If your puppy is straining to urinate or defecate, that's a problem. Diarrhea is also a problem; it can be a symptom of disease, a dog-food issue, or an indicator your puppy ate something she shouldn't have. Report any blood in the urine or feces to your vet right away.

Activity level: Pay attention to changes in your Yorkie's activity as well as any limping, soreness, or lack of desire to play she exhibits. Yorkshire Terrier puppies like to stay close to their owners as a matter of course, but if your puppy seems clingier than normal, that might be a sign something hurts or she doesn't feel well.

Limping or lameness: Your puppy might jump off something too high or fall while playing and just be a little sore. If she won't put any weight on a limb or limps for more than a few hours, call your veterinarian.

Temperature: By this age, your puppy's normal temperature is the same as an adult Yorkshire Terrier's—about 100°F to 102°F. If your puppy isn't acting normal, take her temperature. If it's either lower or higher, call your vet.

Don't hesitate to call your veterinarian if something concerns you. He won't laugh at you if it turns out to be nothing important. Most veterinarians are happiest when their clients pay attention to their dogs.

When you do call, be able to explain exactly what concerns you. Tell your vet what your puppy's appetite is like, how her stools are different from normal, or what her temperature is. Even if you just have a feeling something is wrong, think of how to explain that. A description such as, "My Yorkshire Terrier puppy doesn't seem to be eager to eat and isn't playing like she normally does. Her temperature is 101.5, and her stools are normal. But her expression looks sad and she's hiding under the sofa" can be just what your vet needs to evaluate what's wrong with your puppy.

The more details you can provide, the better. Your veterinarian can sift through all those details and then may have more questions or will ask you to bring in your puppy for an examination.

Dealing with Fleas

A flea is a tiny insect that lives by biting its host—in this case your Yorkshire Terrier puppy. Each time the flea bites, it takes a drop of blood. One flea isn't going to do a great deal of harm, but where there's one flea, there are apt to be hundreds more, and your puppy can potentially lose a drop of blood for each one of these insect pests. A Yorkie puppy could quickly become anemic if infested with fleas.

The bites can also be a problem when the puppy is allergic to the flea's saliva, as are many Yorkshire Terriers. This causes severe itching, and the puppy will scratch, chew, and even lose hair in the area of the bites.

> **TIPS AND TAILS**

If you see some salt and pepper material on your puppy's bed, that's an indication your Yorkshire Terrier puppy has fleas. The dark bits are excreted blood, and the white specks are flea eggs.

To prevent a flea infestation on your puppy, you must control the fleas on your puppy as well as in your home and yard. In years past, that meant using pesticides and insecticides everywhere. However, that's much too toxic and has fallen out of favor with most pet owners and veterinarians.

Instead, it's better to begin controlling fleas *before* they become a problem. The new topical products usually work well, although not all products are safe for puppies or tiny dogs, so choose wisely. And talk to your veterinarian about what she suggests.

A good vacuum cleaner is an indispensable tool in your fight against fleas. Vacuum the house daily during flea season. That means getting the floor, the carpet, your pup's bedding, and the furniture. Don't forget to do your car, too. Throw out the sweeper bag or empty the vacuum container afterward because the fleas could escape from the vacuum and the eggs could hatch in the bag.

Diatomaceous earth and boric acid are also often recommended for use in the house. Sprinkle liberally, leave down for a little while (according to package directions), and vacuum. Sentry makes a spray called Natural Defense Household Spray that can be used in the house, in crates, on bedding, in cabinets, and more. It uses peppermint, cinnamon, lemongrass, and thyme oils and is considered safe for use around puppies.

Although garlic and brewer's yeast were once recommended for discouraging fleas from biting, these have fallen out of favor with many pet experts. Garlic has been found to be not as healthy for dogs and cats as once thought, and brewer's yeast alone isn't very effective.

> **TIPS AND TAILS**

Pennyroyal oil is often recommended as a natural means of flea control. However, cases of toxicity have been recognized recently, so don't use it on your puppy or her bedding.

If your Yorkie is having a reaction to the flea bites and is scratching, chewing, and acting miserable, call your vet. Your puppy might need some veterinary care to overcome the flea-bite reaction or dermatitis.

Taking Care of Ticks

The two most common types of ticks found on dogs are deer ticks and dog ticks, and both are blood-suckers. They can be the cause of several serious diseases, including Lyme disease, Rocky Mountain spotted fever, ehrlichiosis, canine babesiosis, and canine hepatozoonosis. Tick paralysis is also a potential problem with tick bites.

Ticks are usually found on tall grasses or bushes, and when your puppy (or you!) walks past, the tick grabs on. The tick works its way through the coat to the skin on any part of the body, inserts its head into the skin, and begins to engorge on blood.

The most effective way to find ticks is to examine your Yorkshire Terrier puppy often, especially in the spring and fall when ticks are more active. As you work over your puppy, feel for bumps on her skin. When you find something, part the hair and look at the skin. An engorged tick full of blood will be about the size of a pencil eraser or slightly larger.

Use a pair of tweezers to remove a tick. Grasp the tick down near the head, close to your puppy's skin, and gently pull the tick straight out. (You can also use a commercial tool made specifically for removing ticks.) Don't yank or twist the tick, or the head could break off and remain lodged in your puppy's skin, which could cause an abscess. If you later see some redness at the site where the tick was and it doesn't clear up in a couple days, call your veterinarian.

> **TIPS AND TAILS**
>
> If you find a tick, don't squeeze it with your fingers. Many of the diseases ticks carry can also be transmitted to people.

Nutrition

Feeding a small-breed puppy such as a Yorkshire Terrier can be a challenge. Not only does your Yorkie have a very small stomach that can only hold a limited amount of food, but your puppy is also quite active and needs food for energy. Add in the fact that Yorkies can be prone to hypoglycemia (as mentioned last month and discussed in greater detail in Month 6), and feeding can be quite a challenge.

Yorkie Nutrition Tips

Ideally, your puppy should still be eating several small meals throughout the day. Four or five meals are great, although if you and your puppy are going to have a busy day, you can add a couple snacks, too.

Your Yorkie's calorie needs at this age depend on her weight and activity level. As a general rule, a 1-pound Yorkie needs about 120 calories per day while a 5-pound Yorkie needs 150. However, an active puppy may need 10 percent more, say 132 calories for the smaller puppy and 165 calories for the larger one.

To calculate how much to feed, you need to know the calorie count of the food you're feeding your puppy. Let's look at some examples. The Honest Kitchen's food, Zeal, has 437 calories per cup of food. That means one day's ration for an active 5-pound Yorkie is about ⅓ cup. Wellness' Super 5 Mix has 407 calories per cup, so an active 5-pound Yorkie needs between ⅓ and ½ cup per day. And Innova's puppy food has 454 calories per cup, so an active 5-pound Yorkie needs about ⅓ cup per day.

> ### TIPS AND TAILS
>
> Finding the calorie count for commercial pet foods isn't difficult. Manufacturers must, by law, list the calorie count on the food label. If you want to compare foods, go online to the various manufacturers' websites and look for the calorie counts.

Every puppy has his or her own nutritional needs, however, so these calorie counts are simply a place to start. Just keep an eye on your puppy's weight and energy levels. If she's thin and running out of steam, add more food to her meals.

Few Yorkies of this age are chubby, but if your Yorkie has a tendency to that, and you're feeding the recommended amount of food, try to increase your puppy's activity and see if that helps her slim down.

Appetite and Growth Spurts

Yorkies are such tiny dogs that most people, even Yorkie owners, don't think of them as having growth spurts. They do, but a Yorkie's growth spurt just isn't as obvious as one in a larger-breed puppy. Proportionately, however, a growth spurt in a Yorkie affects her body as much as one does in a larger-breed puppy.

Your Yorkshire Terrier puppy's appetite will probably increase just before she begins a growth spurt, so if your puppy suddenly acts famished, don't be surprised. Increase her food slightly, and spread the increase among her meals. If you're feeding five times a day, divide that increase in food among all five meals. If you give the increase in just one meal, it may be too much and your puppy might not eat it. Even if she did eat it, she might develop diarrhea, a common side effect of overeating.

There's no way to predict how much food your Yorkshire Terrier puppy will need during a growth spurt. Each puppy has unique nutritional needs and grows at his or her own rate. Plus, each food or diet is different.

After the growth spurt has slowed, your puppy's appetite may decrease a little. This is normal, so don't worry about it. If she leaves food in her bowl or isn't quite as hungry as she was, just cut back on the amount you're feeding. A slight decrease is okay. Just be ready to increase the food again when the next growth spurt happens.

The Basics of Nutrition

Dogs are carnivores. They're naturally designed to eat and thrive on meat and animal protein. Even though few dogs today actually have to catch prey animals to survive as their wild cousins do, their nutritional needs remain the same.

Good nutrition, however, is much more than just feeding your pet meat. There are many components of nutrition, all of which need to be met if your puppy is to thrive. Some Yorkshire Terriers have food sensitivities, especially as adults. Others may have digestive issues, while some might have slower (or faster) metabolisms. Good nutrition must take into account all of your Yorkie's individual needs.

These are the nutrients important for your Yorkshire Terrier puppy:

Proteins, amino acids, and enzymes: Proteins are necessary for building muscles, producing hormones, fighting disease, aiding growth and reproduction, and many other bodily processes. Proteins can be found in animal products such as meats and eggs as well as in some plants. Proteins found in meats and eggs are called complete proteins because they contain a balanced and complete assortment of amino acids necessary for good health. Many plants, including cereal grains and legumes, contain proteins, but these plant-based proteins are called incomplete proteins because they don't contain all the needed amino acids.

Dogs need 22 amino acids, and they can synthesize 12 of those in their body. The amino acids synthesized within the body are called nonessential amino acids because they don't need to be present in the food the animal eats. The remaining amino acids must be provided by the animal's food, and because of this, they're called essential amino acids. The essentials are arginine, histidine, isoleucine, leucine, lysine, methionine-cystine, phenylalnine-tyrosine, theonine, tryptophan, and valine.

Enzymes are also proteins. These are catalysts involved in many functions within the body, including healing, cell functions, brain functions, and digestion.

Most pet-nutrition experts agree that the best sources of proteins for dogs come from animal sources. Muscle meats, organs, cheeses, yogurt, and eggs are all sources of excellent digestible proteins.

Carbohydrates: Carbohydrates are derived from plants and are found in two forms: simple and complex. Simple carbohydrates are made of simple sugar molecules, and complex carbohydrates are comprised of several sugar molecules joined together in a chain. The body breaks down carbohydrates into glucose, and glucose is used as energy for a variety of bodily functions.

Complex carbohydrates are also dietary fiber. Fiber is needed in the intestinal tract to move foods through and to form stools. Without fiber, your Yorkshire Terrier puppy could easily become constipated.

Your puppy can easily eat and metabolize tubers (carrots, potatoes, sweet potatoes, and yams) as well as greens (green beans, spinach, broccoli, and collard greens) as long as they're chopped into smaller pieces and cooked or steamed. Dogs can also eat some fruits, especially apples, bananas, blueberries, and strawberries.

> **TIPS AND TAILS**

Although simple sugars aren't a necessary part of your Yorkie's daily diet, they can be a lifesaver if your puppy becomes hypoglycemic. Rub some corn syrup on her gums so her saliva dissolves it. This will restore her blood sugar back to acceptable levels.

Fats and fatty acids: Fats are vital for the absorption of fat-soluble vitamins. Fats are also needed for hormone processes, healthy skin and coat, and energy. There are three essential fatty acids: omega-3, omega-6, and arachidonic acid. These are needed for cell structure, development, and function. They also support the immune system and help with the movement of oxygen in the bloodstream. They must be in the correct balance to be of use to your puppy.

Your pet's diet often provides adequate amounts of fats, especially from sources such as meat, fish, poultry fat, avocados, and nuts. Commercial kibble-type foods often add fat to the food—in the recipe or sprayed on after cooking—to enhance the flavor of the food.

Vitamins: Vitamins are organic compounds found in foods that perform essential functions in your Yorkshire Terrier's body. These can range from helping maintain healthy vision to keeping her coat shiny. There are two types of vitamins: fat soluble, which require fats in the diet for metabolism of the vitamin, and water soluble, which use water in the body for vitamin metabolism.

Fat-soluble vitamins are A, D, E, and K. If your puppy consumes excess fat-soluble vitamins, they're stored in her fat cells until they're needed. If she gets too much, these vitamins can create a toxic situation in the body, blood thinning and bleeding, or a variety of other undesirable side effects.

The water-soluble vitamins include the B vitamins and vitamin C. You puppy will excrete the excess water-soluble vitamins in her urine.

Minerals: Minerals are originally from the earth, but a good source for your Yorkshire Terrier is from the meats she eats as well as raw or slightly steamed vegetables.

Calcium is one of the most abundant minerals in the body. Most of it is found in the bones, but it's also necessary for nerve functions and as a co-enzyme for many body functions. You'll find calcium in bones, cheese, seeds, nuts, and dark-green leafy vegetables. Too much calcium can cause constipation, so monitor how much your puppy gets.

Calcium and phosphorus really should be listed as a single mineral because one isn't effective without the other. Together, they are vital for strong bones, for DNA and RNA structure, and for energy. Meats and eggs contain phosphorus.

> **TIPS AND TAILS**
>
> A proper ratio of 1.0 to 2.0 parts calcium to 1.0 part phosphorus is needed to ensure their correct utilization. If the amount of phosphorus far exceeds the amount of dietary calcium, the dog may develop bone abnormalities. Too much calcium with too little phosphorus causes large bone growth but the bones are less dense.

Another important mineral is zinc, which is a co-enzyme for more than 25 different processes during digestion. It also supports the immune system, is important for healthy skin and coat, and aids in healing. Meats and eggs are rich in zinc.

Not all foods contain these nutrients, so be sure you read the label thoroughly to ensure you're feeding your puppy the best food you can.

Dealing with Eating Disorders

Yorkshire Terriers have been known to develop two different eating disorders—*anorexia* and *pica*. These often begin when the puppy starts losing her puppy teeth and her adult teeth grow in.

> **DOG TALK**
>
> **Anorexia** is the lack of an appetite or inability to eat. **Pica** is the practice of eating nonfood items.

In people, anorexia is usually related to a psychological condition regarding weight and appearance. Your Yorkshire Terrier has no concept of her weight or appearance, but anorexia in dogs can still either have a psychological trigger or a medical cause.

Some will stop eating when they're teething because their gums hurt. Although teething is certainly a natural stage of your puppy's life, the pain and discomfort can cause some puppies to avoid eating.

Yorkies can also be quite sensitive to what happens around them, and disruptions in the normal routine can cause your puppy to stop eating. For example, guests in your home can cause a change in the normal household routine. Even though your puppy may enjoy the guests, she may not stop playing with them long enough to eat.

If there haven't been any changes in your puppy's life and she still isn't interested in eating, look for some signs of a health problem, as outlined earlier in this chapter.

If the anorexia has a psychological cause, adding something good-smelling and tasty such as grated cheese or shredded cooked meat to her normal food will usually tempt your Yorkshire Terrier to eat. However, if there's a medical reason for the anorexia—such as liver, kidney, or pancreatic disease—even the good food probably won't tempt her. If you're concerned about the anorexia, don't hesitate to call your veterinarian.

Pica can be quite common in Yorkshire Terrier puppies of this age, especially when they're teething. Many puppies begin chewing on (and swallowing) anything they can get a hold of when they're teething because their gums and jaws hurt. If the pica is actually caused by teething, it will go away when the adult teeth are in. Between now and then, preventing your puppy from chewing on anything inappropriate is the best way to deal with it.

Pica can also have a nutritional cause. Some puppies, especially those who get a less-than-optimal diet or who aren't metabolizing their food well, will have a craving to satisfy that nutritional need. Malnourished puppies will eat dirt, rocks, compost, wood, and other obviously nonfood items. When changed to a better diet or when the food is supplemented with something to aid the puppy's digestion, this disorder often goes away.

Puppies who develop pica because of teething or a nutritional disorder need to be distracted from eating strange things. Swallowed items could cause a blockage in the intestinal tract or perforate intestinal walls. Other items might be toxic.

A verbal interruption can often stop a puppy from grabbing something, but this means you need to closely supervise your pup. Keeping the house and yard puppy-proofed is important, but because puppies eat strange things even the most careful owner can't predict, supervision is still important.

Grooming

Grooming is a fact of life for Yorkies and their owners. Although the Yorkshire Terrier's coat is her glory, it's also a lot of work. Regular grooming is needed to keep her healthy and prevent health problems from happening.

Last month, you began introducing your Yorkie to the very basics of grooming, including a body massage and a pin brush. This month builds on those exercises.

Teaching "Stand on a Table"

It'll be much easier to groom your Yorkie if you teach her to stand on a table. Although you can groom her just about anywhere, even on your lap, the easiest for her, for you, and for your back is to have her stand on a table where your grooming tools are within easy reach.

The table should be tall enough you don't have to stretch or bend to reach her. Yorkies aren't tall, and if you groom her on a standard-height table, you'll probably have to bend over her. It won't take long before your back will be protesting.

Specially designed grooming tables are available. These have nonskid tops so your Yorkie won't slip, and you usually can adjust the table's height according to your needs and your height. Grooming tables also have an arm with a leash attached so you can put a loop of the leash around your Yorkie's neck to help keep her still. This can help your grooming efforts, but the loop can also get in the way when you're combing around your Yorkie's head and neck.

> **TIPS AND TAILS**
>
> Never leash your Yorkie on a table and walk away from her. If your Yorkie tries to jump off the table, she could easily hang herself, potentially break her neck, or suffocate. Always, always stay with her when she's on the table.

Teaching your Yorkie to stand nicely on the table is important—not just for the ease of grooming, but also to help keep her safe. If she's unleashed and jumps off the table, she could severely hurt herself. And if she is leashed, she could also hurt or even kill herself by jumping.

Here's how to teach her to stand nicely:

- 🐾 Have some tiny bits of a good treat in your hand.
- 🐾 Lift your Yorkie to the top of the table, and lightly hold her collar. As she stands still (with your help) tell her, "Sweetie, stand. Good!" and pop a treat in her mouth.

❧ Repeat three or four times and then take her off the table. Come back later, and repeat the exercise.

❧ After a few simple sessions like this, have the pin brush on the table. Ask your Yorkie to stand and run the pin brush through her coat three or four times. Praise her and give her a treat.

❧ Repeat this training step three or four times, stop, and take her off the table.

Over the next couple weeks, gradually increase the time you ask her to stand still on the table. At the same time, increase the combing, too. Always stop before she reaches the end of her patience and begins fighting you. If she begins fighting or struggling, distract her, help her hold still for a few seconds, praise her, and lift her off the table.

> **TIPS AND TAILS**
>
> Don't stop grooming her in the midst of her struggles. If you do, this teaches her that fighting you stops the grooming session. Instead, teach her with praise and treats that cooperating with you is fun.

Gathering Your Grooming Tools

The grooming tools you need to keep your Yorkie looking nice vary depending on your goals for her coat. If you keep her trimmed short (we discuss this more next month) and you have a professional groomer do her haircut, you'll need fewer tools.

Here are the basic tools you'll need now, during puppyhood:

Pin brush: This type of brush has metal teeth topped with a tiny round bead or bit of rubber or plastic. This bead ensures the brush's teeth don't scratch your puppy's skin. This brush is a good tool for introducing grooming.

Bristle brush: You use this brush to smooth the coat after you've brushed or combed it and no tangles remain. It has bristles rather than pins or teeth. The bristles can be nylon or natural hairs, such as from boars.

Rat-tail comb: This plastic comb has teeth on one end and a long narrow handle, or tail. You can use it to work on tangles, but it's most often used to part the Yorkie's hair down the back.

Metal combs: Get a wide-toothed metal comb and another one with the teeth closer together. You'll use the wide-toothed comb first to eliminate tangles, and then the narrower-toothed comb to ensure no tangles remain.

Small comb: You can use a smaller comb, preferably metal, when combing your Yorkie's face. A smaller comb is often easier to use on the face than a larger one, and you need to be careful around your puppy's eyes.

Scissors: You need a pair of scissors with blades 4 to 5 inches long. Don't buy a cheap pair; hair is tough on scissors, so get a nice pair made specifically for cutting hair. You can find them at a beauty-supply store or online.

Round-tipped scissors: If you aren't comfortable grooming your puppy, you might want to buy a pair of round-tipped scissors for trimming close spots such as your puppy's paws. As with regular grooming scissors, get a good pair because cheap scissors will become dull quickly.

Blow dryer: If you have a blow dryer you use on your own hair, you can use it on your Yorkie, too. Opt for the low to warm rather than the hot setting to avoid burning your puppy's skin.

Nail clippers: The scissors-type nail clippers are much easier to use than the guillotine type. Don't get a pair made for cats because they won't be strong enough for your Yorkie's toenails when she grows up.

Shampoo: Get shampoo that's safe for puppies. Many brands are available, so look around, sniff the scents, and choose one that appeals to you.

After-shampoo conditioner: The shampoo you choose may be sold with an accompanying conditioner, and if it is, that's fine. Or you can use the conditioner you use for your hair because it's very similar if not exactly the same as ones made for puppies and older dogs.

Leave-in conditioner: You're going to need a conditioner you can spray on your Yorkie's coat and leave it in. Most conditioners need to be rinsed out, so look for a children's detangler spray conditioner or a leave-in conditioner for dogs.

These supplies are the basics and will get you started. If you decide to leave your Yorkie's coat long, you'll need some additional supplies, but we discuss this in coming months.

Keeping Her Paws Neat

Your puppy's paws are hairy little things that can grab bits of grass, dirt, and other debris and carry it into the house. Hairy paws tend to slip and slide on the floor, too, so keeping your pup's paws trimmed and neat should be a part of your regular grooming regime.

To begin, hold your puppy in your arms or on your lap. Later, when she's used to this, she can stand on the grooming table.

☙ Hold one leg down close to the paw.

☙ Using the round-tipped scissors, trim the hair around the outside of the paw so none of the hair folds under her paw. Ideally, the hair on her paws won't touch the floor when she's standing. Don't make the hair too short, though. Just trim it so it's nice and neat.

☙ Now look at the bottom of her paw. Carefully trim the hair between her pads. If you're worried about accidentally cutting her, here's a trick: Hold the scissors parallel to the bottom of her foot, rather than pointed into the bottom of the foot, and trim the hair that way. Again, trim the hair so none of it folds under her pads.

> **HAPPY PUPPY**

Your puppy's paws are probably ticklish, just like human feet, and if handled lightly, your puppy will try to jerk her paw away. So handle her paws firmly enough so you don't tickle but not so roughly that she protests.

Repeat this process with her other paws. If your puppy begins to protest or gets antsy, do one paw and give her a break. Then bring her back to do another paw. When all four paws are done, play with her and tell her what a wonderful puppy she is.

Trimming Under the Tail

As your Yorkie's coat becomes longer, you'll notice that it can get dirty under the tail as bits of feces stick to the hair. Not only is this dirty for your puppy, but she can then come inside, sit on the furniture or your lap, and spread the dirt around. If you keep the hair under her tail trimmed, you can prevent this.

Many Yorkie owners begin trimming the hair under the tail when their puppy is young to keep things clean right from the beginning. Others wait until the coat starts to get long. You can use either the pointed scissors or the round-tipped scissors.

Here's how to trim under her tail:

☙ Have your puppy stand on the grooming table.

☙ With one hand, hold her body securely under her belly. Or if she's clamping her tail tightly to her hips, lift her tail and hold that.

☙ Hold the scissors sideways to her anal region (rather than pointed toward her). Carefully trim the hair around her anus.

How much you trim depends on you and your puppy. If you're having a hard time keeping her clean and her coat tends to catch a lot of feces, you might want to trim a larger area. Just keep in mind that if you trim too much, she's going to look very funny. Hair does grow back, though, so even the worst haircut in the world will eventually disappear.

Start Cleaning Her Teeth Now

This month is a good time to introduce your Yorkie puppy to easy dental care. She's going to start losing her puppy teeth soon—usually sometime this month—and her adult teeth will be growing in. She's going to need ongoing dental care all her life, so introducing it now and making it a pleasant experience will pay off. (See Month 7 for more about caring for her adult teeth.)

- 🐾 Start by making a paste of a tiny bit (¼ teaspoon) of baking soda and a little water. Ideally, the paste should be a consistency similar to toothpaste.
- 🐾 Wrap a piece of gauze around your index finger, and dip it in the paste.
- 🐾 With your puppy on your lap, gently touch her teeth with your finger. Rub very softly.
- 🐾 After about 30 seconds, release your puppy, praise her, and offer her a drink of water.

At this point, don't worry about actually cleaning the teeth or rubbing each individual tooth. Instead, for now, you're just teaching her that this process isn't evil and won't hurt her.

As she gets used to you touching her teeth, you can begin touching each tooth, both the outside and the inside. Again, don't worry too much about actually cleaning it; just touch it and move your gauze-covered finger on the tooth. Later still, maybe in a couple weeks, you can begin rubbing each tooth so you actually clean it.

> ### TIPS AND TAILS
>
> When you see that your Yorkie's puppy teeth are falling out, stop this brushing process for a few weeks. Her gums are going to be sore, and she's apt to be grumpy. Doing too much with her mouth now could make her hate having her teeth worked on.

Social Skills

The fourth month of your Yorkie's life is an important one for socialization. This is the time to get her out of the house and introduce her to the world she lives in. This socialization can help your puppy deal with everything she faces from puppyhood through old age. Without socialization, she could become fearful and timid, or fearful and potentially aggressive. Neither scenario is a good life for your Yorkie. Socialize now, when it can make a difference.

"Would You Like to Meet My Yorkie?"

Introduce your Yorkie to people of all ages, sizes, shapes, and ethnic backgrounds. If she only meets a few people, perhaps people just like you, she's not going to be able to generalize that all people are nice and friendly. Puppies who never meet young children, for example, may potentially think young kids are creatures from another planet.

Here are some of the people your puppy should meet:

🐾 Babies, including babies held in an adult's arms and babies in strollers

🐾 Toddlers and young children

🐾 Short people, tall people, thin people, heavy people, people in casual clothes, and people all dressed up

🐾 People wearing flip-flops, women in heels, and people in boots

🐾 People wearing ball caps, people wearing cowboy hats, and people with no hats and no hair

🐾 People from ethnic backgrounds different from your own

It's not going to be hard to introduce your puppy to people; just go to places where you'll find people. Walking around with a Yorkie puppy will draw people to you. Have a few tiny bits of dog treats in your pocket, and let one person at a time greet your puppy and give her a treat.

> ### TIPS AND TAILS
>
> Don't let people overwhelm your puppy. Let one person at a time pet her, and don't let anyone get rough. If things get out of hand, grab your puppy and walk away. Don't worry about being rude; it's your job to protect your puppy.

When you want to introduce someone to your puppy, ask the person, "Would you like to meet my Yorkie?" Not only will this give the person a chance to say yes or no, but your puppy will learn this is an introduction. She'll learn to recognize that phrase.

Then you can either kneel or bend over, to prevent your Yorkie from jumping on the person, or pick up your Yorkie. Your puppy can greet people when on the ground or in your arms. Try to have both happen so your puppy gains confidence in both positions. Many Yorkie owners (as well as the owners of other small breeds) have their puppy in their arms so much that the puppy doesn't know how to behave when on her own four paws. (We talk more about this later this month.)

Maintain control of the introduction. Be sure no one gets too rough, and don't do anything you're uncomfortable with. Most dogs dislike having their head grabbed, fingers wiggled in their face, and other rough or disrespectful treatment. If anything like that happens, don't hesitate to move your Yorkie away.

Introducing Puppies and Dogs

Yorkshire Terriers are very small dogs, but they're still dogs. That means your Yorkie puppy needs to socialize with other dogs. This helps her learn how to get along, understand how to communicate, and pick up other social skills that will be important in your puppy's future relations with dogs and people.

Obviously, though, you have to be careful when choosing who your puppy plays with. The other puppy doesn't have to also be a tiny puppy, although two small puppies playing together is certainly easier and there's less chance of a puppy getting hurt.

Many larger puppies can still be gentle and be a good playmate for a Yorkie puppy. At a recent puppy-class play session, a Great Pyrenees puppy was playing with a Papillon puppy and doing so quite nicely. The Great Pyrenees was lying on the ground, and the Papillon was bouncing all over him. The big puppy would open his mouth and hold it open while the Papillon stuck her head in it. He was being very gentle and kind so both puppies were having a blast.

When choosing playmates for your Yorkie, ask some questions:

🐾 Are the puppies or dogs up to date on vaccinations and healthy?

🐾 Are they well socialized with other dogs and puppies?

🐾 Have they played with other small dogs and puppies, and are they known to be gentle?

When possible, choose playmates of other breeds, not just other Yorkies. Your puppy needs to know dogs come in all shapes and sizes.

When the puppies are playing, supervise them but try not to hover. If your puppy senses your anxiety, she may well react to it and stand on your feet or try to climb up into your arms. Instead, walk around, talk to the other puppies' owners, and watch the play. If the play gets too rough, pull out the puppy who has become the bully and let the others continue playing.

> **TIPS AND TAILS**
>
> Teach your Yorkie to walk up to other puppies and dogs nicely without barking and lunging. In canine language, that's considered rude, and many adult dogs may bark or growl at her and her bad manners. If she's pulling, turn and walk the other direction. When she's calm, she can greet friendly dogs.

Socializing with other puppies and dogs is important, but it doesn't mean your Yorkie needs to greet *every* dog she sees. Instead, good socialization means she can handle herself around a variety of dogs in different situations. Sometimes she needs to walk past a dog without greeting him or sit and stay while a dog walks past. This requires training and practice.

Meeting Other Pets

The Yorkshire Terrier is classified by the American Kennel Club and other registries as a toy-breed dog, but historically (and by name) this breed is a terrier. You've probably already noticed your puppy likes to chase moving things, whether a cat or a cat toy on the end of a fishing pole.

Your tiny Yorkie, with a bow in her hair, may be adorable, but given the chance, she is also a mighty (albeit small) hunter. She can be taught to ignore the cat, but the cat is also well armed and able to defend himself. Don't allow the two to get into skirmishes. The cat could hurt the puppy as much as the puppy could hurt the cat.

> **TIPS AND TAILS**
>
> If you have a cat in the house, be sure the cat has some safe places where the Yorkie cannot go, such as on top of furniture or another room blocked off with a baby gate. When necessary, use the leash to keep your Yorkie from chasing your cat.

Never trust your Yorkie with other small pets such as mice, rats, gerbils, ferrets, or rabbits. Reptile pets aren't safe, either, as many Yorkies enjoy chasing any small critter in the yard or garden.

As your Yorkie grows up and you both practice obedience skills, she can be taught to ignore these pets. However, the hunting instinct can override training, so these pets need to be kept in an area your puppy cannot have access to.

Finding New Things

Your biggest challenge for socialization this month is to find new things to introduce to your puppy. Choose items that sound, smell, or look different or new. Pay attention to textures, too, so your puppy can walk on different surfaces.

Be sure your Yorkie sees the following:

🐾 Billowing skirts, floppy hats, or raincoats blowing in the wind

🐾 Flapping sheets or open plastic bags

🐾 Balloons and kites

🐾 Brooms, mops, rakes, and shovels

🐾 Things out of place, such as a lawn chair upside down in the living room or the laundry hamper on its side in the driveway

Let your puppy hear the following:

🐾 A leaf blower running outside

🐾 Household appliances in use

🐾 Loud kids playing

🐾 Music of different genres at different volumes

🐾 Loud cars, trucks, and motorcycles

Search out new smells, too:

🐾 Walk past different restaurants that serve a variety of foods, including fish and various ethnic foods.

🐾 Walk by a full trash dumpster on a hot day.

🐾 Hike past a pasture with livestock.

Don't forget new surfaces such as the following:

🐾 Slippery floors

🐾 Gravel and sand

🐾 Dirt and grass

🐾 Paving stones, cobbles, and bricks

Try to introduce your Yorkie to one new thing each day this month. That's 30 new sights, smells, and surfaces. That really isn't hard but will go a long way toward teaching your puppy how to deal with new experiences. That skill will serve her well all her life.

Make the introductions fun. Don't drag your puppy up to the new thing; instead, talk to her as she looks at or sniffs the new item. Reach out and touch it yourself if you can. When your puppy is ready to investigate it, praise her.

Behavior

When your Yorkie begins teething, you may see some changes in her behavior. She may be sociable one moment and worried the next. You may wonder about your puppy because her moods change so often, but don't worry because this is normal right now.

A Yorkie this age is more aware of her world and everything in it and is alternately a silly puppy and a watchful Yorkie. She wants to play yet is discovering that the world also contains things that concern her. Plus, as she's teething, her jaws and gums hurt. All this creates some unsettled moods.

Surviving Teething

As mentioned earlier this month, your Yorkie will begin losing her puppy teeth sometime this month. When she does, she may be grumpy, irritable, and unhappy because her gums are sore and her jaws hurt.

She'll try to chew anything she can fit in her mouth, including your hands, feet, shoes, remote controls, and cell phone. She may be more defiant than you've seen her before, and she may throw a temper tantrum when things don't go her way. You may look at her in disbelief and ask yourself why you got a puppy when you could have gotten a kitten instead. Don't worry. As the saying goes, "This, too, shall pass."

To survive teething, be sure your house remains puppy-proofed. Be sure everything is put away, nothing is within her reach, and baby gates block off areas you want to keep her out of.

Keep toys within easy reach of your puppy. Hand her a toy and praise her when she takes it from you. Rather than yelling at her when she picks up something she shouldn't, praise her for making a good choice. Don't be angry or impatient with your puppy during the teething stage. She's not being bad on purpose. Remember, she doesn't feel well. So help her through this stage as much as you can, and keep telling yourself it, too, will pass.

Understanding the Yorkie Personality

Yorkshire Terriers are adorable dogs. That lovely coat, the bow on the topknot, and the unique coloring all make for a cute little companion. Yorkies are much more than just their appearance, however. Many Yorkie owners get their first Yorkie because of the breed's appearance but add a second, third, or subsequent Yorkie to the family because living with these little dogs is so much fun.

Some of the most-often-seen Yorkshire Terrier personality traits include the following:

Bold: Yorkies are courageous and bold—sometimes to the point of getting into situations they shouldn't be in. Many a Yorkie has chased a cat only to have the cat back the little dog into a corner. Although her courage is admirable at times, protect your puppy from herself. Don't let her get into situations where she could get hurt.

Bright: Yorkies are bright and intelligent. They can be great problem-solvers when they're motivated to work at the problem.

Independent: Your Yorkie may be quite smart, but she might not always be willing to follow your rules. It's your job to make the training fun so your puppy *wants* to cooperate with you.

Affectionate: Yorkies love to cuddle—when they're not playing—and they're loyal and dedicated to their family.

Standoffish: Although they're very affectionate with their family, Yorkies are often aloof and reserved with strangers.

Stubborn: A Yorkie chasing a lizard in the backyard shows all the traits of her working-terrier ancestry. She is determined, persistent, and yes, stubborn in the pursuit of that lizard.

Although these are breed traits often seen in Yorkshire Terriers, your Yorkie is not every other Yorkie. What her personality is when she grows up will be determined by her genetics (nature) and her experiences during puppyhood and with you (nurture). She will share characteristics with all other Yorkies, but she will grow up to be a unique individual.

Unhappy Alone

With her unsettled moods of this age, you may find your Yorkie is unhappy when left alone. She may whine, pace, or tear up the towel left in her crate. When you leave the house, you may hear her barking.

It's important that she can stay at home without you and be warm, safe, and secure. If she frets, worries, paces, and barks when left at home, neither you, your dog, nor your neighbors will be happy.

Here are some suggestions for helping your puppy feel better when home alone:

🐾 Take her for a walk or play with her before leaving her alone. A tired puppy is more apt to nap.

🐾 Give her a chance to relieve herself before you leave.

🐾 Leave her in her crate and give her a food-dispensing toy with a snack inside. This will keep her busy, keep her mind otherwise occupied, and keep her blood sugar up.

Leave her in her crate like this for half an hour when you're home so she can hear you moving around the house even if she can't see you or isn't in the same room with you. If done on a regular basis, she should get used to being alone in her crate, whether you're home or not, and it won't be as stressful for her when you're not home.

> **HAPPY PUPPY**

Help your Yorkie be comfortable in her crate by giving her a stuffed toy or a shirt or pillowcase that smells like you. Leave the radio or television on when you leave to provide some background noise, too.

If your puppy barks, whines, or howls, don't let her out of her crate. Let her out only when she's calm and quiet. Be matter of fact and calm yourself. If you're excited or feel guilty and apologize to your puppy, she's going to think being in the crate is a problem. Instead, be calm and smile.

As soon as you open the crate door, take your puppy outside. Tell her to relieve herself, and praise her when she does.

Barking Barking Barking Barking Barking

Yorkshire Terriers can be barkers. In fact, barking is one of the most common complaints about this breed. Even though Yorkies are small, they have a big bark and can be quite persistent with it.

You'll never stop all the barking, and you don't want to do that anyway. Your Yorkie should be able to bark a certain amount during play and when someone comes to your house. After all, dogs communicate by barking just as humans speak.

You do want to be sure the barking doesn't turn into a bad habit, and it's nice to be able to ask your Yorkie to stop barking when you've heard enough.

🐾 Don't yell or scream at your barking Yorkie. If you raise your voice, your puppy will think you're barking, too.

🐾 Use something else to distract her from the barking. Drop a book to the floor or slam a cupboard door.

🐾 When your puppy stops barking to turn and see what that was, praise her, "Good to be quiet! Yeah!" Emphasize the word *quiet*.

Barking is instinctive to most dogs but more so in some breeds, and Yorkies are instinctive barkers. So you must be consistent. Interrupt her barking, praise her for stopping when you ask her to stop, and be consistent with your training.

Sleeping Through the Night

As you've learned the last few weeks, your Yorkie has a tiny bladder. She needs to go outside to relieve herself often during the day and, up to now, once or twice during the night. However, by now—or very soon—you'll notice that your puppy will be able to sleep through the night without needing to make a trip outside.

If your puppy hasn't yet reached this point, you can help her. First of all, be sure she eats dinner and has some water early enough in the evening so she has a couple chances to go outside and relieve herself before bedtime. Aim for feeding her dinner by 7 P.M.

After she eats, take her outside. Let her dinner settle for an hour and then have a play session with her. Let her run and play and use up some energy. Then take her outside again.

Now it's time to relax. Pet her, give her a massage, and comb her if you want, but keep everything calm and quiet. Take her outside one more time just before you both go to bed.

> ### TIPS AND TAILS
>
> If your Yorkie is having a hard time holding her urine all night and you've seen some changes in her housetraining habits, don't hesitate to have her checked by her veterinarian for a urinary tract infection (UTI). UTIs are more common in puppies than adults, but in general, it's not a problem for the breed.

Four Paws on the Floor

When you share your life with a tiny puppy, it's easy to get in the habit of carrying her everywhere. After all, being tiny, she's vulnerable. In the house, if she dashes around your feet as you're walking, you could easily kick her or step on her. When out on a walk, kids could step on her or frighten her, and other dogs are just so much bigger. Picking her up seems like a good solution.

Well, it is but it isn't. Picking her up can temporarily keep her safe from being stepped on or accidentally kicked. Having her in your arms can also protect her from rowdy kids or other dogs.

But having her in your arms too much can also lead to problems. For example, she won't learn how to avoid people's feet to keep herself safe. If she's constantly picked up when she circles feet, she'll continue to circle. After all, being picked up becomes rewarding because she likes it.

She also won't learn how to walk on a leash when distracting things occur. If she's picked up when anything happens—kids on skateboards come close, for example— she won't learn how to deal with distracting circumstances. She won't learn how to greet well-behaved children or ignore kids going by on skateboards.

And she'll never learn how to greet friendly dogs while out on a walk. If she's picked up each time the two of you come upon another dog, she won't learn canine social skills. She may assume that because she's being picked up (saved) it must mean other dogs are a problem, and, she will begin barking at them from the safety of your arms. She also won't learn that she doesn't need to greet (or bark at) all dogs encountered on a walk.

Being carried all the time—or even for a great deal of time—gets uncomfortable. Many Yorkies who are carried a lot get restless and squirm—a sign the dog is uncomfortable.

In addition, the more she walks on all four paws, the more exercise she gets, and that's a good thing for an active terrier puppy. Your Yorkie is very small and can be fragile and vulnerable, but she's still a dog. Protect her when she needs protecting, but at other times, let her be a dog with all four paws on the floor.

> ### TIPS AND TAILS

Many celebrities use tiny dogs—including Yorkies—as fashion accessories. Dog owners need to remember that these celebrities are not experts on dogs and shouldn't be emulated.

Training

Your Yorkie puppy's brain is ready to learn right now. In fact, she's at the best age to introduce training. If you wait, she's apt to develop bad habits that will be harder to change later. So don't procrastinate.

Keep the training fun for both you and your puppy. After all, if it's fun, you'll be more apt to do it. And if it's fun for your puppy, she'll be more likely to cooperate.

Working Through Housetraining Problems

The first goal of housetraining your Yorkie is to teach her where you want her to relieve herself. If you want her to go in a doggy litter box in the house, that's fine. If you prefer she go outside, that's good, too. Just choose a spot.

Some dog owners prefer that their dog relieve herself in one specific area in the backyard, such as a back corner, rather than anywhere and everywhere. This is especially nice if there are people in the family who also make use of the backyard.

It's also nice when your puppy will try to relieve herself when you ask her to do so, such as before you bring her inside or when you're traveling. When you stop for gas, you could take her for a walk and ask her to go.

No matter where you want your puppy to relieve herself, just keep these goals in mind as you train your Yorkie puppy and work through any problems.

Accidents in the crate: Be sure she isn't spending too much time in the crate. She can spend the night in the crate and some time here and there throughout the day. But she cannot spend all day and all night in it. She needs to get out, move around, exercise, play, and spend time with you.

Dislikes the crate: If your Yorkie puppy doesn't like to go in the crate, be sure something positive happens each time you put her in it. Give her a food-dispensing toy, such a Kong with treats inside it when you put her in.

Punishment: Don't use the crate to punish your puppy. Don't put her in the crate and then stand there and yell at her. Remember, your puppy's crate should be a place of security and safety.

> ### TIPS AND TAILS
>
> If your puppy is overstimulated, you can put her in the crate as a timeout so she can calm down. But don't yell at her or punish her as you do so. Just be calm and quiet and put her in the crate.

Doesn't go on command: If your puppy doesn't understand your command for her to relieve herself, don't worry. She'll catch on. Just continue taking her outside, and when she begins to go, quietly say the command. When she's done, tell her what a good dog she is—"Good to go potty!"—using whatever word or phrase you decide to use.

Having accidents: Preventing accidents from happening is a huge part of house-training your puppy. After all, every time she relieves herself inside the house, she learns she can. Yelling and screaming after she has already done it isn't going to change future behavior. So limit your puppy's freedom as she's learning housetraining. Keep her very close to you so you can see when she needs to go outside. Then maintain a schedule of feeding, play, and naps so you can let her out regularly.

Housetraining takes patience. Your puppy will get it, but all puppies develop at their own pace. Just stick to your routine and schedule, teach your puppy what you want her to do, and praise her when she does it.

Using the Leash Inside

You've already discovered that your tiny puppy is very fast. If she wants to run away from you, she can. It's tough to catch a tiny dog who doesn't want to be caught.

Unfortunately, running from you is bad behavior, and you don't want this to turn into a bad habit. It's hard to live with a puppy who runs from you, plus it's annoying, and it's dangerous for her safety. So use the leash in the house. When you're moving around the house, perhaps tidying up, putting away the laundry, or checking on the kids, have your puppy walk with you. This way she's not dashing away, you're teaching her to stay close, and you can ensure she's not getting into trouble. You can hold the leash during these times or let her drag it, depending on how apt she is to dash away from you!

If she's in a room with you, with the door closed or baby gates across the doorway, let her drag her leash. If she tries to dash, the doorway is blocked and you can step on the leash to stop her.

> **TIPS AND TAILS**
>
> Never leave the leash on your Yorkie puppy when she's unsupervised. It's too easy for it to become tangled, and she could choke. The leash is a training tool to be used only when you are there to supervise.

When you call your puppy and she comes to you, or when you ask her to do something and she responds, praise her. If she's dragging the leash and has no choice but to respond, that's okay, praise her anyway. Remember, you're teaching her behaviors you want her to do for the rest of her life, so praise her.

Using the Leash Outside

Your Yorkie puppy has become your shadow, and she's following you all over the house, from room to room. She doesn't like to be left behind. So does that mean she'll do the same thing outside? Maybe for a few minutes, but as soon as anything interesting pops up, your puppy will get distracted.

Many Yorkie puppy owners develop a false sense of security when they discover they have a small Yorkie shadow. They think their puppy will follow them anywhere, anytime, no matter what, and they mistakenly let their puppy run free, off leash, when they're outside the fenced-in yard.

While your puppy may follow you, far too many times something distracting or exciting will distract her, and she'll be off like a flash to investigate. That could mean she dashes across a busy street. Or she could be off after a cat or a squirrel and ignore you when you call her to come.

As with so many aspects of puppy training, every time your puppy ignores you, she learns she can. So if your puppy dashes away and ignores your repeated calls to come, she learns she doesn't *have* to respond. This makes teaching the "Come" much more difficult.

Instead, keep your Yorkie puppy on leash whenever you're outside a fenced-in yard. She can still investigate a squirrel or a gopher hole; you'll just be holding the other end of the leash.

Most Yorkies are not mentally grown until they're about 2 years old, so definitely keep your puppy on leash until she's at least that age. And even at that age, before you give her too much freedom, she should be well trained and be able to demonstrate she'll come when you call her, every time you call, no matter what the distractions.

Teaching "Sit"

The "*Sit*" is the first obedience exercise to teach your Yorkie puppy because it helps her learn self-control. After all, if she's sitting while being she's petted, she's not jumping up and scratching your legs. If she's sitting while you fix her food, she's not underfoot. Self-control is a good skill for all Yorkie puppies to learn.

> **DOG TALK**
>
> "**Sit**" is the command that means "Lower your hips, keep your front elevated with your front legs straight, and hold still until I release you."

Here's how to teach the "Sit":

🐾 Put your puppy on her leash so she can't run away from the lesson.

🐾 With your left hand, hold the leash close to her collar.

🐾 Have a treat in your right hand, and let her smell it.

🐾 Move your hand with the treat up from her nose and slightly back over her head. As her head comes up, her hips will move downward. Tell her, "Sweetie, sit."

🐾 As her hips touch the ground, tell her, "Sweetie, good to sit!" Then give her the treat.

As she eats the treat, pet her and help her remain in the sitting position. After a few seconds, tell her, "Sweetie, *release*," and walk her forward a few steps.

> ### DOG TALK
>
> "**Release**" is the command that means "This is the end of this exercise for the moment."

After you've practiced the sit several times a day for a few days, begin saying "Sit" as you begin to move the treat from her nose rather than waiting until her hips hit the ground. Later still, after a lot of practice, you'll be able to simply say, "Sweetie, sit," and you won't need a treat. But that's months from now.

Collar Touch

Far too many puppies learn to play keepaway when someone tries to touch their collar. Perhaps they learn that a person grabbing their collar means they're going to their crate or that punishment will follow. That's a bad habit, though, and potentially dangerous. After all, you need to be able to hold your puppy's collar in many different situations. So it's important to teach your puppy that touching her collar is good. Here's how:

🐾 Have the leash attached to your puppy's collar so she doesn't dash away. Have some good treats in one hand.

🐾 Let your puppy sniff the treats, say her name in a happy tone of voice, and touch her collar. Jiggle it, and as you do, pop a treat in her mouth.

🐾 Repeat this several times, take a break and play with your puppy, and repeat the exercise.

Do this often. You can do it during every training session, during walks, or even when you're playing with your puppy. Let her know that when you touch her collar, good things happen.

Teaching "Stay"

Right now, you can teach your Yorkie puppy to stay while in the sit position, but eventually, she can do the stay while sitting, in a down position, or even while in a standing position.

Here's how to teach the "*Stay*":

> **DOG TALK**

"**Stay**" is the command that means "Hold still, in this position, until I release you."

🐾 Put the leash on your puppy so you can help her hold still.

🐾 Ask your puppy to sit, and praise her.

🐾 Hold the leash close to her collar with your left hand and then with your right hand, palm toward your puppy's nose, move it up and down a few inches as if building an invisible wall. At the same time tell your puppy, "Sweetie, stay."

🐾 If your puppy pops up or lies down, tell her, "No. Sit. Stay." Help her do it.

🐾 After just a few seconds, praise her, pet her, and release her.

Over the next few weeks and months, gradually increase the time you ask her to sit and stay. Begin by asking her to hold still for just 5 seconds, then 10 seconds, and then 20. If your puppy begins making a lot of mistakes, you may be pushing her too hard. Ease back on the time you're asking her to stay and try again.

Also, over time, you can begin taking a step or two or three away from her. But just as with the time, if she makes mistakes, you're probably moving too far away too quickly. Don't rush; you have lots of time to teach her this.

Teaching "Watch Me"

At this age, your puppy will be distracted by just about everything in her world. Birds, butterflies, and even ants are fascinating to her. You can't teach her if she isn't paying attention to you, so you need to help her pay attention.

Teaching her to look at you when you tell her, "Sweetie, *watch me,*" helps teach her focus. Plus, because you're going to be sure she likes the rewards for this exercise, paying attention to you will be fun.

> **DOG TALK**
>
> **"Watch me"** is the command that means "Ignore all distractions and look at my face," preferably making eye contact.

Find a few really good treats that have a good smell that your Yorkie puppy really likes and normally doesn't get—such as Swiss cheese. The treats have to be special.

- With your puppy on leash, ask her to sit facing you.
- Hold the leash in your left hand and have a treat in your right hand.
- Let your puppy smell the treat in your hand and then move the treat toward your chin as you tell her, "Sweetie, watch me."
- If she jumps up to get the treat, have her sit again and this time use your left hand to hold her collar. Then repeat the verbal command and hand motion.
- As soon as her eyes move to your face, praise her, "Good to watch me! Yeah!" and pop the treat in her mouth.

Repeat three or four times and then play with your puppy for a few minutes. Then repeat the exercise.

As your puppy gets better at this, challenge her a little. Take a step to the left and then to the right while asking her to watch you. Then back up a few steps, encouraging her to follow you while watching you. Praise her as she watches you.

Learning the First "Come" Technique

"Come" is one of the most important obedience exercises your Yorkie can learn. A reliable response to the come helps make life easier because your puppy will come when called rather than you having to chase her down.

"**Come**" is the command that means "Look for me and proceed directly to me, quickly, without stopping, no matter what the distractions might be."

The "Come" also has the potential of saving her life. If she's heading into danger—toward a street where cars are, for example—being able to call her back to you is vital.

Because come is so important, there are many ways to teach it. The first technique is easy for puppies to learn and understand. In the next section, we explain a second technique.

The first technique uses a sound stimulus to make the come exciting. Many trainers use a clicker that makes a sharp clicking sound. When paired with treats, the clicker marks or identifies the behavior you want your puppy to repeat in the future. Other trainers use whistles because it can be heard over a longer distance.

Here, we suggest using a small shaker that contains some dry dog-food kibble to mark good behavior. Most puppies already know the sound is equated with food, so they'll respond to it.

🐾 Have your puppy on leash and have some really good treats (not the dry kibble—that's just for noise) in your other hand.

🐾 Make a noise with the shaker, and immediately give your puppy a treat. Don't say anything at this point; you want her to associate the sound with a really good treat.

🐾 Do this three or four times, take a break and play with your puppy, and repeat the exercise.

🐾 After 2 or 3 days, add the word "Come." Again with your puppy on leash and close to you, shake the noisemaker, say, "Sweetie, come," in a happy tone of voice, and pop a treat into her mouth.

Up to this point, your puppy isn't really coming to you—after all, she's with you on leash. But you are teaching her first that the sound equals a treat and then that the happy word "Come" and the shaker mean a treat, too. These are both important first training steps.

❧ After several days of practicing this, you can move on to the next step. Keep your puppy on leash, but let her get distracted. Shake the noisemaker, tell your puppy, "Sweetie, come!" and back away from her for several steps so she has to follow you. If she dashes toward you, praise her enthusiastically and give her a treat.

❧ If the distraction keeps her attention, use the leash to move her toward you. Then back up several steps and praise her for following you.

As your puppy learns this exercise, keep her on leash and vary the distractions. Practice with the family cat in the same room or while the kids are playing. But always keep the exercise fun and rewarding for your puppy.

And don't be in a hurry to stop using the noisemaker. Remember, you want these obedience exercises to become new habits, and that takes time. So over the next few months, keep repeating this exercise, varying the treats and the distractions.

Teaching the Second "Come" Technique

When your Yorkie puppy understands the first come technique, after a couple weeks of training, you can add this second technique. For this technique, you need the noisemaker, some good treats, and a longer lightweight leash. A 20-foot-long leash is great but a 30-foot leash is even better.

This technique teaches your Yorkie puppy that even when she's bold and wants to investigate things at a distance from you, she still needs to come when she's called.

❧ Attach the long leash to your puppy's collar. Have the shaker and a few treats in your other hand.

❧ Walk around your yard and let your puppy get distracted. Hold on to the leash but don't say anything to her or even pay attention to her. You want her to be distracted.

❧ When she's distracted, back away from her, shake the noisemaker, and call her to come. Praise her and pop a treat in her mouth when she comes right away.

❧ If she doesn't come immediately, don't stand there and repeat the command. You want your puppy to respond right away instead of taking her time, so back away from her and tug on the leash to be sure she comes directly to you. Then praise her for coming.

Never scold your puppy for not coming to you. She might easily misunderstand and think coming to you is bad. So let the leash enforce your command and keep your voice, your facial expression—smile!—and your posture happy.

Teaching "No Pull"

Puppies like to pull. They're always in a hurry to see and smell new things, and people just walk too slowly.

Unfortunately, when puppies pull, they can hurt their neck, shoulders, and joints. Yorkies who pull can develop throat problems, including but not limited to a collapsed trachea. Using different collars, harnesses, and no-pull equipment isn't the answer because as soon as your puppy isn't wearing that equipment, she'll go back to pulling.

Instead, your puppy needs to learn to walk nicely on the leash without pulling. Luckily, this isn't hard to teach.

- ☙ Put the leash on your puppy and have some treats in your pocket.
- ☙ Without saying a word to your puppy, simply begin walking forward.
- ☙ If she dashes ahead and begins pulling, simply turn around and walk the other direction.
- ☙ When she catches up with you, praise her, "Hey, look at you!" and give her a treat.

Each and every time she pulls, repeat the exercise. When she decides to walk with you, praise her enthusiastically and give her a treat.

The key to this exercise is consistency. If you practice this exercise sometimes but let her pull at other times, her behavior won't be consistent, either. Yorkies are smart dogs; she can learn to walk without pulling.

Enrolling in Puppy Class

The beginning of this month is a great time for your puppy to enroll in a puppy-training class. Most trainers require puppies to have two distemper/parvo combination vaccinations prior to starting the class, and by 13 or 14 weeks of age, most puppies have had those shots.

Most puppy classes combine training, socialization to other people, and socialization to other puppies in their curriculum. The class is also good for you because you can talk to other puppy owners. It can be a relief to find out your puppy isn't the only one trying to chew up everything in the house or having some housetraining problems. It's good group therapy.

Most puppy classes include the following:

- 🐾 Introduction to the basic obedience skills: sit, down, stay, come, and walk on a leash without pulling.

- 🐾 Problem-prevention tips for common puppy issues such as jumping on people and biting with those needle-sharp puppy teeth.

- 🐾 A chance for your puppy to meet and be petted by other people, including the trainers in the class and other puppy owners.

- 🐾 Most puppy classes also let the puppies have a play session so they can run, chase, and interact with other puppies in the class.

If you've already selected a trainer to work with, contact him and ask when he's starting a puppy class. If you don't yet have a trainer, call your veterinarian and find out who he recommends.

You and Your Puppy

Yorkshire Terrier puppies are playful little things. Anything can be turned into a game, and that includes pouncing on your wiggling toes or chasing the family cat. This playfulness makes having a Yorkie a great deal of fun. You'll laugh until you cry while watching your energetic little puppy.

With everything that's going on right now—housetraining, obedience training, and socialization—be sure you take time to play with your puppy. Not only is this great fun for both of you, but it helps build your relationship with your puppy. Through play, your puppy learns to trust you and that spending time with you is fun.

If your puppy begins biting during play, say, "Ouch!" in a high-pitched tone of voice and get up and walk away. The game stops when she bites. If she chases after you, biting at your feet, pick her up and give her a time-out in her crate.

You can also use play sessions to make your training more exciting. Intersperse play sessions in between training exercises. This helps keep your puppy's attention on you and the training, too.

It really doesn't matter what you do to have fun with your puppy as long as it's enjoyable for both of you, isn't frightening your puppy, and isn't teaching your puppy to fight you. Retrieving games are fun, as is hide and seek. Just enjoy your Yorkie's puppyhood. It'll be over before you know it.

Month 4	Month 5	Month 6
	Socialization in public	
	Teething begins—heavy chewing period	
	Ready for basic commands	
	Rapid growth	
	3rd DHPP vaccines	
	Switch to a food for all life stages	

Month 5 encompasses weeks 17 through 20 of your Yorkshire Terrier's life. So many changes take place this month, both physically and mentally. Teething continues, and his puppy coat is giving way as his adult coat grows in. His appearance is gradually looking more adult.

Your puppy is curious and interested in everything right now. He's more independent and yet at times is quite cautious about things he doesn't understand. That's normal at this age.

Grooming

During the last couple months, you've been introducing your puppy to the basic grooming skills. By letting your puppy get used to these things slowly and with lots of massage, praise, and a few treats, grooming becomes a pleasurable activity rather than something to be detested. This is very important because grooming is a fact of life for a Yorkie.

Continue to massage your puppy on a regular basis, and do it daily if you can. Not only does this give you a chance to get to know your puppy's body (we discuss this more in the "Health" section later in this chapter), but you can also catch any grooming problems.

Your Yorkie's Coat

The Yorkshire Terrier is known for several characteristics, including the breed's tiny size, their big-dog attitude, and of course, their glorious coat. The Yorkie *breed standard* says the quality, texture, and quantity of coat are of prime importance.

> **DOG TALK**

The **breed standard** is a written description that describes a breed's perfect dog.

Yorkie puppies are born black and tan with a short, and often fuzzy, coat. The coat colors are not clear during early puppyhood, and black hairs may be mixed in with the tan. As the puppy grows up, the colors become clearer and more defined with less mixing. When he's an adult, there should be no mixing of the colors at all.

An adult Yorkie's coat should be dark steel-blue from the back of the neck to the base of the tail. The tail is a darker blue. The head is covered in golden-tan hair, as are the legs.

On adults, the hair on the top of the head often is gathered into a topknot. The hair on the body is parted from the back of his head to the base of his tail. The coat continues to grow and will reach the floor and still continue to grow. The coat is shiny, glossy, and truly glorious.

Caring for a Long Coat

It takes 2 or 3 years for a Yorkie to fully grow out a floor-length coat. If you plan on showing your Yorkie in dog shows, he'll need that coat. If you don't plan on competing in conformation dog shows but you love the look of the long coat, you can certainly let it grow out, but it does take some special care.

A long, silky coat attracts debris, whether it's bits of dried grass or burrs and foxtails from outside. The coat will also pick up dust and dirt from the floor. You'll have to comb a long-coated Yorkie each and every day to remove the dirt and debris. Otherwise, the coat tangles and matts will form. Debris can also cause individual hairs to break.

> **TIPS AND TAILS**

Dogs who compete in conformation dog shows have their hair wrapped up between shows to protect it. The coat is divided into small sections, folded into wax paper, and secured with rubber bands to protect it from dirt, debris, and breakage. Ask your puppy's breeder to show you how to do this.

To comb a long coat, you need a pin brush, metal comb, and spray bottle. Mix together some conditioner (yours or some made specifically for long-coated dogs) in a ratio of ¼ conditioner and ¾ water in the spray bottle.

Here's how to care for your Yorkie's coat:

- 🐾 Place your puppy on the grooming table. Have him stand on a towel to catch the excess conditioner spray.

- 🐾 Dampen one section of his coat—one shoulder, for example—with the spray.

- 🐾 Lift that section of the coat in your hand, and with the pin brush, begin brushing the underneath section first, from his body to the ends of the coat. Follow up with a metal comb to finish the section.

- 🐾 When any tangles are worked out, section the coat above what you just did, and brush and comb that layer. Then brush and comb the top layer.

- 🐾 Move on to the next section of the coat and repeat the process. Then do the legs, the tail, and the head. This all should take about 3 to 5 minutes if you don't run into any matts.

You don't have to brush and comb in any particular order. You can start at his head and move toward his back if you want. Just always start with the coat underneath first and move up. If you brush and comb the top layers of the coat, you could miss tangles closer to the skin.

The Puppy Cut

A long, flowing Yorkshire Terrier coat is gorgeous, but it requires a great deal of care. It needs to be protected, too, so hairs don't break. Many owners find that taking the time to care for the coat can become an issue. Plus, many Yorkie owners would like to take their dog with them on walks or hikes and find the long coat prevents them from doing this. Sometimes owners who enjoy performance dog sports decide that the long coat hampers their dog or their enjoyment of the activities.

If the coat becomes a problem, you can keep it shorter. Many Yorkies have what's called a "puppy cut." In this style, the coat is trimmed to the length of a puppy Yorkie's hair—often about an inch in length. This creates a cute, puppyish appearance.

The good side of a trim like this is that your Yorkie can be involved in many dog (and human) activities without the detriment of the long coat. However, it does create a different look; your puppy will not look like those elegant show dogs. So think this through before you do it.

Most Yorkie owners elect to have a professional dog groomer do the grooming and haircut. You can discuss your options with the groomer, including the length of the coat and whether you want the hair shorter on the belly and under the tail for cleanliness. You may want the hair on your Yorkie's feet a little shorter, too.

Professional grooming normally is done every 6 to 8 weeks. However, depending on the length of your puppy's coat and how quickly it grows, your groomer may recommend bringing him back for grooming more often.

Trimming His Ears

Last month, you learned how to keep the coat under his tail clean as well as how to trim his paws. Even if you have the groomer do your puppy's haircuts, there's one more area that will need regular trimming at home: your Yorkie's ears.

Traditionally, the ears are trimmed outside the ears, inside the ears, and along the edges so the ears stand erect, have a clean appearance, and have a pointed tip. For puppies, keeping the ears trimmed lessens the weight of the coat on the ears, enabling them to more easily stand erect.

Although professional groomers trim the ears with grooming clippers, most puppy owners find a pair of mustache trimmers is much easier to use. They are lighter weight and easier to handle.

Here's how to trim your Yorkie puppy's ears:

🐾 Place your puppy on the grooming table.

🐾 Comb the hair on the ears well, both on the outside of the ears and on the inside. Comb the hair that falls off to the side of the ears so it does, in fact, fall to the side.

🐾 Use the clippers or trimmers to trim the hair on the outside of the ears, trimming just the top third of the hair. Always move clippers in the direction the hair grows.

🐾 Do the same thing on the inside of both ears.

🐾 Using scissors, trim the hair on the edges of both ears to create a neat appearance. Be careful not to cut the edge of the ears. If you're concerned about the edges, catch the coat with a comb so the comb is between the ear flap and the scissors, and trim the hair on the outside of the comb.

There's no set timetable as to how often you should trim your Yorkie's ears. Just keep them neat and trim them as needed.

Cleaning His Ears

One downfall of your puppy's upright, hair-covered ears is that they seem to attract dirt. You'll need to regularly clean your Yorkie's ears.

To clean the ears, you need either some cotton balls or small gauze pads; one or two for each ear are usually enough for one cleaning. Some ear cleaner is necessary, too. This can be a commercial ear-cleaning solution, mineral oil, or witch hazel.

Here's how to clean your Yorkie's ears:

🐾 Place your Yorkie on the grooming table facing you.

🐾 Dampen a cotton ball or gauze pad and squeeze out the excess fluid.

🐾 Holding one ear flap in your hand, gently wipe the inside of the ear flap from the inside out. When one cotton ball or gauze pad is dirty, set it aside and dampen a clean one.

🐾 When the ear flap is clean, gently swab the inside of the ear, cleaning all the folds of the ear. Never try to reach inside the ear canal, and never use a cotton swab to clean into the ear canal.

🐾 When one ear is clean, repeat the process on the other ear. If the ears are damp when you finish, carefully dry them so bacteria doesn't proliferate.

> ### TIPS AND TAILS
>
> If your Yorkie's ear is red and inflamed, if it has a waxy buildup, if he's shaking his head or pawing at his ears, or if there appears to be a discharge from the ear, call your veterinarian right away. Don't clean his ear first because your vet will want to see the problem.

Physical Development

Your Yorkie is still growing, although sometimes it's not as obvious in tiny breeds as it is in larger breeds. Whereas Labrador Retrievers or German Shepherds seem to grow by leaps and bounds—inches and pounds—your Yorkshire Terrier puppy is putting on ounces. But he's still growing.

Plus, your Yorkie has the advantage over larger-breed puppies in coordination. He's more agile and better coordinated at this age than the larger puppies who are still tripping over their own paws.

He's Still Teething

Although many of your Yorkie's puppy teeth are gone now, his adult teeth are still growing in. His premolars and molars especially are still coming in, so his gums and jaws will still be bothering him at times.

Offer him ice cubes, broth cubes, and toys to chew on. Food-dispensing toys are great because they work better to keep his attention off his sore mouth.

> **HAPPY PUPPY**
>
> To make your puppy a fun teething treat, place some small carrot slices, some bits of shredded chicken, and other good foods in an 8-ounce paper cup. Fill the cup with water, and freeze. To serve, peel off the paper cup and give the frozen treat to your puppy in a safe place outside or on a towel in his crate or exercise pen.

Some puppies suffer from nausea when teething, and when they do, they won't want to eat. This can be a problem with tiny Yorkies because they can suffer from hypoglycemia when they don't eat. Keep some corn syrup or Nutri-Cal on hand, and give him a little if he doesn't eat. Don't hesitate to call your veterinarian, either, if your puppy is skipping meals.

All About the Tail

Both the American Kennel Club and Canadian Kennel Club Yorkshire Terrier breed standards call for a tail that has been docked to a moderate length. In the past, most breeders or veterinarians would dock the tail where the tan color meets the black on the underside of the tail, usually one third to halfway from the base of the tail. However, most tails are now about a ½-inch longer to present a more balanced look when the dogs are shown as adults.

Docking usually takes place when the puppies are about 3 days old. Breeders state that after the docking, the puppies fuss for a few minutes and then quickly begin to nurse on their mother.

> ### TIPS AND TAILS

Docking is controversial, and many countries outlaw the procedure. Some provinces in Canada, the United Kingdom, Australia, France, Germany, Greece, Sweden, and Switzerland—to name just a few—have made docking illegal, condemning it as animal cruelty. Many experts feel that in the future, both the American Kennel Club and Canadian Kennel Club and the breed parent clubs will have to address this issue. No one is willing to guess whether the standards will be changed or how long it will take before Yorkies will all have natural tails.

A Yorkie usually carries a short tail in a fairly upright manner. Not straight up in the air, but higher than the level of the back. A longer tail is usually carried over the dog's back, somewhat curled, much like a Shih Tzu's tail. The tail's coat hangs over the back.

There are no health or behavioral issues related to the Yorkie's tail being either shorter or longer. However, the longer tail does carry more coat and needs more grooming.

Health

Although it's still too early to spay or neuter your Yorkshire Terrier puppy, it's definitely time to begin thinking about it. Research the subject, perhaps talk to your puppy's breeder, and discuss the subject with your veterinarian.

Your puppy is also old enough now to begin heartworm preventatives if these pests are a problem in your region. Unfortunately, the territory where these pests are found has spread considerably in recent years. If you don't know whether they're a problem or not, call your veterinarian.

Should You Spay or Neuter Your Pup?

Not every Yorkie needs to be bred. Only the best of the best—those Yorkies with breed championships and/or multiple performance sport titles, and those who are healthy and sound both physically and mentally—should be bred. Obviously, any dog with physical, structural, or health problems should not be bred. Dogs with any temperament flaws should not pass along their genetics.

As you're thinking about this decision, keep in mind that breeding dogs is a tough endeavor; not only does it require a thorough knowledge of the breed, researching and reading pedigrees, and knowing the breed genetics, but there's also the actual breeding, whelping, raising the puppies, and finding the best homes possible for them. Breeding dogs—and doing it correctly, as it should be done—is not for the faint of heart. There's a lot more to it than playing with cute little puppies.

If you're curious as to whether your puppy has the possibility to be bred in the future, talk to your breeder and have her take a look at your puppy. She may be able to tell you right away that your puppy needs to be spayed or neutered and she can explain why. Or if you're seriously planning on competing with your puppy in the future, both in *conformation dog shows* as well as obedience or performance sports, she may tell you to hold off a little while to see how your puppy grows up.

> ## DOG TALK

Conformation dog shows are competitions where dogs are compared to their breed's description of a perfect dog as well as against the other dogs competing on that day. The Westminster Kennel Club dog show, televised every February, is a conformation dog show.

Spaying a female dog consists of a surgical ovariohysterectomy. The ovaries and uterus are removed through a small incision in the abdomen. A spayed female Yorkie will not come into season and will not be able to reproduce. Recuperation is usually very easy. She'll probably have to wear a wide collar or cone to keep her from licking at her stitches and potentially pulling them out. Your veterinarian will recommend keeping your Yorkie quiet for a week to 10 days. You can do this by keeping her on leash and close to you. When you can't supervise her, put her in her crate.

Alternatively, some veterinarians are now performing a simpler surgery that just removes the ovaries. The surgery is easier, as is recovery time. Ask your veterinarian which she recommends.

With males, the surgery consists of castration. The testicles are removed through a small incision forward of the scrotum. As with the females, your veterinarian will tell you to keep your dog quiet for a week to 10 days. He, too, will probably need to wear a wide collar or cone to keep him from bothering the incision. Again, recuperation is usually very fast.

Spaying a female dog tends to decrease the incidences of breast or mammary-gland cancers. The female dog is also protected against cancers of the reproductive system because it's no longer there. Obviously, a spayed female longer comes into season twice a year; the primary reason for spaying a female Yorkie is to keep her from reproducing.

The benefits of neutering a male dog include a lessening of sexually related behaviors, including fighting with other male dogs, trying to escape from the yard, roaming, and other related behaviors. Leg lifting, marking, and urinating on upright surfaces tend to be decreased, too. Testicular cancer is no longer an issue, either, because the testicles have been removed.

Spaying or neutering your dog does have some risks and potential side effects. Surgery and anesthesia always carry some risks. The dog may bleed during surgery, stop breathing, or even die. There can be complications from the anesthesia— although there are options as to different types of anesthesia that may lower the risks. There may be complications from the surgery, and although these are rare—especially with young, healthy dogs—they can happen. Discuss these risks with your veterinarian prior to scheduling the surgery.

Although spaying or neutering your Yorkie does stop the chance of unexpected reproduction, this should be a well-researched decision rather than an automatic one. Some of the potential problems seen in spayed or neutered dogs can be serious. For example, both spayed females and neutered males have twice the risk of developing osteosarcoma and hemangiosarcoma as intact dogs, although toy-breed dogs have a lower risk of this cancer than do larger breeds. Spayed females are more likely to develop urinary incontinence later in life, and males are more prone to urinary tract cancers and prostate cancer. Research is continuing on several other possible issues, including the increased risk of knee injuries.

For most dogs not used for breeding, spaying or neutering does have benefits. However, wise dog owners will make an educated decision on whether to spay or neuter their Yorkie. If you have any questions or concerns, talk to your veterinarian.

If you do decide to have the surgery for your Yorkie, find out at what age your vet prefers to do the surgery. Many veterinarians prefer to wait until your puppy has reached his full growth.

Heartworm and Preventatives

Heartworms are a totally different type of internal parasite. Rather than living in your dog's intestinal tract like roundworms, hookworms, and other intestinal parasites, heartworms live in your dog's heart, as the name suggests. Because of this, testing a stool sample won't give a diagnosis of heartworms; a blood test is needed instead.

Heartworms, like tapeworms, have an insect intermediary host. This time it's a mosquito. When a mosquito draws blood from a dog already infested with heartworms, it also draws in the heartworm larvae circulating in the dog's bloodstream. When it bites another dog, it transfers the larvae to the second dog, infecting that one, too.

As the worms grow inside the dog, the bloodstream carries them to the dog's heart. It takes about 6 months for the larvae to mature in the dog, but when they do mature, they reproduce. The offspring, born alive, are called microfilaria.

> **TIPS AND TAILS**
>
> Heartworms have been found in all 50 states, although they're most common along the Eastern seaboard from New Jersey south to Florida, along the Gulf of Mexico to Texas, and up the Mississippi River.

Thankfully, preventatives can ward off an infestation, but a blood test must be done first to be sure your Yorkie doesn't have heartworms to begin with. The preventatives must be given throughout mosquito season; your veterinarian can provide some guidance as to when that should be. In some regions, the preventives should be given all year.

Getting to Know Your Yorkie's Body

We've mentioned the importance of a daily massage a few times in the past few months, especially in relation to your Yorkie's grooming needs. But there's another good use for the daily massage. When you massage your Yorkie each day, your fingers learn what your puppy's body feels like. Because you can't trust your eyes to notice a problem—especially when your puppy's longer adult coat grows in—your fingers need to know what's normal so when a problem appears, you will feel it.

For example, if your puppy plays too hard and twists a knee, you will feel it if it's swollen. Plus, when you touch it, your puppy will wince and pull away his leg. If a tick has attached itself to your puppy's neck, you'll feel it as you massage him.

Continue giving your puppy that daily massage. Feel for grooming needs, especially tangles and debris in the coat, but also let your fingers learn what's normal on your Yorkie.

Nutrition

Hardly anything in the dog fanciers' world causes more arguments than a discussion about dog foods. Talk to 50 dog owners, and you'll get 50 different ideas about what's a good dog food and what isn't.

Unfortunately, this lack of a consensus makes it tough because your puppy's growth, good health, and longevity depend on good nutrition.

The Industry

More than $8 billion worth of pet food was sold in 2010. This is a gigantic industry designed to provide mass-produced and, for the most part, relatively inexpensive foods that adequately nourish as many dogs as possible.

The primary benefit of commercial dog foods is their convenience. Dog owners can buy dog food at the grocery store while shopping for the family or at the local pet store. Then while cooking for the family, they can scoop some dry kibble food or canned food into the dog's bowl. Voilà. The dog is fed.

As a general rule, dog-food companies spend a considerable amount of time and money in research. As a result, they produce puppy foods, weight-loss foods, foods for giant-breed dogs, and foods for older dogs. Manufacturers have created foods with unique proteins such as duck and rabbit and unique carbohydrates such as sweet potato and barley so dogs with allergies can eat without problems.

But remember, the primary goals of these companies—besides feeding dogs—are to sell their products and make money. These goals may not always be compatible with your nutritional goals for your Yorkie puppy.

> **HAPPY PUPPY**
>
> Although commercial dog foods (and dog-food companies) do have some problems, many Yorkies can eat good-quality commercial dog foods with no negative side effects. They will eat their foods eagerly and have bright eyes and a shiny coat as a result.

The dog-food industry isn't perfect, and the recalls of 2007 showed us that. As this book is being written, even more new recalls are being issued, with multiple companies involved, dogs reported sick, and even dog owners hospitalized after they handled salmonella-contaminated food.

The 2007 recalls involved a nonfood substance that was added to pet foods. When the information that was known at the time was compiled together, Menu Foods, which was manufacturing dog foods sold under hundreds of labels, appeared to be the primary culprit. In March 2007, the federal Food and Drug Administration (FDA) belatedly issued a recall of 60 million packages of dog and cat foods made by Menu Foods. These foods contained wheat gluten imported from China that had been contaminated with *melamine.*

In the weeks and months that followed, this initial recall turned out to be just the tip of the iceberg. Corn glutens were found to be contaminated, as well as rice gluten. As testing continued, other contaminants were found in assorted dog foods.

At one point, more than 6,000 dogs were known to have fallen ill and at least 3,000 died as a result of these tainted foods. These figures are the ones known but are nowhere near accurate because some dogs fell ill prior to the official recall and many veterinarians were so busy treating sick dogs they never reported any numbers.

In the spring of 2012, it appeared that one dog-food plant had manufactured foods for several dog-food companies. The foods produced at that plant became contaminated by salmonella. As a result, dogs and their owners became sick. As of this writing, new illnesses are still being reported, and the final totals are as yet unknown.

If anything good could come out of incidences such as these, it's that dog owners cannot be complacent. Pay attention to the commercial foods you feed your puppy. A number of websites and blogs post dog-food recalls when they're issued. One is expertrecall.com. Check in often with this and other sites.

A Quick Look at Commercial Foods

Trying to determine the best food for your Yorkie can be confusing and even frustrating. Everyone has an opinion, and most of those opinions are different. So what can you do?

First of all, read the labels on the foods and then understand what they say. For example, know that if a label says "Beef, wheat germ, wheat middlings, and wheat flour," that's really a wheat-based food rather than a beef food even though beef is listed first. By breaking the wheat ingredient into three different types or forms, the wheat can be listed three times, each of which is less in weight than the beef, but when combined, are most likely much more than the beef. Ingredients in the food are listed by weight, not volume.

Know what the ingredients are and what they are not. The American Association of Feed Control Officials (AAFCO) maintains a website that lists what ingredients are allowed in dog foods and exactly what each includes. For example, the AAFCO states that chicken by-product meal consists of the ground, rendered parts of the carcass of slaughtered chickens and includes necks, feet, undeveloped eggs, and intestines. There are no guidelines as to how many feet or eggs may be included in each batch for example, so each batch is variable and may differ in nutritional value from other batches.

Don't pay too much attention to the guaranteed analysis that lists the percentages of protein, fat, fiber, and moisture in a food. Although many people may tell you your Yorkie should eat a food that's a certain percentage of protein, the protein percentage on the package isn't necessarily a good guide. For example, melamine was added to foods to boost the protein, as determined by laboratory analysis. However, it wasn't digestible protein and was, as we now know, toxic. But legally, dog-food companies cannot put on the packaging how digestible the ingredients are. The guaranteed analysis can be, and often is, misleading.

Therefore, the best thing you can do is look for a good-quality meat as the primary ingredient, followed by either a second-quality meat or good-quality carbohydrates such as sweet potatoes, yams, green vegetables, apples, bananas, papayas, mangos, or other digestible and good foods.

A variety of different types of commercial foods are available, each with advantages and disadvantages:

Dry foods: Generally, these foods have a moisture content of between 6 and 10 percent—hence the description "dry." These foods are easy to store and use, and, depending on the recipe and formulation, may have a moderate shelf life—perhaps 6 months. Dry foods may consist of a variety of ingredients, including meats, carbohydrate sources, and added vitamins and minerals.

> **TIPS AND TAILS**
>
> Cheaper commercial dry dog foods usually contain a high percentage of cereal grains, which usually include rice, corn, and wheat. These ingredients are known to cause allergy problems with many Yorkies.

Canned foods: These are generally meat-based foods with a moisture content of 80 to 85 percent. They may or may not have vitamins or minerals added. They have a long shelf life, sometimes even a couple years.

Dehydrated foods: Dehydrated dog treats, especially those made from liver, have been available for many years. Dehydrated foods, however, became available only in the past decade. These foods can be dehydrated raw or lightly cooked foods. The primary advantage to dehydration is that the slow processing doesn't destroy the nutrition in the ingredients like the high temperatures in other forms of processing can. When kept in cool dry conditions, these foods have a moderate shelf life—usually up to a year.

Frozen foods: These are available in raw-food form or cooked. As with any frozen foods, handling is very important. If the food is allowed to thaw at any point, it may become contaminated with bacteria. Therefore, buy a reputable brand name and feel free to contact the manufacturer and ask at the store where you buy the food any questions you have about distribution and handling procedures. These foods usually have a fairly short shelf life, although it varies by food and manufacturer.

Although these are the most popular types of commercial foods, others are available, too. Some foods are now packaged in long tubes, like bologna or sausage, and you can cut off a slice or chunk for feeding. Refrigerated fresh foods or cooked foods are also available. As dog owners continue to demand better-quality foods, manufacturers are responding.

Feeding Your Yorkie a Raw-Food Diet

Many Yorkie owners prefer to feed their pups homemade foods. Yorkies have a very small stomach, and the food they eat must be good quality to provide good nutrition. If the tiny dog is eating a commercial junk food with a lot of fillers, he may eat as much food as his stomach can hold and yet still be malnourished.

Some owners who have dogs with allergies or other health problems fix their own dog foods. Other owners are concerned about the quality of commercial dog foods and prefer to know what exactly their dog eats.

Raw-food diets have become very popular in the last 20 years. They're usually based on raw meats and bones, with vegetables, fruits, and other good foods mixed in. Although proponents claim these diets are more natural than commercial foods—and they are—they're not without risk. Raw meats are commonly contaminated with bacteria that can make both dogs and people very ill, sometimes fatally so.

If you want to feed your Yorkie puppy a raw diet, here are some guidelines:

🐾 Use a recipe designed and tested by a canine nutritionist, and adhere to that recipe exactly.

🐾 Find a local source of clean, unadulterated meat.

TIPS AND TAILS

Use safe handling techniques with raw meat, including cleaning all tools, dishes, and the counters with bleach. Wash your hands well afterward, too. Store all meats in the refrigerator or freezer.

- Find a farmers' market or other source of clean, pesticide-free vegetables and fruit.
- Supplement with a good-quality vitamin and mineral supplement that contains calcium. Feed according to directions for a growing puppy. Do not oversupplement, though. More is not better because it can affect your puppy's growth, especially his bones, and his overall health.

Raw-food diets can be very good for your Yorkie if done safely and with good-quality ingredients. However, feed him this diet with caution because salmonella and other bacterial and parasitic contaminations are serious business.

Feeding Your Yorkie a Home-Cooked Diet

Home-cooked meals are somewhat safer than raw-food diets if only because the ingredients are cooked, and the cooking process kills any bacteria or parasites in the raw foods. A balanced diet is just as important with home cooking as it is with other diets, so if you decide to feed a home-cooked diet, this, too, should be formulated and tested by a canine nutritionist.

If you decide you'd like to avoid commercial dog foods, talk to your veterinarian first and get her opinion. If you're both of the same mind that this would be advantageous for your Yorkie puppy, ask for a referral to a canine nutritionist.

You can feed your pup a home-cooked diet safely, but you do need to take care while doing it. Keep in mind that your Yorkie puppy is dependent on these foods for his energy, mental well-being, physical health, and growth.

Paying Attention to Feces

This might seem like a disgusting subject to discuss, especially in the nutrition section, but it's an important one that's directly related to your puppy's food as well as other nonfood items he might consume. In addition, your puppy's feces are a reflection of his overall health, especially his digestive health, but many diseases can cause changes to the stools.

Although most adult dogs have two bowel movements per day, it's not unusual for a Yorkie puppy to have three or four, primarily because he eats several small meals per day. After he's 6 to 8 months old, when you decrease his meals to three a day, he'll have fewer bowel movements, too.

Constipation can be a problem by itself, or it can be a symptom of a disease. It's rare but not unknown for a confused puppy to force himself not to pass any stools, especially if he has been disciplined for housetraining accidents. By not passing stools, the intestinal tract continues to absorb moisture from the stools, they become hard and dry, and soon the puppy needs veterinary help.

Puppies also chew on things they shouldn't, and these foreign objects can cause constipation by becoming lodged in the intestinal tract. If your puppy has been chewing on something he shouldn't and isn't moving his bowels, call your veterinarian right away.

Diarrhea is more common in puppies than constipation. Because dogs—and puppies even more so—tend to eat many things they shouldn't eat, diarrhea is often the result. The foreign substances, which may include grass, leaves, sticks, garbage, and other debris, can irritate the stomach and intestinal tract, causing diarrhea.

> **DOG TALK**
>
> **Constipation** means infrequent, difficult, or a lack of defecation. **Diarrhea** is a bowel movement that passes soft, watery, unformed feces. There are often many more than normal bowel movements in a short period of time.

Your puppy's feces should be pretty much the same every day, especially if his diet remains pretty much the same. Abrupt changes to his diet can cause changes to his feces, too, including the color, odor, shape, and firmness of his stools.

Normal stools don't contain mucus. They also should not have fresh blood (bright red) or partially digested blood (black and tarry) in them. Foreign objects or parasites are also problems.

Never try to treat constipation, diarrhea, foreign objects, parasites, or other problems on your own. Instead, take a stool sample directly to your veterinarian, and let her decide how your Yorkie needs to be treated.

Social Skills

Continue socialization this month. Your pup needs to continue to go different places with you so he can meet new people, see different sights, and encounter new situations. He's going to be interested in everything; his curiosity has no limits.

At times he's going to be extremely bold during these outings. In fact, he may seem too bold at times, even to the point of putting himself in danger. However, don't be surprised if sometimes he becomes a little cautious during these outings. Both of these emotions, even though they conflict with each other, are normal right now.

As you take your puppy out and about, it's important for you to understand his perception of the world around him. Knowing his body language gives you a better understanding of what he's feeling.

Your Puppy's Conflicting Emotions

How can your puppy be curious and bold one moment and reserved and cautious the next? Although this might seem strange, it really is normal.

Your puppy is curious about the world because he has more confidence now, both in himself and in you. This confidence enables him to be bold and put himself in situations he wouldn't have tried a month or two ago. He might interact more with unknown dogs, for example, or chase a strange cat. Actions like these can get him in trouble, so it's your job to help keep him safe.

His caution and reserve also kick in because he has also been startled or frightened at some point. He realizes that not everything in the world is safe and secure. That sense of caution can help keep him safe.

One of the hardest things for you to do is to keep him safe without overprotecting him. You need to allow him to grow and develop and gain more confidence without letting him get hurt or scared. It's a tough balancing act.

> **HAPPY PUPPY**
>
> Should your Yorkie be frightened or even overly cautious, jolly him out of that mind-set. Act silly and talk to him like there's no problem in the world you can't solve.

Understanding His Body Language

Over the last few months, you've learned to understand what your Yorkie is trying to tell you when he barks, whines, and howls. Dogs are pretty good at communicating with their humans.

Dogs also communicate through facial expressions, postures, and body language even more than they do through verbal sounds. When you can look at and listen to your puppy and see all his ways of communicating with you, there will be fewer misunderstandings.

Happy and relaxed: Your Yorkie's mouth is open and his tongue may be out. His eyes and ears are relaxed and in a normal position. His tail is wagging. He may roll over on to his back, baring his tummy, and he may squirm back and forth, soliciting a tummy rub.

Playful: His mouth is open so he looks like he's smiling. His tongue may be out but not always. His eyes are wide open, and his ears are up and facing forward. His tail is wagging, too. He also may be doing a *play bow*.

> ### DOG TALK
>
> A **play bow** is a posture where your puppy's rear end is up while his front end is lowered to the ground. His head may be lowered, too. His tail will be wagging. This is an invitation to play, and he'll give it to other dogs, people, or even the family cat.

Curious: His mouth is closed, although not tightly clenched. His eyes are open, and his ears face forward. His tail is in a normal position but probably not wagging. Your puppy's posture is upright and probably leaning toward whatever has his interest. If he walks toward it, his step might be slightly cautious or stiff.

Confident: His mouth can be either open or closed, his eyes are open normally, and his ears are facing forward. His tail is upright and probably not wagging. His head is held upright, usually with attitude. He'll also be standing up, square, with his feet planted, again with attitude.

Angry or aggressive: His mouth is slightly open, with his lips pulled tight and wrinkled at the back corners of his mouth. His teeth usually show behind a snarl. His eyes are staring hard at the object of his anger. His ears are facing forward and stiff. His feet are planted, and he's facing forward, often leaning forward.

Anxious or fearful: His tongue may be licking his nose or lips, and he may turn his head away and yawn. His mouth may be slightly open with his lips pulled back. He can be blinking more than normal, and his pupils are dilated. His ears are back, too. His tail is tucked and may be tight to his hips. His head and body are lowered and tucked tight to his body.

As you live with your Yorkie, watch his emotions as he expresses them through his facial expressions, postures, and body language. Get to know your puppy better by learning how he communicates. This doesn't mean you have to give in to his every whim just because you understand him—that's not good for him. But it is fun to know what he's trying to communicate.

Behavior

You're apt to see some changes in your Yorkie's behavior this month. They won't be abrupt changes, usually, but more gradual ones.

Most Yorkies of this age tend to become a little more independent than they previously were. Their prey drive—that urge to chase anything that moves—is stronger now, too. The chewing isn't new, but because your puppy is still teething, that urge is strong right now.

Little Mr. Independent

One of the characteristics most puppy owners enjoy is that canine shadow they have. Puppies tend to follow their people around. Granted, they can get underfoot and become a nuisance, but most puppy owners enjoy that feeling of being important and needed.

Sometime during this month, however, most Yorkie puppies go through an independent phase. When this hits, you'll find that your Yorkie is more interested in exploring on his own than following you. He's more apt to chase the lizard in the backyard or the neighbor's cat than remain close to you.

Although a normal stage of puppyhood, this aloofness often catches owners off guard. Puppy owners get used to their puppy's compliance and tend to think their puppy is well behaved or more attached than other puppies. In reality, baby mammals are, for the most part, genetically programmed to follow their mother. We see it on wildlife shows all the time. The wolf cub, antelope baby, or wild horse foal follows his or her mother, even in times of danger. Puppies are the same way. But as your puppy gets older and approaches adolescence, that programming breaks down and he becomes more independent.

The best way to deal with this is to use the leash and training to keep your puppy close and prevent bad behaviors. Put the leash back on in the house, and don't let your Yorkie puppy wander off into rooms that might not be puppy-proofed. Keep him on leash when outside your yard especially. Don't take him off leash and expect him to stay close and listen. He might, but it's more likely he won't.

Continue with obedience training. Remember, the goal of obedience training is to teach your puppy good habits that will last a lifetime.

Dealing with That Pesky Prey Drive

The Yorkshire Terrier is one of the smallest breeds, and the AKC classifies the breed as a toy-breed dog rather than a terrier. However, as the breed's name implies, Yorkies are terriers at heart.

Terriers are hunters. Most are thrilled to chase lizards in the yard, mice in the woodpile, and even bugs in leaves. It's great fun to watch a lovely Yorkie with his top-knot tied with a lovely bow … hunting a lizard.

The *prey drive* is what fuels this hunting instinct. The prey drive is what makes Yorkies tiny but efficient hunters. The urge to hunt is usually triggered first by movement and then by sound or smell. So if your Yorkie sees the flash of a lizard moving, he'll look and focus on where he saw the motion. He'll also listen, sniff, and dash toward it.

> **DOG TALK**
>
> In dogs, **prey drive** is that instinctive desire to chase something that moves. It's related to the behavior of a predator chasing, hunting, and catching a prey animal.

Prey drive can cause problem behaviors. If your Yorkie decides to hunt and ignore you when you call him to come, he could get into trouble. If he decides to chase the neighbor's cat across the street, he could get hit by a car. Instincts are powerful motivators for dogs.

However, training can give you more control so you can call your puppy back to you if he takes off. However, the training needs to be consistently practiced and applied. Plus, you need to know your puppy and keep him on leash in situations where he could get into trouble.

Using the Prey Drive

Although Yorkies haven't been working terriers for many generations now, they still have that terrier prey drive to chase small things that move. More than one Yorkie owner has been horrified to find a dead mouse or rat killed by their adorable little dog with a bow in his topknot.

Prey drive is something your puppy is born with, and some Yorkies have a stronger prey drive than others. The prey drive can be annoying at times, especially when your puppy brings you a dead mouse or a lizard's tail.

> **TIPS AND TAILS**
>
> Many generations ago, the ancestors of today's Yorkshire Terriers were mousers and ratters. They were fearless little hunters.

Working-dog trainers specifically choose dogs with a high prey drive because they can channel this into obedience and occupational training. The most successful law-enforcement and drug-detection dogs, for example, all have a strong prey drive. You can turn your Yorkie's prey drive into a desire to play and to work for you, either through obedience, flyball, or agility training or something fun such as trick training.

Your puppy's prey drive can be used as a reward for cooperating with you. To do this, make a fishing pole toy, much like one for exercising an indoor cat. The ones for cats aren't sturdy enough for a Yorkie, though, so if you have one for your cat, make another one for your Yorkie. Here's how:

🐾 You'll need an inexpensive fishing pole without a reel or any other equipment attached to it. A length of a bamboo pole works, too.

🐾 Fasten a 6- to 8-foot length of sturdy twine or lightweight rope to one end of the pole.

🐾 Tie a small, lightweight fuzzy toy to the other end of the twine or rope.

To introduce this to your puppy, just drag it in front of him slowly. Encourage him to chase it, and when he does, praise him. When he catches it, make a big deal over him. "Good boy! What a mighty hunter!" As he figures out the game, gradually move the toy faster, continuing to praise and encourage him. Soon, the game itself will become the reward.

> ### TIPS AND TAILS
>
> If your Yorkie doesn't want to give up the toy after catching it, trade him a treat for the toy. Offer a high-value treat that has a good smell, and when he drops the toy, praise him, "Give. Good to give! Yeah!" and give him the treat.

Once your puppy understands this game, begin offering him a chance to play when he has cooperated with you during training. Let him play for 30 seconds after a good sit and stay or after coming to you when you call him to come. Or let him play for a minute or two after he has stood still for grooming. Play is a great reward, especially when the game is something he enjoys.

He's Chewing Everything!

This month, your puppy's adult teeth are growing in, and his gums hurt, his jaws hurt, and he has an uncontrollable urge to chew anything or everything so he'll feel better.

Unfortunately, chewing on the TV remote, your cell phone, your shoes, and the rungs on the dining room chair really don't make him feel better. But he still has an urge to chew. You have to approach the chewing from three different directions:

First, keep your house puppy-proofed. Be sure everything is put away, including shoes, socks, cell phones, electronic power cords, and anything else that can fit in his mouth. Don't assume he won't chew on something; right now he's not thinking, so just keep the house puppy-proofed for both your sakes.

Second, continue to restrict his freedom. Don't let him have free run of the house, or he'll get into trouble. He can be in the room you're in while you can supervise him, but when you're going to be busy, put him in his crate or exercise pen.

Third, be sure he has appropriate things to chew on. Give him chew toys, broth or regular ice cubes, or food-dispensing toys. If he can satisfy his need to chew with the right things, he'll be less apt to chew on the wrong things.

When your puppy does chew up something he shouldn't, don't yell at him. Instead, yell at yourself for letting it happen and make a vow you'll be more careful from now on.

Bad Behaviors Aren't Outgrown

Recently we overheard a puppy owner say, "I'm not going to do anything about his barking because he'll outgrow it soon." That's the wrong approach to take.

Puppies and dogs do the things they do for a reason. Dogs repeat the behaviors or actions that have a positive result for them. This is also why positive reinforcements—praise, petting, food treats, and toys—are so powerful when training your puppy. When he learns that coming to you when you call him results in praise and a treat, he's more apt to come the next time you call him.

But the positive reinforcements don't have to come only from you:

- 🐾 If your puppy barks and gets either attention or an adrenaline rush from barking, he's going to bark again in the future.
- 🐾 If your puppy chews up a leather shoe and it tastes good and relieves some of his teething pain, he's going to chew on any other shoe he can find.
- 🐾 If your puppy raids the bathroom trash can, tears up some tissue paper, and has a great time, he will do it again.

Any behavior that produces any kind of a reward at all won't be outgrown and can instead become a bad habit. Therefore, you must address any behaviors you don't like now. Don't ignore them.

The best way to deal with bad behaviors is to identify exactly what he's doing wrong. Let's say he's raiding the bathroom trash can. When is he doing it? When you're busy and not supervising him. Why is he doing it? Because at that moment, he's bored and you're not paying any attention to him. Plus, it's fun to tear up paper.

So what should you do about this? First of all, put the trash can away where he can't reach it. Then, supervise the puppy more closely. When you can't watch him, put him in his crate or exercise pen. Then, put him on his leash and bring him to the bathroom with you. When he sniffs the trash can, interrupt him, saying "Leave that alone!" Praise him when he backs away, "Good to leave it! Good boy!"

> ### TIPS AND TAILS
>
> With most behavior modification and dog training, it's important to be *proactive* rather than *reactive*. Teach your dog what to do rather than what not to do. However, once in a while, you need to deal with a bad behavior. Communicate clearly with your puppy, saying "Oh no!" or another sharp word, and always finish by praising him for doing something right.

Training

Although you began training your puppy when he came home with you, this month, really amp it up because your Yorkie puppy's brain is like a sponge right now. He can soak up everything you teach him. Just be sure to keep your training sessions short and fun. Show him what to do, help him do it, and praise and reward him for doing it.

When he figures out that cooperating with you makes him happy, he'll beg to do things for you. You'll find him sitting in front of you offering behaviors, bringing you a toy to throw, spinning circles, or rolling over. Enjoy this because it's great fun for your puppy and for you.

Establishing Household Rules

We've discussed the importance of not allowing bad behaviors to continue. If they're the least bit rewarding to your puppy, they'll turn into bad habits rather than go away.

The same applies to behaviors around the house. What canine behaviors do you enjoy, and which ones would you rather not have happen? What household rules you decide to establish depends on you, your family, your house, your household routine, and so much more. What's comfortable for one family might not be right for yours.

No matter what household rules you establish, it's important that everyone in the household enforces them uniformly. If one person ignores the rules and encourages your puppy to break them when no one else is around, your puppy will be confused. For example, if your teenage son likes the puppy to get up on the sofa with him, the puppy will try to get up with other people, too. Consistency is important.

What household rules should you establish? Again, it's up to you, but here are some ideas:

Do you want your Yorkie in the kitchen? A tiny Yorkie can easily get hurt when underfoot in the kitchen. You could trip over him or drop something on him. Use your obedience training to stop him at doorways; sit and stay work well. Then if he steps inside the kitchen, stop him and move him back to the doorway.

Would you like to keep him off the furniture? Many toy-breed owners enjoy having their tiny dog on the furniture, but if you'd like to keep dirt to a minimum, it's fine to teach him to stay off.

Would you like it if your puppy didn't dash out open doors and gates? This really could be a safety issue because a dog who dashes out doors and gates could get hit by a car. He could charge a larger dog walking by and be injured or even killed by the other dog. Have your puppy sit and stay at every door or gate. After a few seconds, either give him permission to go outside or not.

Teach him to ignore trash cans. Trash cans are attractive to puppies because they often contain food or other interesting things. However, they can also have things that could make your puppy sick or hurt him. Plus, he makes a huge mess when he knocks down a trash can and rummages through it. If you think a toy-breed dog is too tiny to knock over a trash can, think again. He might be too small to push over large outdoor cans, but he can dump over inside cans. Plus, he can easily jump *into* the can. Use the "Leave it" command to teach him to ignore trash cans.

TIPS AND TAILS

To teach "Leave it," put your puppy on his leash. Use a full-to-overflowing kitchen trash can with something smelly on top, such as an empty tuna fish can. Walk your puppy past the trash can. When his nose goes to the trash can, quickly turn the other direction, using the leash to turn him away as you tell him, "Sweetie, leave it!" Praise him when he turns toward you, "Yeah, good to pay attention to me!" Repeat this several times. Later, when he understands, train him with other distractions, too.

One very important part of teaching household rules is to reward good behavior. Puppy owners get so focused on saying "no" to their puppy they often forget to acknowledge good behavior. Your puppy has to be praised for good behavior, or he'll regress. After all, "No, no, bad dog," is still attention from you, even though it's not fun attention. But you don't want him working for negative attention; you want him trying to get those positive rewards from you.

Here are some suggestions for when you can praise your puppy:

🐾 If he sniffs the sofa, looks at it, and then lies down on the floor, praise him.

🐾 If he walks past the overflowing kitchen trash can and looks away from it as if it weren't there, praise him.

🐾 When he sits at an open door and looks at you for permission, praise him.

🐾 When he picks up his toy rather than your shoe, praise him.

🐾 When he watches the cat amble down the hallway and doesn't chase her, praise him.

Although interrupting bad behavior has a place in puppy training, your rewards are much more powerful. So watch him and praise him for good choices.

Teaching "Down" and "Stay"

When your puppy learns to lie down and hold still when asked, he's following your instructions but he's also developing more self-control. This can be effective at many times and in many places, such as when guests come over and spoil your puppy, letting him jump and climb all over them and develop bad behaviors. So if you leash your puppy before the guests come in your home, you can invite them in, ask them to have a seat, and then have your puppy do a *Down* and "Stay." Later, when your puppy is calm, your guests can greet him.

> **DOG TALK**
>
> **"Down"** is the command that means "Lie down." Don't use it to ask your puppy not to jump on you. Keep in mind each command you teach your puppy should have only one definition.

Here's how to teach the "Down":

- Have your puppy on leash and hold the leash in your left hand. Have a treat in your right hand.
- Ask your puppy to sit, and praise him.
- Let him sniff the treat in your right hand, and move the treat slowly from his nose to his front paws, letting his nose follow your hand. As his nose comes down, move the treat forward.
- As he lies down, praise him, "Good to down!" Give him the treat.
- If he's wiggly, keep your left hand (with the leash) on his shoulders.
- When you're ready for him to get up, pat him on the shoulder and tell him, "Sweetie, release!"

The hand signal you're making is an L shape—moving the treat from his nose to his toes brings his head down—and then moving the treat forward gives his body room to lie down. These are small hand signals, and your hand moves just inches down and inches forward.

When you've practiced the "Down" for a week or so and your puppy is doing it well, you can add the "Stay," just as you did last month with the sit exercise. In the beginning, sit or stand next to your puppy when you tell him stay just in case he pops up. He shouldn't have any trouble, though, because he has already practiced this command with the sit.

You and Your Puppy

This is a great time of puppyhood. Not only is your puppy ready to learn and you both can enjoy his training, but he's also eager to play. He's physically stronger and more coordinated, his prey drive has kicked in, and he's well bonded to you. Playing with him is going to be great fun for both of you.

You can play many games, including retrieving games. Just be sure your puppy enjoys the game as much as you do. Don't throw the toy too far, and always praise him for bringing it back to you. If he doesn't want to give the toy back to you, offer to swap the toy for a treat. Then praise him when he cooperates.

Playing Tug Games

Tug games, often called tug-of-war games, have a bad reputation, and many trainers discourage dog owners from playing them. If not played correctly, your puppy can take advantage of the game and learn some bad habits. For example, if your puppy plays tug, grabs the toy from you, and runs off to hide it, he has learned he can do this and get away with it. If he tries to do this with your car keys or even one of your dirty socks, you'll have a problem.

But tug games are fun, especially for breeds with a strong prey drive like your Yorkie. So it's important to have some rules when you play tug with your Yorkie.

Always remember how small he is. He may sound ferocious, but he is tiny and has an equally tiny jaw. Don't play rough, never pick him up by the toy when he's holding it in his mouth, and let him do the shaking. You should never shake the toy and him.

Should he touch his teeth to your skin during the game, stop the game immediately. Take the toy away, and walk away from him. If he's jumping at your legs, pick him up and put him in his crate for a few minutes.

Teach him to give you the toy, as described earlier. If he won't drop the tug toy and stop when you ask, stop the game right away. If he won't stop, put him in his crate so he can calm down.

Don't let children play tug games with your Yorkie puppy because there is too great a potential the kids will play too roughly. This could result in a hurt puppy or an overexcited puppy who could forget his training and bite the child's hands.

> ### HAPPY PUPPY
>
> When playing tug games, your Yorkie puppy can growl and snarl and act like he's killing lions. That's why the game is so much fun for him. He's using those natural hunting instincts of his.

Use tug games to play whenever you want, or use them as a reward for good behavior. Between obedience exercises during a training session, for example, play some tug. Praise him and let him tug for a while.

Giving Him Some Alone Time

We've placed a lot of emphasis on teaching your puppy housetraining skills, household rules, obedience training, and socialization. We've also stressed the importance of play. All these are things you work on or do with your puppy.

Your puppy also needs to spend time alone. We mentioned this last month, but don't forget to continue practicing it this month and in future months.

Although most puppy owners prefer to spend most of their waking hours with their puppy (and maybe even some sleeping hours), it's important for a puppy to learn to spend some time alone. Then when your Yorkie is left alone, such as when you're at work or out running errands, he won't panic.

Dogs who have developed *separation anxiety* are absolutely miserable. Plus, this behavioral problem is very difficult to solve or change. It's better to be sure your puppy learns to be comfortable alone when he's a puppy than to try to change a problem behavior later.

> ### DOG TALK
>
> **Separation anxiety** is a behavioral problem characterized by a dog's extreme fear or anxiety when left alone. Dogs with this issue may chew their way out of dog runs, crates, and even rooms. Some have broken through doors, windows, and fences—even to the point of hurting themselves.

Leave your puppy for an hour or two now and then in his crate or in an exercise pen. Be sure he has relieved himself first, had a chance to play with you, and had something to eat. Leave some gentle music playing, and give your puppy a couple toys, a warm towel, or a big stuffed toy to cuddle up with.

Make leaving and coming home calm and quiet events. Leave the high emotions for another time. If you're calm and matter of fact, your puppy will tend to be that way, too.

Protecting Your Puppy

Your Yorkie is gaining more independence now because he's beginning to grow up, but he's still mentally immature and physically very small. He still needs your protection.

He needs to be protected from himself because he has no idea how tiny he is or how vulnerable. Protect him from barking and lunging at other dogs. If he's challenging or being rude to another dog, that dog might take offense. One grab by a larger dog could kill your puppy, and it wouldn't be the larger dog's fault.

Birds of prey also target tiny dogs. Many a Yorkie, Chihuahua, and Papillon have been grabbed and carried away by hawks and other birds of prey. If outside in an area where birds of prey are common, keep your Yorkie on leash and close to you. If you hear a hawk call or screech, look for the bird and keep an eye on your puppy.

Unfortunately, you also have to protect your puppy from some people. Don't let people get rough with your Yorkie. When people get rough, they could frighten him, and that's not right. He should be able to trust the people in his life.

Remember, this is *your* puppy, and he needs you to watch out for him. If anyone attempts to do anything with your puppy that you know is wrong or you're not comfortable with, stop it. Don't let it happen. If that means you need to grab your puppy and walk away, do it. You can always explain yourself later, if you even want to do that.

Taking Time to Enjoy Him

This is a lovely time of your puppy's life. He's bright, alert, smart, and ready to do anything you want to do. So if at all possible, don't let other things deprive you of time with your puppy. Puppyhood disappears so quickly; in just months your Yorkie puppy will no longer be a baby and will be an adolescent instead.

Make time for him. For example, go for walks in different places. Check out the local tourist areas in your region. Find dog-friendly parks, motels and hotels, and other attractions. Play games with him, too. Remember hide and seek from childhood? Your puppy will love playing this with you. Invite him to cuddle with you on your lap as you read or watch television, and when you're at the computer, give him something to chew on so he remains close to you. Talk to him once in a while so he's aware of you.

Remember, you brought this puppy home for companionship, so take the time to enjoy him and have fun with him. You'll never regret it.

Month 5 | Month 6 | Month 7
Socialization in public
Teething begins — heavy chewing period
Enroll in basic obedience class
Rapid growth
Rabies vaccines
Switch to a food for all life stages

This month, which includes weeks 21 through 24, is a fun one. Your Yorkshire Terrier puppy is learning quickly and is a lot of fun to play with. You're probably also seeing more of her soon-to-be adult personality.

In addition, you'll see the puppy terrier zoomies this month! The zoomies can be hysterical to watch, but you've got to be sure they don't get out of control.

Physical Development

The biggest change during your puppy's sixth month is sexual maturity. Puberty has arrived in your Yorkie puppy, with all the changes it brings.

Your puppy's senses have been active for months now, but she's learning to use them better now. It's fun to watch her follow a trail or track a butterfly overhead. Plus, her increased use of her sense of smell can lead to some fun games, which we talk about later in this chapter.

Female Sexual Maturity

Female Yorkies tend to hit puberty this month. But don't worry if she's a little late. As with people, this is variable. It's not unusual for some puppies to reach sexual maturity at 7 or even 8 months. Sexual maturity generally refers to the age when your puppy would *come into season*.

If your Yorkie hasn't been spayed, the first signs that signal she's getting ready to come into season are usually behavioral. She may be flirty, or she may try to mount other dogs of her size. She may mount stuffed toys, too. Some female dogs also get grumpy.

When she's in season, she'll have a bloody discharge. This isn't very much; after all, she's a tiny dog. Most females keep themselves quite clean, so the only signs you may see are some spots on her blanket or bed. You can use a tiny feminine pad and some panties tied up to fit her, or commercial products are available.

An in-season female Yorkie's pheromones are quite attractive to any *intact* male dogs in your neighborhood. Be vigilant about protecting your tiny Yorkie during this time because larger male dogs could kill her when trying to mate with her or in frustration when they couldn't.

> ### DOG TALK
>
> **Coming into season** is the term for when a female dog is receptive to breeding. **Intact** refers to male or female dogs who have not been spayed or neutered.

Once your Yorkie comes into season, she's considered sexually mature, but that has no bearing on whether or not she's physically or mentally mature. Neither of those will happen for several more months, so even if you're planning on breeding your Yorkie, don't do it yet.

A mentally immature mother dog may not accept her puppies, may not be willing to care for them, and may even harm them. After all, she's just a puppy himself. She's much too young and immature physically to care for puppies, too, if she was even able to carry a pregnancy to term. She might not produce milk, or produce enough milk, and the pregnancy itself could harm her.

Experts agree that a Yorkie shouldn't be bred until she's at least 2 years old and is of good health. Even then, she should have passed any health tests necessary for the breed. (See Month 12 for more information.)

Male Sexual Maturity

Your male Yorkie can also reach sexual maturity this month, although there's no definitive sign as there is with females. However, during the past month or so, your male puppy's testicles have been growing larger, and he's started producing sperm.

At this age, many boys begin lifting their leg to urinate and *mark* their territory. Unfortunately, leg-lifting can turn into problem behavior with the male marking in the house as well as outside. Some females also mark.

The owners of leg-lifting Yorkies need to be conscious of marking and put some restraints on it. Your puppy does not have to mark every vertical object in his world.

Let your Yorkie know that this is not acceptable by using a verbal interruption in a sharp tone of voice, such as, "Hey! Not allowed!" Then take your puppy to the place where you do want him to relieve himself, use his command to go, and praise him when he does.

If you notice that your male Yorkie has only one testicle, bring that to your veterinarian's attention at the next vet visit. Your puppy will need to be neutered and that wayward testicle found. *Cryptorchidism,* or a retained testicle, could turn cancerous and must be removed.

> ## DOG TALK
>
> **Marking** is generally the behavior of a male to show all who come his way that this is his property or territory. **Cryptorchidism** is a condition in which only one (or sometimes neither) testicle has descended.

The Yorkie Nose

Your Yorkie puppy has a very good nose and sense of smell. Although Yorkshire Terriers aren't one of the best at scenting, like Bloodhounds or German Shepherds, her nose is still far superior to yours.

Your puppy has a nasal cavity that runs the length of her muzzle. This cavity is divided in half so each nostril has its own passageway for air and scent. These passageways contain many nerves that connect to the olfactory center in the brain. This center is more than 40 percent larger relative to the same portion of the human brain.

As your puppy finds and inhales a scent, say of that gopher in the yard, the odors dissolve in the moisture on the nose and in the nasal cavity. Signals are then passed on to the brain.

Your puppy can detect and sort through numerous different scents inhaled in the same breath. Your puppy is still immature, however, and her concentration isn't the best right now, so she's not going to be able to process all this information yet. But as she matures, she'll get better at it. Within a few months, her scenting abilities will be impressive.

> ## HAPPY PUPPY
>
> Your Yorkie has good vision, excellent hearing, and good scenting abilities. However, she doesn't have a good sense of taste. Her scenting abilities tell her more about food than her sense of taste does.

Yorkie Eyes and Vision

Your Yorkie has very good vision, although as a rule, dogs can't focus as well as you can. A person with excellent vision sees at what's measured at 20/20 vision. Your Yorkie sees at about 20/75 to 20/80. However, your puppy has a wider field of vision than you do and sees moving objects much better. That's why your puppy will react to the sight of a moving rabbit or even just a gopher poking his head above ground much more quickly than you can.

Dogs also see color differently from how you see it. Although not quite as color-blind as dog owners have long been told, dogs don't see color the same way we do. Your Yorkie has fewer cones in the retinas of his eyes, so although she does see color, it's not the same palette of color you see.

Dogs can see yellows and blues but not reds and greens. Your Yorkie sees grays best, from a light gray to a darker, almost black gray—much like with a black-and-white television.

Yorkie Ears and Hearing

Your Yorkie's upright ears act as a funnel, catching sound vibrations and directing them down into the ear canals. The ear canals are proportionally larger than what people have.

The upright ears as well as the muscles that support and move the ears all come in to play to help your puppy determine where sounds originate. People have to move their head to locate sounds; your puppy has only to twitch her ears.

Your Yorkshire Terrier has significantly better hearing than you do. People can generally hear sounds between 20 and 20,000 Hertz (Hz), while your puppy can hear between 67 and 67,000 Hz. We can hear lower sounds, although she can feel the vibration of those sound waves, but she can hear significantly more and higher sound vibrations.

Health

Your Yorkie will finish her puppy vaccinations this month. Usually the distemper and distemper combinations vaccinations finish earlier, perhaps last month, but the rabies vaccination is often given this month. She shouldn't need any other vaccinations until a year from now. In Month 12, we discuss the vaccination schedule for adult shots.

Last month, we talked about spaying and neutering. Your veterinarian may have recommended it be done this month, or the two of you may have decided to wait. There is no right or wrong time because many variables are involved.

One of the most common reasons for a trip to the veterinarian this month, after vaccinations and spay or neuter surgery, is accidents. Yorkies are tiny and can be sat on, stepped on, kicked, or dropped. Yorkies will also jump from places that are much too high—off furniture or out of your arms, for example—and hurt themselves. Yorkies can also get sick or eat something they shouldn't. These situations can also be emergencies.

Learning to recognize an emergency is important. Knowing what to do once you recognize an emergency situation is important, too. Knowing what to do gives you peace of mind, even if you never have to use that knowledge.

Recognizing an Emergency

A veterinary emergency is a situation in which immediate action must be taken to prevent a worse outcome. If your Yorkie puppy is having trouble breathing, that's an emergency. If she's bleeding and it won't stop with direct pressure, that's an emergency.

Several veterinarians compiled this list of potential emergencies:

Allergic reaction: Your puppy has been stung by a bee or bitten by an insect or has been exposed to something that causes redness and swelling, especially around the muzzle, face, or throat.

Bleeding: Your puppy has a wound that's bleeding in spurts (arterial bleeding) or the bleeding is steady and won't stop with direct pressure.

Breathing difficulties: Your puppy is gasping for air, her breathing is impaired, or she cannot breathe.

Burns: Major burns that cause loss of fur, loss of skin, blackness, swelling, and blistering need immediate care.

Choking: Your puppy is pawing at her mouth, is struggling or gasping, or has something stuck in her mouth or throat.

Dislocated joint: A dislocated joint will be nonfunctional, it will look wrong, and your puppy won't put any weight on it.

Heat stroke: Symptoms include body temperature over 104°F, bloody diarrhea and/or vomiting, depression, stupor, difficulty breathing, increased heart rate, and red mucus membranes.

Heart or circulation problems: Symptoms include a slow heart rate, one that's much too fast, or an undetectable pulse.

Hypoglycemia: A sudden loss of coordination, paired with sleepiness and general weakness.

DOG TALK

Hypoglycemia is a sudden drop in blood sugar (glucose) that can occur in Yorkie puppies after exercise or during stress.

Hypothermia: An overly cold puppy may have a body temperature of less than 95°F, a slowed heart rate, stupor, unconsciousness, pale or blue mucus membranes, and extreme shivering.

The first thing to do in any emergency is to calm yourself. If you are in a panic, you won't be thinking clearly and your puppy will react by panicking, too. She'll then be more apt to struggle and fight your efforts to help her. So take a deep breath and calm yourself.

Then you need to assess the situation:

- 🐾 What has just happened?
- 🐾 What caused the problem?
- 🐾 What is your puppy's condition?

Now call your veterinarian or the local emergency veterinary clinic. They will want to know the following:

- 🐾 What happened?
- 🐾 Is your puppy breathing? Is she breathing with difficulty? Be able to describe it.
- 🐾 Does your puppy have a pulse? What is it?
- 🐾 What is her temperature?
- 🐾 Has she vomited or passed any stools? What do they look like? Did she pass any foreign objects in her stool?
- 🐾 Is your puppy bleeding? How much? And from where?

TIPS AND TAILS

A Yorkie puppy's normal temperature is between 101°F and 102.5°F. Anything above or below that is abnormal. Normal respirations are between 10 and 30 breaths per minute. A normal pulse is between 90 and 160 beats per minute; an excited or small Yorkie will have a higher heart rate.

If your puppy has no pulse and is not breathing, you need to perform cardiopulmonary resuscitation (CPR). This will keep oxygen in your dog's system until you can get her to help or someone else can assist you in getting her help. Never do CPR on a dog who has a heartbeat or is breathing; you'll only cause more harm.

Here's how to give your Yorkie CPR:

❧ Check your dog's airway and be sure nothing is obstructing it. If she's got a ball stuck in her throat, for example, pull it out using your fingers, needle-nose pliers, tongs, or anything else you can grab it with.

❧ Inhale a good breath and blow into your dog's nose, cupping your hands around her muzzle to make it airtight. You can wrap her lips around her mouth and hold them with your hands to seal them. Remember to blow gently; she's a tiny dog with tiny lungs.

❧ Watch to be sure her chest rises with your exhale.

❧ Then place your hands, one above the other, over your dog's heart where her elbow touches her chest. Place your other hand below her rib cage. Gently squeeze five times and breathe for her again.

Meanwhile, try to call for help from someone else in the house or nearby. It's tough to perform CPR or stop bleeding and call the veterinarian for guidance all by yourself.

Your veterinarian may have additional questions depending on the circumstances. He'll also provide some guidelines about restraining your puppy and instructions for what you need to do immediately and when and how to bring your puppy to the clinic.

Enrolling in Pet First-Aid Classes

Pet first-aid classes are a great idea for all pet owners. Not only will the classes teach you how to recognize an emergency, but you'll also have a chance to practice CPR on a canine CPR dummy. That alone can give you some peace of mind because you know what to do should something happen.

The American Red Cross offers first-aid classes for people and pets (dogs and cats). Other programs are available, too, although many are based on the Red Cross program.

To find a class near you, contact the Red Cross, your veterinarian, or a dog trainer in your area. The classes are usually very reasonable in cost and are only 3 or 4 hours long. The Red Cross class includes a small book and a DVD.

Assembling a Pet First-Aid Kit

Liz has maintained three first-aid kits (in her home, work, and car) for many years. In fact, it's been a standard joke with friends and family that if anyone needs anything—bandages, ibuprofen, or a cold pack—check with Liz! She doesn't mind because that's why she has them.

Liz's first-aid kits include items for people and for pets, but if you already have one for the people close to you, it's easy to put one together for your Yorkshire Terrier puppy.

A basic first-aid kit should include the following things:

🐾 Gauze sponges and pads of various sizes for cleaning wounds and to put pressure on wounds

🐾 Bandaging tape to hold gauze pads in place

🐾 Stretch tape or wrap to cover bandaging or immobilize a wound

🐾 Antibiotic ointment

🐾 Benadryl for allergic reactions

🐾 Cold compresses to reduce swelling

🐾 Scissors (both round tipped and pointed tipped)

🐾 Tweezers (metal ones are better than plastic)

🐾 Disposable razors to shave hair away from a wound

🐾 Nail clippers small enough for Yorkshire Terriers

🐾 Nutri-Cal or other nutritional supplement for hypoglycemia

🐾 Rectal thermometer and petroleum jelly

🐾 Sterile eye wash

🐾 Antiseptic cleaning wipes

🐾 Styptic powder to stop bleeding from a broken toenail

🐾 Pen or pencil and paper to jot down information for the veterinarian or advice from the vet

It's also a good idea to have a towel or two at hand, and a blanket, depending on where you live and what activities you do with your Yorkie puppy. The towel can dry off a wet dog or clean up after bleeding or vomiting, and a blanket can immobilize a hurt dog or keep her warm.

You should also have a muzzle that fits your puppy. Your Yorkie is tiny, but if she's frightened or hurt, she can still hurt you should she bite.

Practice muzzling your puppy during grooming or training sessions so she'll be used to it prior to an emergency. Hold a treat in the opening of the muzzle, slide the muzzle over her face, and give her the treat. Praise her, slide the muzzle off, and tell her how wonderful she is.

Yorkie Health Challenges

Yorkshire Terriers are, overall, a healthy breed. But they do have some health concerns. In this section, we cover those concerns that might appear in puppyhood. Month 12 has more information on health challenges that can appear in adulthood.

Hypoglycemia: Tiny-breed dogs such as Yorkies can suffer from low blood sugar if the puppy goes too long between meals. Hypoglycemia can also result from strenuous exercise or stress. Symptoms include sleepiness, lethargy, weakness, and, if it progresses, convulsions and death.

Yorkies of this age should eat four or five times a day. If you suspect low blood sugar, offer her food. If she won't eat, give her a nutritional supplement immediately.

Legg-Calve-Perthes disease: This is a disease of the hip joints. When the head of the femur loses its blood supply, it will deteriorate and die. The puppy will begin to limp or refuse to use the leg because it's so painful. This can be caused by an accident such as a fall from a height. A forcefully dislocated hip can also cause it.

Your veterinarian will x-ray the joint to confirm the diagnosis. Surgery will remove the affected ball of the femur, and the puppy's muscles will then form a false joint. A hip replacement is also often an option.

Lymphangiectasia: This is a condition in which lymph fluid, when collected from the body's tissues, is not returned to the blood stream but instead is leaked into the intestinal tract. It is then excreted in the feces. The puppy may have stunted growth, swollen legs and abdomen, and trouble breathing.

Diagnosis is made through laboratory tests, and the condition can be treated through diet and veterinary care.

Patellar luxation: This is an inherited disorder of the patella, or kneecap, of one or both hind legs. The patella normally slides up and down in a groove on the femur when the hind leg moves and bends. However, if the groove is too shallow or the tendon of the quadriceps muscle is too tight, the patella will move out of place. If this happens repeatedly, the groove wears down more, making it happen even more.

The puppy will cry when this happens. She will also hop on one back leg, carrying the hurt one bent under her, or she'll extend the injured leg. When the leg is straight, the patella will often pop back into place. However, in more severe cases, the patella may not stay in position. The severity is graded from 1 to 4, depending upon the severity of the disability. Your veterinarian will need to evaluate the degree of disability. Surgery may be needed for severe cases.

> ## TIPS AND TAILS
>
> The Orthopedic Foundation for Animals (OFA) maintains a patellar luxation registry and issues a certificate for those Yorkies who palpate normal at 12 months of age.

Tracheal collapse: When the rings that make up the trachea are soft, or less rigid than they should be, the rings can collapse. If it happens in the chest area, the Yorkie will have trouble exhaling. If it happens in the neck area, the puppy will have difficulty inhaling.

This can be made worse if the puppy coughs, has a respiratory infection or an enlarged heart, or has suffered from inhalant allergies. Obesity is also a factor. This can also occur when the puppy is eating or drinking.

One of the first symptoms is a cough with a unique, harsh honking sound. In extreme cases, the puppy will turn blue from lack of oxygen and may pass out. This requires veterinary care.

Dealing with Mites and Mange

Mange is caused by mites, tiny insects that live on and in the skin. There are several different kinds of mange that can torment your Yorkie.

Demodectic mites are transmitted to puppies from their mothers. However, an outbreak of mange usually doesn't occur until the puppies are under stress, such as during teething. More males seem to get it than females. There also appears to be a predisposition or inherited tendency toward this but exactly how that happens is unknown. This is not contagious to people. During an outbreak, the skin is red, scaly, and infected with hair loss. Your pup would need veterinary care for this, as this can be serious.

Sarcoptic mange (often called scabies) is caused by a tiny, spiderlike mite. It's very contagious and is transferable to people and other pets. It causes severe itching. This must be treated under a veterinarian's supervision.

Chyletiella mange affects puppies and is often called walking dandruff because the mites can be seen moving under flakes of skin. This may or may not cause itching. This mite can also be transmitted to people. Flea preparations often prevent mite infestations, but once infested, treatment usually consists of several baths over 6 to 8 weeks with pyrethrin shampoo.

If you see any thinning of the coat, red skin, or your puppy is scratching and itching, call your veterinarian. Your vet can diagnose the problem and recommend treatment. He can also let you know whether the problem is contagious and what kind of care needs to be taken with family members or other pets.

Combating Dangerous Insects

At this age, your puppy is busy exploring his world. She may look for lizards in the firewood pile or chase a critter into some bushes. Unfortunately, she can then get bitten or stung by an insect. Insect bites and stings can be frightening as well as painful for your puppy.

Ants: More than 22,000 species of ants inhabit every continent of the world, except Antarctica. Most ants bite, and for their size, they have amazingly powerful bites. Fire ants also have a toxin that can be harmful and cause an allergic reaction in many dogs.

If your Yorkie is bitten by fire ants, she'll need immediate veterinary care. Call your veterinarian before leaving for the clinic because he might want you to give your puppy a Bendadryl first. He might also want you to go to the nearest emergency clinic.

Bees: There are more than 20,000 species of bees, and although not all of them sting, many do. Most of those that do sting can cause an allergic reaction. Africanized bees in particular are very defensive of their territory; once they perceive a threat, many will come to the hive's defense, therefore multiple stings are common.

If your puppy is stung just once, scrape out the stinger, give her a Benadryl, put ice on the stung place, and watch her. If there's little swelling and no swelling of the face or throat, she'll probably be fine. However, if she appears in distress, pacing and uncomfortable, or if she has any swelling around her face or throat, take her to your veterinarian.

If Africanized bees sting your puppy multiple times, she's going to need immediate help. Give her a Benadryl, and go directly to your vet or the emergency clinic, whichever is closer.

Scorpions: Scorpions tend to be more common in warmer climates, but with more than 1,750 species worldwide, they also cannot be called uncommon. These eight-legged, clawed insects have a large stinger at the end of their tail. Their venom is poisonous, although only 25 species are considered deadly. Many only sting when stepped on or disturbed in their hiding spots.

If you see the scorpion that stings your puppy, get a good look at it so you can describe it to your veterinarian. Call before heading to the vet's clinic because he might want you to give your dog a Benadryl first.

> ### TIPS AND TAILS

If you can safely catch the insect, do so and bring it to the veterinarian's clinic so the vet can identify it. This can help your veterinarian plan the course of treatment.

Black widow spiders: These spiders with their trademark red hourglass on the underside of the abdomen are well known throughout North and South America. However, not all black widows are black, and not all have a red hourglass. Some are brown, some may have red spots, and some might have yellow and white markings. These spiders will bite readily and are potentially lethal.

Your puppy will need immediate veterinary care if bitten. Call your veterinarian, and go directly to his clinic unless he recommends the closest emergency clinic instead.

Wasps: There are more than 100,000 species of wasps (sometimes called yellow jackets or hornets) worldwide, and although they normally don't swarm to protect their hive, they do readily sting, especially when disturbed.

Wasp stings are quite painful and often trigger an allergic reaction. Immediately give your puppy a Benadryl if she's stung. Put ice on the stung spot, and if there's no swelling, she'll probably be fine. If you see any swelling, especially around the face or throat, call your veterinarian immediately.

The vast majority of insect bites and stings are annoying and can be painful but are not deadly. However, a few can pack quite a wallop. So pay attention, watch for a reaction, and contact your veterinarian if you have any doubt whatsoever about what's going on with your puppy.

Nutrition

Yorkshire Terriers have some very specific nutritional requirements, much of which is based on the fact that the breed is so tiny. As your Yorkie continues to grow and becomes more active this month, excellent nutrition is even more important.

Nutritional Needs Now

We can't emphasize enough that your Yorkie needs good nutrition, not just more food. Feeding your Yorkie more food shouldn't be your goal. After all, many commercial foods contain a lot of filler—usually fiber and cereal grains. That's not the nutrition your puppy needs. With a physically small stomach, your puppy could eat and get full without getting the calories he requires.

The food she eats should be at least 25 percent protein, at least 17 percent fat, and less than 5 percent fiber. It should contain 1.0 to 1.8 calcium and 0.8 to 1.6 percent phosphorus. The food should be at least 80 percent digestible, but by law, the digestibility levels are not allowed to be posted on the dog-food label.

Unfortunately, experts don't agree on how many calories a Yorkie in her sixth month should consume. Recommendations for a 5-pound puppy range from 150 calories per day for a sedentary Yorkie to 375 calories per day for a very active one. As a general rule, an average active 5-pound, 6-month Yorkie needs about 224 calories per day.

If your puppy is eating a puppy food, you can gradually switch her to a food labeled for all life stages this month. Begin the change by offering ¼ of the new food and ¾ of the old food. Then after a week, go to ½ old and ½ new. On the third week, give her ¼ of the old food and ¾ of the new. By the fourth week, you can eliminate the old food. Take several weeks to change her over. Should she get soft stools during this time, slow the change even more.

Creating a Good Eater

Many Yorkie owners are so worried that their puppy eats well to avoid hypoglycemia that they turn their puppy into a finicky eater. If the puppy doesn't eat, the owner panics and offers the puppy something different. After all, the puppy must eat, right?

Well, yes and no. Hypoglycemia is a potential problem, but not all Yorkie puppies develop it. And if your puppy eats a good diet and is fed scheduled meals, chances are she'll be just fine.

> **TIPS AND TAILS**
>
> If you're going to be doing something more active than normal or potentially stressful with your puppy, keep some nutritious snacks on hand. Give your puppy one every so often to keep her blood sugar from dropping.

If your puppy learns that when she turns up her nose at her food you offer her something even better, you'll create a finicky eater. Your Yorkie puppy can't eat volumes of food—her tummy isn't big enough—so eating a good-quality food is important. Being a good eater is even more vital.

To help your Yorkie be a good eater, you and your puppy both need to build some good habits:

- ❧ Feed your puppy three or four times a day, depending on her activity level.
- ❧ Feed her at the same times each day. A schedule is important.
- ❧ Feed her in the same place.
- ❧ Feed her a good-quality food or diet.
- ❧ Feed her about an hour after exercise, after she's relieved herself, and not right after a nap. She needs to be awake and hungry.
- ❧ Feed her away from other dogs.
- ❧ Hand-feed her a portion of her food. This makes eating more exciting and involves you in the process.

> **HAPPY PUPPY**
>
> In the past, dog owners were told not to hand-feed their dogs, that it would spoil the dog. However, that feeling has changed. Hand-feeding your puppy a portion of her food makes eating more exciting, involves you in the process, and can significantly reduce food-guarding behaviors.

- ❧ Don't make frequent changes to your puppy's food or diet. Constant changes may temporarily tempt your puppy to eat, but they can also build expectations for new foods.

If your puppy is and remains a finicky eater, call your veterinarian and have a thorough examination done. Be sure there's no health reason for her lack of appetite.

Using Training Treats

As training your Yorkie becomes increasingly more important, you'll be using quite a few training treats. The size of the individual treats needs to be tiny, not just because your Yorkie is tiny but also because you don't want the treats to upset the nutritional balance of your puppy's food.

As a general rule, anything added to your Yorkie's diet should never amount to more than 10 percent of the daily food. That means all the training treats, chew treats, and supplements you give your puppy cannot total more than 10 percent.

It's usually a good idea to avoid many of the commercial treats that contain additives, artificial flavorings and preservatives, sugar, and salt. However, if you prefer using commercial treats, read the ingredients carefully and avoid treats that contain a lot of additives and junk foods.

The following table lists some calorie counts for foods you can use as healthy treats for your Yorkie. The calorie counts are for the measured amount; obviously you won't be feeding that much during a training session or even throughout a day. But you can break down the calorie count according to how much you give during the training session.

Food	Amount	Calories
Beef, liver, cooked	¼ cup	198
Chicken, gizzard and heart	4 ounces	150
Cheese, cheddar, cubed	¼ cup	133
Cheese, American, cubed	¼ cup	132
Cheese, Swiss, cubed	¼ cup	125
Popcorn, popped, plain	1 cup	80
Yam, cooked, cubed	½ cup	80
Carrots, sliced	½ cup	25

Avoid foods that could upset your puppy's gastrointestinal tract, such as greasy or spicy foods or foods high in salt or sugar. Instead, use foods that are potentially good foods, such as those listed in the preceding table.

No matter what you feed your Yorkie and what you use as treats, just be aware of everything your puppy eats and how much. Too many treats could interfere with your puppy's appetite. Too many can upset the good nutrition provided by her food. It's definitely a balancing act.

Grooming

The Yorkshire Terrier's coat is certainly one of the reasons why so many people choose this breed. The flowing hair, the unique colors, and the topknot all provide a lovely picture. That appearance requires some care, however, as we've discussed in the previous months.

Brush Thoroughly

It's worth repeating: You have to groom your Yorkie. There's no getting around it. But there are ways to make it easier on both of you.

You can brush and comb your Yorkie anywhere, even on your lap if you want, but it's much easier if you have a table you can use. Grooming tables are especially nice because you can adjust the height so you don't strain your back, and they have a non-slip surface.

The process is also easer if you keep all your supplies together so they're readily at hand. For brushing and combing your pup's coat, you need a pin brush, a wide-toothed comb, and a spray bottle with a combination of $\frac{1}{4}$ hair conditioner and $\frac{3}{4}$ water.

- ♣ Spread a towel on top of the table, lift your puppy up, and decide where you're going to start. Let's say you're going to begin with your puppy's right side.
- ♣ Spray the water-and-conditioner mix on the area until the hair is damp. (Dry hair tangles more and is brittle.)
- ♣ Begin with the hair coat lower on the right side, at the belly. Lift up the coat so the belly is showing. Brush with the pin brush first and then the comb. When all tangles are gone and the coat is silky, part the hair farther up on the side, pull it down, and repeat the process.
- ♣ When the side is finished, do the legs on this side of your puppy.

Then turn your puppy around and do the other side. Then brush and comb the tail, the chest, and then the head. Just make sure you don't forget any portions or parts. When you're all done, a comb should glide nicely through her coat all over her.

Tangles and Matts

A tangle is when the hairs become wrapped around a foreign object such as a burr or grass seed, and get knotted. A tangle can also form in a friction spot, such as under or behind the legs. A collar or harness or dog clothes can also cause friction and then a tangle.

Matts form when tangles aren't brushed out. The tangle will attract more hairs, which in turn join the tangle, and then the tangle gets thicker. Pretty soon, a solid matt has formed.

You can comb out most tangles using a wide-toothed comb. Be gentle as you comb hairs out of the tangle. If combing alone doesn't get out the matt, use a little hair conditioner or detangler from the grooming section of your local pet-supply store. Work this into the tangle, and then comb it again.

If the tangle or matt cannot be combed out, you may need to cut it out of the coat. This is often the better solution than continuing to pull on your puppy's hair, but be very careful when you cut it because you could cut the underlying skin.

To trim out a matt, place the wide-toothed comb in the coat between the matt and your puppy's skin. Trim with the scissors parallel to your puppy's skin on the outer side of the comb. Trim with tiny snips just to be safe.

> ### TIPS AND TAILS
>
> If your puppy has several matts, you will need the help of a professional groomer. He'll probably recommend your puppy be shaved short because trying to comb out a number of matts will be uncomfortable for your puppy.

Tangles and matts are more than a cosmetic problem; they are also uncomfortable for your puppy. As the tangles and matts grow by incorporating more hairs, they pull on your puppy's skin. The skin under the matt can be sore, red, and inflamed, too. Dirt, moisture, food, and even fecal matter can get caught in the matt, and it can become quite disgusting.

Groom Often

In Month 4, we discussed the importance of establishing—and following—a grooming schedule, and we want to emphasize that again here, especially now that your puppy is growing more coat. You need to comb your puppy each and every day, without fail.

It only takes one run outside in the rain or one play session with another puppy for a tangle to form. That doesn't mean your puppy shouldn't play; these activities are necessary for a healthy mind and body. Instead, daily grooming can take care of these minor tangles before they grow into major matts.

Hopefully, you have established a grooming routine. Just be sure you keep to that schedule. This is an appointment with your puppy that you have every day. But that doesn't mean you can't run the comb through your puppy's coat at other times, too. Many Yorkie owners have a comb with them at all times. When watching TV, they'll comb their dog. Keep to your regular grooming schedule, but also comb your puppy any time you want.

Social Skills

Your Yorkie puppy's emotional and mental faculties are constantly evolving right now. She's not a baby puppy anymore, but she's not yet a teenager either.

She is at an in-between stage, and that can be tough for many puppies—and their owners. She's going to need your help to get through this stage in one piece.

Living with People

Your puppy was born into the world surrounded by people; she's familiar with people and yet she's a dog. A tiny dog, but still a dog. She was born with the instincts to bond closely with people, but nothing in her heritage has told her how to live with people.

Your Yorkie will be devoted to you, but she will always be a dog first and a terrier second. She will be happy to be with you, but she'll also be happy chasing lizards in the backyard and hunting for mice in the woodpile.

Living with people can be confusing for your puppy. She won't understand when children wrestle, run around wildly, and yell. She may bark at them and may even snap at them out of concern or in protectiveness. Help her stay out of trouble by removing her from those situations. At the same time, teach the kids to be calm around dogs.

She also won't understand when a child is being disciplined. She may bark or growl or try to protect the child. Again, remove her from the situation. Don't yell at her or get angry.

She won't understand if two adults in the household have a disagreement, either. She may again bark, try to interfere, or run away and hide. If at all possible, put her in another room.

Your Yorkshire Terrier has probably become a vital part of your family, and it's often hard to imagine that she doesn't understand how the family works. But she will often be confused, especially at this stage of her life.

Help her understand by providing clear communication. Praise her when she's reacting or acting correctly, and interrupt her when she's making a mistake. Remove her from any situations that are too loud, scary, or intimidating for her.

Working Through Unsocial Behavior

Don't get upset if your Yorkie puppy misbehaves in public. Again, she's got to learn the expected social behaviors, and even though you've been teaching her for the past few months, she's still immature and will make mistakes.

If she starts barking at people, kids on skateboards, or other dogs, distract her, turn her away from the cause of her barking, and tell her, "Sweetie, leave it!" Praise her when she stops.

Watch her body language, and when you see her begin to stare—which is usually the first thing she's going to do before erupting in a flurry of barks—distract her. Don't wait for her to begin barking. Praise her when she looks at you.

If you find your Yorkie challenging other dogs, especially much bigger ones, stop that immediately. It isn't funny, it isn't cute, and it could get your tiny dog killed. And it wouldn't be the bigger dog's fault.

In a dog's world, a challenge is a challenge, and dogs don't measure other dogs to see if they're the appropriate size to respond to. If your Yorkie gets in another dog's face and barks furiously at him, that big dog could reach down, grab your Yorkie, shake her, and even kill her.

So don't let her develop that horrible habit. Should she begin to bark at another dog, stop her immediately, saying, "That's enough!" Turn her away from the dog and praise her for being quiet. If you pick her up, don't let her bark while in your arms.

Limiting Socialization

Socialization is still important and will continue to be important as your Yorkie grows up. She still needs to go places, hear strange sounds, smell different smells, and do all sorts of different things.

However, as she approaches adolescence next month, you may find that she's not going to be as comfortable having everyone pet her. That's fine; respect your puppy's feelings, and don't allow everyone to pet her. This breed is so tiny and adorable, everyone wants to pet her, but that's not necessarily good for your puppy. Yes, socialization is important, but even socializing your puppy to a variety of people doesn't mean *everyone* needs to pet her.

Let half of the people you meet pet her. Tell the others, nicely, "No, thanks, we're just out for a walk." But if you notice your puppy is a little uneasy with even that many people petting her, cut the number down even more. Let one third of the people you meet pet her and have a few of those people give her a special treat. That way, she'll be happier about being touched.

Behavior

Housetraining is an ongoing process, and hopefully it's going well. But in case it's not, let's take a look at what's going on, what might be happening, and what you can do if you run into some problems.

You'll also see the zoomies begin this month, if they haven't already started. The zoomies can be vastly entertaining, but they can also turn into a bad habit. Let's see what they are and what causes them.

Housetraining Revisited

As we've mentioned in earlier months, housetraining can take a while with Yorkies. It's not that your Yorkie is being bad on purpose, but remember, she has a very tiny bladder. It often takes a while to develop bladder control.

> **HAPPY PUPPY**
>
> Your continued praise and positive reinforcements for her housetraining efforts are necessary for good reliable housetraining skills. Don't forget about housetraining until she has an accident.

Many different things can cause housetraining problems:

Schedule inconsistencies: It's important to maintain your housetraining schedule and to be sure she gets outside (or to her indoor potty area) on a regular basis. Continue to ask her to go and then praise her for going.

Submissive urination: If your Yorkie leaks some urine when she's excited, don't yell at her or get mad at her. This is called submissive urination and is the result of her excitement. This is more common in females, but males also do it. If you scold your puppy for this, it will only get worse because now she'll be excited and stressed.

To overcome this, keep homecomings calm and quiet. Don't greet your excited puppy until she calms down. And even then, greet her with a towel for a while. Most puppies outgrow it by about 1 year old.

Urinary tract infections: It's not uncommon for a puppy to develop a urinary tract infection, and when she does, she'll have urges to relieve herself often. She may not have time to find you or ask to go outside; she just squats where she is.

Medications: Some medications can cause housetraining accidents, urinary or fecal. If your veterinarian prescribes a medication, ask what side effects you should expect.

Other causes: Many other factors can cause housetraining accidents, including illnesses, intestinal parasites, or food allergies.

If your Yorkie has been doing well with her housetraining and then regresses, call your veterinarian first. If all health causes are eliminated, treat this as a training problem.

The Zoomies!

After you've finished dinner, fed your puppy, cleaned the kitchen, and turned on the television, you'd probably enjoy some peace and quiet for a few minutes. However, this is usually when the zoomies begin.

All of a sudden, your Yorkie puppy is tearing around the house, zipping up and down the hall, rocketing around the dining-room table, bouncing off the back of the sofa, and running right up the front of you to give you a lick on the nose. Now you can laugh out loud at the zoomies, and that's fine, but you also need to be able to turn them off if need be.

Being able to turn off the zoomies is important because when she's zooming around, she's not thinking. She's happy, full of energy, and wants to run and play. However, you need to be able to stop her in case it becomes dangerous for her to act in this way. For example, if you dropped a cup and there's broken glass all over her path of travel, you need to stop her. Perhaps you have guests over and you don't want her running up the front of them as she does with you.

The best way to control the zoomies is to put her on leash prior to the time she usually begins—while she's eating dinner, for example. Then hold on to the leash, and should she try to pull or zoom, let her know, "No. Not now." When she relaxes, praise her.

Then, after she's calm and quiet, take off her leash and tell her, "Okay! Zoomies!" Toss her a toy to let her know she can run and then praise her. Put the zoomies under your control, and teach her she can do it when you give her permission to do so.

Jumping on People

A Yorkshire Terrier jumping on you isn't going to cause nearly the problems a larger dog will cause, but it can still be an annoying behavior. If you wear hose, for example, you're not going to appreciate those sharp nails putting run after run in them. If you're dressed for work and take your Yorkie outside to relieve herself, you don't want her jumping up on your slacks.

So the first decision you need to make is whether this is a problem or not. Then everyone in the family needs to abide by the decision. One person cannot encourage jumping while someone else tries to stop it.

If you decide to stop it, teach your Yorkie to sit for petting and attention. Teach her she doesn't get any attention when she jumps; just walk away from her. Then ask her to sit, lean down to pet her, and praise her. Be consistent with this. If jumping occasionally results in attention, that will be enough to keep her jumping.

> ### TIPS AND TAILS
>
> Slot machines in Las Vegas draw in gamblers not because they pay out every time but because they pay out *sometimes*. If your Yorkie's behavior gets a reward sometimes, she'll try even harder to do it.

Training

There's a lot of motivation to train a large dog. A Labrador Retriever, Great Dane, or German Shepherd could hurt you, knock down the kids, or destroy your house if he isn't trained. Tiny dogs are so cute, it's hard sometimes to see that they, too, need training. Tiny dogs can get in just as much trouble as larger breeds, and even though they often don't cause the vast amounts of damage a large dog can, they can do enough damage to hurt your belongings or even themselves.

This month your Yorkie is becoming more able to concentrate and learn. She still may have a short attention span, but it's getting better. Several training options are available for you and your puppy, and each comes with pros and cons.

Training Tips

Remember, your Yorkie puppy is not a fur-covered person. Even though she has become a well-loved member of the family and at times does seem very human, she's not. Her thought processes, her view of the world, and how she responds are always going to be different.

In addition, no matter how intelligent your Yorkie is, she's never going to be able to think like a human. That means you have to try to decipher what she's thinking and why she does what she does. This is tough because although we can guess how a dog thinks, we'll never really know for sure.

Here are some other training tips to keep in mind this month:

- Continue to limit your Yorkshire Terrier puppy's freedom in the house using her crate and baby gates.

- Don't give your puppy off-leash freedom outside your fenced yard. She's not going to be mentally mature enough, or well trained enough, until she's 18 months to 2 years old.

- Continue to try to prevent bad behaviors from occurring rather than trying to deal with them after they've happened. Preventing the bad behaviors can help build good habits, and that's your goal.

- Teach your Yorkie that "Sweetie, good!" or "Sweetie, thank you!" are words that make you happy. Say them with a smile and a happy voice.

- Timing is very important. Praise your puppy as she does something right, and interrupt bad behaviors as they happen.

- Continue trying to help your puppy succeed both in her training sessions and in life in general. She learns much more from her successes than she does from her mistakes.

- Punishments given after the problem behavior has already occurred don't work and could potentially damage your relationship with your puppy because she won't understand why you're scolding her.

Have fun with your training. If the training is fun, you're going to be more apt to do it, and if both you and your puppy have fun, she's going to cooperate more. Plus, it's fun watching your puppy learn, understand, and do what you ask her to do.

Enrolling in Basic Obedience Class

If you and your puppy enrolled in a kindergarten puppy class, also often called a puppy socialization class, you've both probably graduated by now. The next level of classes is a basic obedience class. Some trainers or training clubs also call these pre-novice or novice classes.

The difference between puppy class and basic obedience is easy to see if you think about classes for young children. The kindergarten puppy class is like kindergarten for kids with lots of socialization, learning to get along with others, basic social rules, and an introduction to the concept of self-control.

Basic obedience is like first grade. More emphasis is placed on self-control and learning about skills the youngster will need in the future.

Don't think of dog-training classes as boot camp. Although that might have been the case in years past, because of recent changes in training techniques, dogs today tend to approach training class with tails wagging wildly.

Even though you and your puppy have begun learning many of the basic commands, including sit, down, stay, come, and leave it, in class, your puppy would be expected to do them alongside other puppies and their owners. That means many more distractions than your puppy is probably used to. Although it can be hard, your puppy is certainly capable of this.

Should You Go It Alone or with Help?

You started training your puppy when she first joined your household and have been adding to those skills each month. Many Yorkshire Terrier owners teach their dogs at home and do well without the services of a professional trainer. But if you're having problems or you and your terrier are butting heads, a trainer can help you.

Here are some of your options:

🐾 Group classes are usually quite economical when compared to private training.

🐾 Group classes have a set curriculum, although the instructor usually addresses individual issues, too.

🐾 A group class can provide distractions you don't have at home. This provides both you and your puppy a chance to learn and work with other people and other dogs.

🐾 Private or one-on-one training can take place in your home or at the training facility. With these lessons, only you and your dog meet with the trainer so you have her undivided attention.

🐾 Private training is more expensive than group training.

🐾 Private training lessons can be centered around your puppy's individual needs.

🐾 Private lessons are great if you have a variable work schedule and can't make a group class.

🐾 Behavior consultations are held by *behaviorists* or *behavior consultants*.

🐾 Behavior consultations usually focus on problem behaviors.

A **behaviorist,** or veterinary behaviorist, is a veterinarian who specializes in behavior. A **behavioral consultant** is a behavior specialist, and often also a dog trainer, who is not a veterinarian.

Each of these forms of training is beneficial. If you have any doubts as to what you and your puppy need, talk to your dog trainer.

Before enrolling in the class, talk to the trainer and be sure the class will be safe for your tiny puppy. Although most classes do have dogs of various breeds and sizes, the trainer should be aware of the need to protect the tiny ones. Of course, the trainer will also ensure you protect your puppy without spoiling her.

You and Your Puppy

Your puppy is a lot of fun at this age. She's past the very young months of puppyhood when she was so incredibly fragile. Although you may still be having some house-training issues, she's been doing well with that, too. She's also sleeping through the night now.

This month, she's playing and learning. You're getting to know her better, and you've figured out she's really a nice little dog.

Teaching "Roll Over"

The trick "Roll over" is an easy one to teach and is fun for your Yorkie to do. Here's how to teach it:

- 🐾 Sit on the floor with your puppy and have a handful of tiny tasty treats with you.

- 🐾 Ask your puppy to lie down, and gently roll her on to one side. Keep a hand on her shoulder to keep her from popping up.

- 🐾 Let her sniff a treat. Hold the treat close to her nose, and move it in a small circle from her nose to her shoulder and toward her back.

- 🐾 As you move the treat toward her shoulder and back, tell her, "Sweetie, roll over!" Keep moving the treat slowly so she rolls all the way over.

- 🐾 When she rolls over, give her the treat and praise her, "Sweetie, good to roll over!"

For the first few times, you might have to give her a little help to get all the way over. When she does it entirely on her own, enthusiastically praise her.

Once she knows "Roll over" means to move one specific direction, have her lie on her other side and teach her to roll the other way. Use the command, "Sweetie, roll the other way," and use the same training technique.

Putting a Stop to Biting

You may have discovered there are certain times when your puppy wants to play-fight with you. Perhaps this happens when you interrupt the zoomies or when you're trying to groom her. It's hard to take this play-fighting seriously—after all, she's so tiny! It's not like a German Shepherd is trying to bite your hands.

However, this is still a bad habit that you should never encourage and, in fact, you need to stop. Whenever a dog, of any age or size, tries to use her mouth on people, in play or when protesting something like grooming, there's a potential for the puppy to bite. If the puppy gets in the habit of using her mouth during every grooming session, it will change from play-biting to serious attempts to bite while protesting the grooming.

Play-biting: Never play-fight with her. Don't wiggle your fingers in her face, and don't let her grab your hands, fingers, or sleeves. If she does, stop her immediately with an "Ouch! No bite!" Play-biting is accompanied by a wagging tail, running and bouncing around, dashing away and back, and repeated nips or bites.

Aggressive biting: If you're trying to brush your Yorkie and she doesn't want to be groomed, she might try to bite your hand to stop you. Or she might grab one of your socks and want to keep it, growling, snarling, and trying to bite when you take it away. Her body language will be all up front: She'll be standing tall and leaning forward, with her tail straight up and her teeth bared. Aggressive biting is a problem, and you need the help of a dog trainer or behaviorist to work through this.

Fearful biting: If your Yorkie is placed in a situation where she's afraid and can't get away, she might bite. If you keep in mind this is a very small dog in a very large world, you can understand that at times she'll be afraid. To prevent fearful aggression, protect her from situations where she has no recourse except to bite. The fearful dog will be crouched and pulled in tight with a tucked tail, and she might be whining.

If you feel her biting may be increasing or becoming a problem, get some professional help. Never ignore biting in hopes it will go away.

Enjoying Some Quiet Time

With so much going on in your puppy's life right now, it's important to create and share some quiet times. Not only do you need peace and quiet once in a while, but so does your puppy. The two of you can still enjoy each other's company while you watch the news, check your email, or read.

If your puppy tends to be a little calmer at certain times, take advantage of those times first if you can make them work in your schedule. If, for example, immediately after dinner your puppy wants a nap, you can check your email then. Just ask her to lie down in the chair next to you, and praise her when she does. If she tries to climb up your chest, put her back where you had her originally.

Some quiet times should be for both you and your puppy. Find a time that works for you, such as in the evening after you come home from work or just before you go to bed. Sit on the sofa, and invite her up next to you (if you're allowing her on the furniture). Stroke her head, or if she rolls over to her back, give her a tummy rub. Enjoy the quiet with no television and no music, and simply calm your soul by touching your dog. It really doesn't get any better than this.

Month 6 > **Month 7** > Month 8

Socialization in public
Adult teeth are in—chewing continues
Enroll in basic obedience class
Moderate growth
Sexual maturity

At 7 months, your Yorkshire Terrier puppy is becoming an adolescent. He's feeling a little more grown up and may challenge you, other dogs, and even the family cat. He's also barking more now as a result of this new attitude.

This can be a difficult time for puppy owners. They often can't believe their adorable Yorkie puppy can be so, well, difficult! Don't worry. This is a natural part of growing up, and your Yorkie's personality and temperament aren't changing. It is, however, important that you continue your puppy's training. Don't allow these bad puppy behaviors to turn into bad habits.

Behavior

Adolescence is the stage of growth when the young—be they human, canine, or any other species—transition to adulthood. The youngster is trying to see if the rules his or her parents have established still apply. Teenagers challenge authority as they strive toward independence and leaving childhood behind.

Most youngsters go through this stage to varying extents, and human and canine adolescents share many adolescent characteristics. Both can be wonderful in childhood or puppyhood and then be horrible in adolescence. A human teenager may tell her mother, "I hate you," one moment and then want affection from her mother the next. Likewise, a canine adolescent may chew destructively one moment and act like an angel the next.

Experts have discovered that during adolescence, the brain goes through some major changes. This is why teenagers, no matter what species, don't always make good decisions. While the teen is striving for independence, these physical changes in the brain cause havoc.

Unfortunately, as a result of these behaviors, and because many owners don't understand canine adolescence, more dogs are turned in to shelters for behavioral problems during adolescence than any other time during the dog's life. That's too bad. Adolescence can be unsettling for puppy owners and can be a lot of work, but it's normal and just a passing stage of life.

Surviving Yorkie Adolescence

Most Yorkshire Terrier puppies hit adolescence during their seventh month. This is an average, however, and some can come into it sooner or later. One of the first signs of adolescence owners see is when their shadow disappears. As a puppy, your Yorkshire Terrier's instincts told him to follow an adult who could protect him and keep him from harm. When adolescence hits, that instinct disappears.

The worst of adolescence for Yorkies is between 7 and 10 months. But once your puppy hits 10 months old, that doesn't mean he's all grown up and mentally mature. As we've mentioned, your Yorkshire Terrier puppy isn't going to be mentally mature until he's about 18 months to 2 years old.

Most puppy owners take this rebellion personally, wondering *Why is he doing this to me?* His behavior really isn't directed at you. Instead, it's Mother Nature's way of preparing your puppy for adulthood.

Even though your Yorkshire Terrier is going to continue living with you and is never going to have to live on his own, as a human teenager will, your dog is still going to need to make some decisions on his own. Those might include whether or not to listen to you and cooperate, or whether to ignore you and go chase the lizard in the yard. During adolescence, his brain is changing from that of a puppy to that of an adult who can make good decisions.

Waning Bite Inhibition

As your Yorkshire Terrier puppy moves into adolescence, he's also growing faster and stronger. He's still very small, but he doesn't realize it. This, combined with the hormones of adolescence and his willingness to challenge authority, means he'll be more casual about using his teeth. He may show less bite inhibition in play, both with other dogs and with people.

Be sure he gets an opportunity to play with friendly, small adult dogs. Ideally, have him play with dogs he considers friends. Then, should he use too much force while playing, they'll let him know with barks, growls, and snarls. They'll also put a stop to the play if he continues to bite inappropriately.

He can also play with younger puppies or smaller adult dogs if he behaves himself. If he starts being a bully and isn't playing nicely, step in and stop the play. Leash him and have him sit or lie down while the others play without him.

When he plays with people, don't let him bite. Ever. If he does, stop the game right away and leash him.

> **TIPS AND TAILS**

Be sure you continue caring for your Yorkie's mouth and teeth during this stage of life. Clean his teeth regularly, and, while doing so, open his mouth to examine his mouth and teeth. This is good grooming and health care, and it also conveys to your dog that you can control his mouth—a good lesson for adolescents.

Dealing with Leg-Lifting

When adolescence hits, leg-lifting can become a problem. Adolescent male puppies will lift a rear leg to urinate. Intact males are the most prone to mark by lifting a leg to urinate, but neutered males will, too. To the surprise of many dog owners, some adolescent females—intact as well as spayed—will also lift a leg to urinate.

Leg-lifting is more than simply urinating. When your puppy urinates, he empties his bladder. When a dog marks, he urinates a tiny splash each time, saving some urine for future marking opportunities. The goal of marking is to show the world this dog was at this particular spot and claims ownership of it. The dog is saying, "I was here, and this is mine!"

Leg-lifting can become a problem when the leg-lifter wants to mark every vertical surface and then each dog following him wants to do the same thing. Fire hydrants become so gross it's amazing firefighters can stand to touch them.

While out on walks, discourage leg-lifting. At the beginning of the walk, tell your pup to relieve himself and praise him when he does. Then, should he begin to sidle sideway to get into position to lift his leg, use the leash and your voice to interrupt him, "Ack! Not here."

Should your adolescent ever urinate on you, any family members, or personal items, and you catch him in the act, be shocked and horrified and let him see that reaction from you. Then leash him, walk him to his crate, close the door, and leave him alone for a while. When you let him out, keep him on leash in the house for a while and closely supervise him.

That Yorkie Attitude

Every breed of dog is unique in its own way—probably one reason why there are so many different breeds loved by so many different people. Yorkshire Terrier owners love the breed's small size, upright ears, intense eyes, and luscious coat. And then there's the breed's lively demeanor.

Yorkies are a combination of sweet and spicy. They're affectionate and loving yet have that terrier feistiness that leads them to challenge anything that doesn't go their way. When combined with the challenges of approaching adolescence … well, this month, your Yorkie's behavior can be a wild ride.

At 7 months, the best description for most Yorkies is self-assured. Maybe even brash. And this self-confident attitude can get them into trouble.

It's also not unusual to see Yorkies at this age challenge bigger dogs. Although it might be funny to see a 6-pound Yorkie standing in front of a much larger dog, barking furiously, that behavior could also get the Yorkie hurt or even killed.

Although this behavior is normal during this stage, that doesn't mean it should be tolerated. Discourage or control this behavior as much as possible. Let your Yorkie be a silly puppy when he's in a safe situation. A lizard in your backyard isn't going to hurt your Yorkie, for example, so he can chase that lizard all he wants. But when you're out in a field where snakes are known to be, keep your Yorkie on leash.

Don't be surprised if at times your self-assured Yorkie shows a fearful side. That's normal right now, too. It's important to keep your Yorkie safe from danger, but he also needs to continue his socialization. So don't hide him at home when he's worried.

Sounding the Alarm!

Many Yorkshire Terriers discover their voice at this age, and when they do, oh boy, can they sound the alarm! Yorkies can be barkers, and in fact, barking is one of the top behavioral problems many Yorkie owners complain about.

Most of the time, Yorkies bark because they see or hear something in the environment that triggers their interest or watchfulness. Perhaps a delivery truck is coming up the street or a strange cat is sitting on the back fence. The barking may even be at a butterfly fluttering by. To your Yorkie, his barking sounds an alarm that there's a perceived problem you need to be aware of.

However, just because your Yorkie thinks there's a problem doesn't mean you should allow his barking to continue. Your neighbors will soon begin to complain, and you're likely to get a headache. Besides, it's not good for your Yorkie to live in a constant state of watchfulness and excitement.

Your goal should not be to stop all barking; that's an impossible goal. Yorkies are watchful terriers and will always have an alarm bark. Instead, your goal should be to set some limits. How much barking will you tolerate? Then teach your dog to stop barking when you ask him to stop, as covered in Month 4.

This training will take some repetition; don't expect instant understanding and cooperation. After all, barking and watchfulness are very natural to Yorkies.

The Importance of Your Guidance

One of the most important lessons you can teach your Yorkie is to look to you for guidance. This is also one of the toughest lessons to teach some terriers because the breed has long been known for its self-reliance. However, when your Yorkie looks to you for guidance, you can either encourage or discourage him from any given course of action.

For example, while on a walk, your Yorkie alerts on something he sees. He stands tall, stares at it, and turns back to look at you for guidance. You can encourage him, "What is it? Let's go see!" and the two of you can go look at it. Or if you see a problem when he turns to look at you, you can tell him, "No, let's leave that alone," and walk away.

This is much easier than having to stop your Yorkie from barking uncontrollably, lunging and pulling on the leash, or exhibiting any other undesirable behaviors.

Teaching your Yorkie to look to you for guidance comes from your relationship with your Yorkie. Practice your training often, and make it fun. Play with your Yorkie and have fun with it. But at the same time, teach your Yorkie that although the two of you do have fun often, he still has to respect you. He's not allowed to bite you during play or lift his leg to mark your items. Respect toward you, as well as the relationship the two of you have, his trust in you, and his looking to you for guidance are all woven together.

Physical Development

Your Yorkie puppy is still growing and changing. He may seem a little off kilter this month because all his parts aren't growing evenly. This is all normal. Not all the body parts grow at the same time or at the same rate, but eventually everything will catch up.

You also may notice he's putting on some muscle. Most terriers, including Yorkies, are muscular dogs. Feel your puppy's upper front legs and shoulders as well as his upper back legs and hips. Feel those muscles? Good! That means he's getting his exercise. If you don't feel those muscles, gradually increase your Yorkie's activities. He should be strong, muscular, and fit.

Looking Like a Miniature Adult

Although your puppy's proportions are still a little off due his growth this month, he's beginning to look more like a miniature adult Yorkshire Terrier rather than a puppy. Yorkie puppies are round and soft; your puppy is now more angular. His facial features are more pronounced, and his body is longer.

Your puppy's posture is also more grown up. When he's paying attention to something, he'll stand with his paws firmly planted, his tail upright, and his head up. He'll look directly at the object of his interest. This stance is so attractive (and grown up) when you see it, you'll probably sigh and ask yourself where your puppy went. Many Yorkie owners do.

His adult teeth are in now—all 42 of them—and they're bright, shiny, and amazingly large for such a small dog. If any puppy teeth remain, talk to your veterinarian about what to do with them. She likely will recommend pulling them. However, she may want to x-ray your Yorkie first to be sure an adult tooth is waiting to come in behind it. If your Yorkie has an adult tooth that's come in right next to the puppy tooth, that puppy tooth will need to be pulled.

Changes in the Coat

You began to see some changes in your Yorkie's coat over the last couple months. Your puppy's short, soft puppy coat began to look unruly between 3 and 4 months of age, and now, at 7 months, you're seeing more and more of the silky adult coat.

The coat doesn't change immediately, and the change isn't evenly dispersed over the body. Normally you'll see the adult coat begin along the spine. It will be silkier than the puppy coat and flat. This new coat will gradually move up and down the back, down the sides, and up toward the head. As the adult coat grows in, it will also begin to hang down along the dog's sides.

At this age, it's not unusual for Yorkie puppies to look somewhat rough, with coats that have some adult coat growing in yet still with some puppy coat remaining. That's okay, though. It's normal, and they'll outgrow it.

The coat's color is gradually changing, too. The black in your puppy's baby coat may be gradually turning a little more bluish. Most Yorkies don't fully have their adult coloration until 3 years of age, but this month you'll see hints of the change to come.

Your Yorkie's tan spots are also changing. Puppies tend to have some black hairs scattered in the tan marking, making them a little duller in color. As the adult coat comes in, these dark hairs disappear and the tan color becomes clearer and more pronounced.

> **TIPS AND TAILS**
>
> The Yorkie coloring—the puppy black that turns to an adult steel blue—is caused by a gene that only this breed carries. Some other breeds change colors as they mature, but it's due to other reasons or other genes.

Health

Your Yorkie puppy is, hopefully, strong, active, and healthy. However, sometimes puppies get sick. Maybe your puppy has eaten something that upset his digestive tract or he's played too hard. By keeping an eye on him, you can react quickly when something upsets him.

Avoiding Tiny Dog Dehydration

Your puppy is very small, and he can become dehydrated very easily. Dehydration primarily occurs when the puppy loses fluids faster than he can replace them. This can happen if he's playing hard and doesn't drink or if he has vomited several times and can't keep water down. Diarrhea can also dehydrate him.

One of the first ways to check for dehydration is to pinch the skin over your pup's shoulders, gently lift it away from his body, and let go. If the skin immediately falls back to his body, he's most likely okay.

Another way to check is to look at his gums. A well-hydrated healthy puppy has warm, pink, wet gums. If his gums are pale and sticky, there's a problem.

If you think your puppy might be dehydrated, call your veterinarian. In mild cases, she might recommend giving your puppy some diluted electrolyte solution such as Pedialyte, available from your local drug store. In more severe cases, your veterinarian will want to examine your puppy to see if intravenous solutions are needed.

Lethargy Isn't Normal

Yorkies are active little dogs, and one who's lying around, lethargic, has a problem. Lethargy can be caused by anything from an injury to an illness.

Pain: An injury can cause even a Yorkie puppy to be still. An injury can be mentally depressing as well, causing the puppy to act lethargic. Give your Yorkie a gentle massage to see if any part of him hurts.

Liver shunt: With a liver shunt, the puppy won't feel well and won't have any energy. See Month 3 for more information.

Nausea: An upset stomach can put anyone out of action, including your puppy. This is usually accompanied by a loss of appetite.

Infection: An injury or illness that's caused by or has caused an infection may also produce lethargy. As with pain, check with a gentle massage to see if anything hurts. Take your puppy's temperature, too, because an infection is often accompanied by a fever.

If you see signs of any of these problems in your Yorkie, or if the lethargy continues, call your veterinarian. Several other problems not necessarily found in puppies such as anemia, cancer, or metabolic disorders can also cause lethargy.

The best thing you can do for your puppy's health is to know what's normal. Know what he looks like, how he acts, and how he feels when you massage him. Then, when there's a change, you can identify it and explain it to your veterinarian.

The Mess of Diarrhea

Diarrhea is bad, both for your puppy and for you. Unfortunately, it can also quickly lead to dehydration, especially when paired with vomiting. Some puppies are more prone to diarrhea than others, and it's hard to tell from one puppy to the next how the puppy will react to life's stresses until diarrhea occurs.

Stress: Some Yorkie puppies will have diarrhea anytime things change. A trip to the veterinarian's office may trigger it, as can a change in the household schedule. Thankfully, many puppies outgrow this tendency.

Change in water: Some puppies don't tolerate changes in their water. If your puppy is like this, introduce bottled water so you can bring some with you on outings or when you travel.

Change in food: If you change foods, always do it gradually over several weeks. Diarrhea from an abrupt food change is very common in Yorkies. To prevent this, puppies should eat more than just their one kibble food. Puppies who are introduced to a variety of foods when they're young often deal better with food changes.

Food allergies: Food allergies or sensitivities can also cause diarrhea. The only way to deal with this is to avoid those foods.

Intestinal parasites: Most intestinal parasites can cause diarrhea, especially if the puppy has a large infestation. If you see worms or worm segments in the feces, take a sample to your veterinarian.

Disease: Many diseases can cause diarrhea. The one that strikes terror into veterinarian's hearts is parvovirus. This disease causes diarrhea with a foul odor.

If your Yorkie has diarrhea, take a good look at it before calling your veterinarian. She'll want to know these things:

🐾 Is it a different odor? How can you describe it?

🐾 Does it contain any red blood? Or darker, partially digested blood?

🐾 Are the stools just softer than normal? Or are they very thin and watery?

🐾 Is there any sign of foreign objects in the stools, as if your puppy ate something he shouldn't have eaten?

🐾 Are there signs of worms or worm segments in the stools?

🐾 How many episodes has your Yorkie had in what time period?

🐾 Is he also vomiting?

Your veterinarian might recommend an antidiarrheal medication. However, if your Yorkie is also showing signs of dehydration, he needs veterinary care.

Nutrition

The subject of nutrition—for people and for dogs—is complex. Remember a few years ago, when people were told to stop eating eggs, or at least cut back on how many they ate? Now we're told eggs are a wonderful food. Food for dogs is just as complex and contradictory.

Hundreds of dog foods are available, and the manufacturers would like you to think their particular food is the absolute best one for your Yorkie. If your Yorkie is doing well—growing nicely with a healthy coat and bright eyes—his diet is probably fine.

However, if you're interested in researching dog foods, the first place to begin is with the labels.

Pet Food: Convoluted Oversight

No one organization or committee oversees pet foods. Instead, a number of organizations share the work, with a different group in charge of a portion of the industry.

The Association of Feed Control Officials (AAFCO) sets the maximum and minimum levels of nutrients in foods. They also make recommendations concerning pet-food labels so information is presented in an understandable format. The Food and Drug Administration (FDA) has a branch, the Center for Veterinary Medicine (CVM), which specializes in what ingredients pet-food companies are permitted to use and how they are to prepare the foods. The United States Department of Agriculture (USDA) states what can or cannot be present on the labels. The Pet Food Institute (PFI) is a lobbying group for pet-food manufacturers. And the National Research Council (NRC) group evaluates ongoing research and makes recommendations for changes within the industry or foods.

In addition, each state has its own regulations, guidelines, and officials that direct pet-food manufacturing in that state, as well as distribution. Without any one organization in charge, it's easy to see why the industry is so confusing.

Understanding Dog-Food Labels

Each and every package or can of dog food must contain the manufacturer's name and contact information, be it a phone number, mailing address, or website.

The package must also have the food name, such as "Beef Chunks Dinner" or "Puppy Food." As with all other aspects of the pet-food industry, regulations define and govern what these names can be.

The package must also state what animals the food is manufactured for, such as dogs, cats, rabbits, ferrets, or other animals. If the food is made for a specific purpose such as weight loss or for a certain life stage such as puppies or geriatrics, the package must state that, too.

A nutritional adequacy statement is also required. This statement details what testing system was used—either feeding trials or laboratory analysis.

Then the guaranteed analysis lists the percentages of several different parts of the food, including the minimum percentages of protein and fat as well as the maximum amounts of crude fiber and moisture. This is for the food as it's packaged, not necessarily as it's fed. For example, if you add water to the food or mix in another ingredient, the proportions of protein, fat, fiber, and moisture may change.

Also, although the percentages of protein, fat, fiber, and moisture are listed, carbohydrates are not. In addition, there's no statement of the quality of the proteins or fats, just that they exist.

> ### TIPS AND TAILS

Nothing on the dog-food label says anything about the digestibility of the food. Laboratory analysis may show that the food has a certain level of protein, for example, but it doesn't guarantee the protein is in a digestible form.

The label must list the ingredients, in decreasing order, from most to least, by weight. That means 1 cup meat, which is often 70 percent water, is going to be heavier than 1 cup of another ingredient with less water, such as barley, for example.

A dog food may potentially have far more barley than meat by weight, yet meat may still be listed first on the label because it's heavier. The consumer—you, the dog owner—might look at the label and see meat listed first and assume it's a meat-based food with barley as a secondary ingredient. In reality, it's a barley-based food with meat. That can make a huge difference, nutrition-wise, for your Yorkie.

This labeling loophole can mislead consumers in another way, too. Say, for example, a food lists the ingredients this way: chicken, wheat germ, wheat flour, wheat middlings, and so on. Because chicken is listed first, you'd assume there's more chicken than wheat, right? Not necessarily, and probably not. By splitting the wheat into several ingredients rather than simply listing it as one ingredient—wheat—the chicken can be listed first even though the food probably contains more wheat than chicken. Although deceptive, it is legal.

Manufacturers aren't allowed to use just anything they want in pet foods. In fact, the ingredients are extensive—many foods and parts of foods are allowed—but they are regulated. The AAFCO's website (aafco.org) has a complete listing of the ingredients that can be used in pet foods.

Making a Good Decision

Yorkies don't eat a lot—remember, their stomachs are tiny! To some owners, it might seem like the foods a tiny dog eats can't be that important because he eats so little of it. But the opposite is true. Because your Yorkie doesn't eat very much, what he does eat is very important. His food should be very nutritious, it should be made of good-quality ingredients, and he should have very little (or no) junk food.

You don't have to study nutrition to choose a good-quality food for your Yorkie. Just read the dog-food labels; be sure you understand what the labels say; and if you don't understand, call the dog-food company representatives and ask questions. Obviously, they are in the business of selling dog food and will try to convince you to buy their food. But ask your questions, and if you can't get a good answer, buy a different food.

Making Homemade Dog Food

If you're unhappy with the dog food you're feeding to your Yorkie, or if you're concerned about the ingredients in commercial dog foods, you can feed your dog a homemade diet. With a homemade food, you have control over what goes into the food and the quality of those ingredients.

Here are some good foods you can include in your Yorkie's homemade diet:

Meats: Clean muscle meats from beef, chicken, turkey, bison, venison, elk, duck, and goose are all good foods.

Fish: You can use just about any deboned fish, including salmon, tuna, mackerel, herring, trout, catfish, or bass. You can also feed your Yorkie shellfish, including clams and oysters.

Dairy: Don't feed your pup cow's milk because many dogs can't digest it well, but goat's milk is good. Aged cheeses from cow's milk are fine, as are goat's milk cheeses. Yogurt and cottage cheese are also good.

Eggs: Eggs are excellent foods because they contain all the essential amino acids dogs need. Use chicken, duck, goose, turkey, or quail eggs.

Vegetables: Pumpkin, squash, sweet potatoes, yams, potatoes, carrots, spinach, zucchini, green beans, and kidney beans can all be good foods.

Fruits: Avoid citrus fruits, but apples, bananas, pears, mangoes, and papaya are excellent additions to the diet.

> ### TIPS AND TAILS
>
> When feeding your Yorkie eggs, cook them first. Raw eggs can be contaminated with salmonella. Plus, raw eggs can interfere with vitamin B absorption.

The foundation of your homemade diet should be meats. Muscle meats are great, as are some organ meats such as beef heart and chicken heart. Yorkies can become picky eaters easily, so vary the meats regularly to add different tastes to your dog's food. Changing the meats also changes the nutritional aspects of the food. Different meats provide different (or different ratios of) amino acids, enzymes, vitamins, and minerals.

Be sure you thoroughly cook meat and fish. Although raw-food diets are very popular, these foods can contain bacteria that could easily make your Yorkie sick. Plus, the easiest way to make a homemade diet for your Yorkie is to make a good-size batch ahead of time and then feed your Yorkie small meals from that batch. If you're feeing your Yorkie a raw-food diet, serve him the raw meat immediately to reduce the danger of bacterial contamination.

Grate or chop and then steam vegetables prior to adding them to meats. Grated or chopped vegetables are a small-enough size your Yorkie can eat them without difficulty. Steamed vegetables are also more digestible for your tiny dog's digestive system. To steam veggies, grate or chop them to the right size, place them on a paper towel, cover with another paper towel, and place in the microwave. You could also steam them in a small amount of water in a saucepan on the stove. For about $1/4$ cup vegetables, cook for 45 seconds to 1 minute; use less time for high-powered microwaves.

How much food your puppy needs depends on several things. The National Research Council has established calorie guidelines for puppies, but these vary depending on how active the puppy is, how much he's growing at the time, and his individual metabolism. As a general rule, a Yorkie puppy needs approximately 44 to 50 calories per day per pound of body weight. An inactive puppy needs less while an active, fast-growing puppy needs more. For example, a 2½-pound Yorkie puppy needs between 110 and 150 calories per day, a 5-pound Yorkie needs between 220 and 250 calories per day, and a 10-pound Yorkie needs between 330 and 350 calories per day.

But again, these are general guidelines. Use the information in Appendix B to keep an eye on your puppy. If he's gaining too much weight, cut back on the calories you're feeding. If he's keeping too thin, increase the calories. If you need to cut back on calories but your Yorkie acts hungry, increase the fiber in his food.

> **HAPPY PUPPY**
>
> Cooked, plain, canned pumpkin (not pumpkin pie mix) is tasty; most dogs like it; and it's high in fiber. It's high in vitamins and minerals, a good food to add fiber to a diet, and gentle for dogs with an upset stomach.

Before beginning any homemade diet, talk to your veterinarian. She may have some concerns as to whether this would be appropriate for your dog, especially if your Yorkie has some health challenges.

Grooming

One aspect of grooming many dog owners fail to do is keep their dog's teeth clean. Many dogs dislike having their teeth cleaned, fight the process, and make the chore a difficult one for dog and owner alike.

It doesn't have to be that way. You can teach your dog to put up with the teeth-cleaning so you can do it regularly and quickly.

Yorkie Dental Problems

Unfortunately, Yorkshire Terriers are born with the tendency to develop dental problems. Their teeth are large for their mouth, which causes crowding, and it's hard to keep those crowded teeth clean.

After eating, plaque—a soft, yellow-brown material comprised of food particles and bacteria—builds up on the teeth. If not cleaned off, within 3 to 5 days, minerals in the dog's saliva turns the plaque into tartar. Tartar is hard, and as it builds up, it irritates the gums, a condition called gingivitis. As it continues to build up, it also extends down between the teeth and the gums. This causes a separation of the teeth and gums, called periodontal disease. This can cause loose teeth, tooth loss, and abscesses.

In addition, the bacteria from the mouth can move into the bloodstream. This can cause problems with various body organs, especially the heart and kidneys.

> ### TIPS AND TAILS
>
> One of the first signs of dental disease is bad breath. Your Yorkie's breath should not smell bad. If it makes you move away or avoid a lick from your dog, dental problems are probably brewing.

To make matters worse, the bone density of a Yorkie's jaw bone is less than it is for larger-breed dogs. This, combined with shallower roots on the teeth, can lead to tooth loss. With some Yorkies, that tooth loss can occur far too young, sometimes even in early adulthood.

But even with these tendencies, Yorkies don't *have* to have dental problems. Good dental health habits, started early in life, are very important. When started early, the teeth, gums, and jaw can remain healthy.

Keeping Your Yorkie's Teeth Clean

The first step in keeping your Yorkie's teeth clean is to feed him a good food. No matter whether you feed him homemade meals or commercial food, it should be high in meat protein and low in (or with no) cereal grains. Meat-based foods attract bacteria at a far slower rate than do foods high in carbohydrates (sugars).

Provide your Yorkie with things to chew on. Hard chewies, like dried parts of beef (tendons, pizzles, and noses) are excellent. As your dog chews, the plaque is scraped off the teeth. Some toys, especially hard rubber ones, work the same way.

It's also important to teach your Yorkie to accept having his teeth brushed. Make a paste of baking soda and water (that's about the same consistency as your toothpaste) or purchase a commercial dog toothpaste. Dip a child's toothbrush (the smallest you can find) in the paste and gently brush the teeth. Praise your Yorkie when he's allowing you to do this, and stop before he's had enough. Then later, do it again. Gradually increase how much you can do in a session until he'll allow you to brush his entire mouth. Be liberal with your praise when he's cooperating.

> TIPS AND TAILS

Shawn Messonier, DVM, a holistic veterinarian in Plano, Texas, says, "CoQ$_{10}$ is often recommended for pets with heart disease but the feeling now is that by acting as an antioxidant, it can also help pets with dental disease."

If you feel your Yorkie's teeth are beginning to look bad, get him into the veterinarian clinic before there's a big problem. After cleaning and treatment, your vet can give you some commercial products that can help keep your Yorkie's teeth healthier.

Social Skills

Your Yorkshire Terrier has now had several months of socialization and training. Ideally, his social skills out in public are coming along nicely. If he can cope with different circumstances without panic and with some confidence and flair, he's doing well.

Unfortunately, at this age, some Yorkies take that confidence and flair and turn it into cockiness and bravado. This can cause problems in your dog's relationships with other dogs, people, and even other pets.

Big Pups and Small Pups

Contrary to popular belief, big dogs and small dogs can get along. In fact, they can be great friends. This is especially true if the bigger dog learns to be cautious around the smaller dog and tempers her strength during play sessions. In addition, the smaller dog has to control his temper and not get mad if the big dog is a little too rough.

This kind of friendship doesn't just happen, though. The two dogs have to make it happen. Jester is a Border Collie and Australian Shepherd mix who weighs about 50 pounds. Her best friend is a Yorkshire Terrier named Bones who weighs about 6 pounds. Despite a 44-pound weight difference, these two dogs are the best of friends. They run together, with Bones trying her best to keep up with Jester—and most of the time she can. They also gently wrestle. When they play tug of war with a toy, Jester simply holds the toy while Bones pulls, growls, and pulls some more.

Jester and Bones got to know each other as puppies. They taught each other what was acceptable play and when it got too rough. If Bones grabbed Jester under the belly and bit too hard, Jester would cry, move away, and not play anymore. If Bones got stepped on, she would cry, growl, and snap at Jester's leg. Although their means of communication varied, it obviously worked for them.

> **HAPPY PUPPY**
>
> As long as two puppies playing are getting along, the occasional growl, snap, or cry is fine. The two are communicating. However, interrupt the play if blood is drawn or if one of the puppies loses his temper.

When introducing your Yorkie to a new puppy, begin with both puppies on leash. Don't let the two lunge toward each other, jump on each other, or otherwise try to wrestle while on leash. In canine communication, as in human communication, invading another's personal space is considered rude.

Instead, have the two puppies sit or relax while you and the other puppy's owner talk for a few minutes. The puppies can see each other, sniff, and watch while you're talking. You can even go for a walk together.

Then, if there's a safe, fenced-in area nearby, let the two puppies off leash to play. If either puppy gets overstimulated, your Yorkie loses his temper, or the larger puppy gets too rough, leash both puppies and let them relax for a few minutes. It may take a few play sessions for them to learn how to play together. If the larger puppy is consistently too rough and you feel he may injure your Yorkie, stop all play right away.

Teaching Good Dog Skills

Yorkies are tiny, but they're still dogs. They aren't, as much as some owners like to believe, human babies in dog suits. It's important for Yorkie puppies to socialize with other puppies for their own good mental health. But at the same time, Yorkies are tiny enough that they often need to be protected. It's a balancing act.

Yorkies are often reactive when meeting other dogs, especially if a bigger dog has previously been rough. They will lunge toward the other dog, bark furiously, and then dash back to hide behind their owner. The Yorkie is often trying to say, "I'm here! Don't step on me!" or "Don't hurt me!' Some Yorkies have a little more attitude and seem like they're saying, "I might be little, but I'm tough!"

This behavior often gets the other dog riled up. The Yorkie, barking, lunging, and dashing, is then often the target, and the other dog will try to catch the Yorkie. Obviously, this then becomes a vicious circle with the Yorkie barking more and the other dog trying harder to catch the Yorkie.

It's important to teach your Yorkie puppy that barking and lunging at other dogs is not allowed. When approaching another dog on leash, ask your Yorkie to sit. Praise him for sitting and being quiet. If he barks or tries to dash toward the other dog, turn him away from the dog, toward you, and again ask him to sit. Help him do it if you need to, and praise him for sitting.

If you're holding your Yorkie in your arms, don't allow him to bark at other dogs. This, too, can cause the other dog to get excited, and she may jump up on you to try to grab your Yorkie. Instead, teach your Yorkie to be calm and quiet in your arms.

Although your Yorkie needs to learn to behave himself while walking on leash, if the other dog appears to be too excited and you feel that your Yorkie might be in danger, pick up your puppy and move away. That "move away" advice is important. Don't stand near the other dog with your Yorkie in your arms. Your Yorkie could still be an attractive target for an overstimulated larger dog.

Making a Good Impression

At this age, your Yorkie is still young, and although he's had some socialization and training, he still has a lot to learn. Continued exposure to the world around him will help him gain more confidence as he grows up.

As an added benefit, the better his behavior out in public, the better the impression he'll make on everyone who meets him. Unfortunately, toy-breed dogs sometimes are looked upon with a less-than-favorable eye because so many are poorly behaved. A socialized, well-behaved, nicely trained Yorkshire Terrier is a wonderful ambassador for the breed.

This month, take some time to combine your Yorkie's social skills with his training. You can do this out on walks, on trips to the local hardware or pet store, or at your local park. For example, have him sit each time you stop at a curb so he doesn't step out in front of a car. Ask him to sit and stay while you get your mail out of the mailbox. You can also ask him to pay attention to you as other dogs walk past, not the dogs. Have your puppy sit as someone pets him, too.

Training sessions such as these teach your Yorkie puppy that his training applies everywhere and not just at home. In addition, you and your puppy can show off! An owner who asks her puppy to behave himself and a well-trained young dog are the best representatives the breed can have.

Meeting Other Animals

Ideally, during the last several months, your Yorkie has met a variety of new people of all ages, sizes, and ethnic backgrounds. Hopefully, he has also met other puppies and gentle adult dogs of various breeds and sizes.

Your Yorkie may have also introduced himself to a cat who wandered into your backyard, or a rabbit or a squirrel. He probably unceremoniously chased those critters out of his yard, too. After all, that's what terriers do, even tiny terriers.

Your Yorkie needs to understand not every animal is fair game to be chased. Many animals are pets and companions, and he needs to respect them. In addition, some larger animals are capable of hurting or even killing your Yorkie if he's rude or aggressive toward them.

Ask some neighbors and friends if they have a dog-friendly cat, a pet rabbit, a ferret, or perhaps a goat or a horse. These are all animals he could see during his life with you, and better he's introduced to them in a controlled situation.

Introduce your puppy when he's on leash. The other animal should also be on leash or held securely by her owner. If the other animal is on the ground, have your puppy on the ground, too. If the animal is in her owner's arms, hold your puppy, too. However, if your puppy gets too bold and feisty when held in your arms, put him on the ground.

When your puppy and the other animal are both calm, walk your puppy up to the other animal. Make your pup walk calmly; if he lunges, barks, or growls, turn and walk him away. Let him turn back and look at the other animal when he's calm and quiet.

When he can approach the other animal calmly, let him walk up to her again. If they can sniff noses, that's great. If either animal appears stressed, walk them away from each other again.

Never let your Yorkie run loose with another animal such as this. Not only is your Yorkie small, fragile, and easily hurt, your Yorkie is also a terrier. That chase instinct and prey drive to chase and catch smaller animals is very strong.

> **HAPPY PUPPY**

If your Yorkie seems to have a strong drive to chase small animals (or lizards in the backyard), take a look at earthdog tests. These were designed as a way for small hunting terriers to use their natural instincts. Yorkies cannot title in this activity, but they can do it for fun. See Month 12 or akc.org/events/earthdog/index.cfm for more information.

Training

You and your puppy have been doing a lot of training over the last several months. You've worked on his housetraining skills, introduced several obedience exercises, and taught him to walk nicely on a leash when you go for walks. You've also been teaching him how to politely greet people as well as other dogs and animals.

In fact, everything you do with your Yorkie teaches him something because he's always learning. For example, if he jumps up on your lap while you're reading, nudges between you and your book, and you stop reading to pet him, he's learned that works. He'll do it again at another time to get attention.

You may think this is cute and appreciate the break to pet your dog. That's fine— as long as you can also tell your Yorkie when it's not appropriate. Perhaps you're studying for a test or are in the best part of the book; you need to be able to tell your dog you don't want his interference at the moment.

Just be aware that everything you do with your dog teaches him something. Be sure it's a lesson you want him to learn … and a behavior you're okay with him continuing.

Practice, Practice, Practice

It's important that your Yorkie know the obedience skills you've been teaching him apply *all* the time, not just when you're having a training session. If you only practice or enforce the skills during a training session, your Yorkie will think that's the only time he has to perform them.

To help him learn, ask him to sit for everything he wants, including his meals, his treats, and when you hook up the leash to go for a walk. Have him sit to pet him.

Ask your Yorkie to sit and stay before you open a door or gate. Use the leash so you can help him keep from dashing out. As he learns to hold the sit stay, he'll also learn he's not allowed to go dashing out and to look to you for permission. Practice this same skill in the car for the same reasons.

Teach him to stay out of the kitchen while you're cooking so you don't step on him or trip over him. To do this, put him on a chair, sofa, or somewhere else outside the kitchen and ask him to down and stay.

Have him down and stay on a dog bed or a chair away from the table while the family is eating. This will prevent him from pawing at people's legs and begging for food while they're eating.

Teach him to ignore the cat, cat food, and cat litter box by using the "Leave it" command. Also teach him to ignore trash cans and the roll of toilet paper by using "Leave it."

Many clumping cat litters can be deadly to dogs if ingested. The litter can cause an intestinal obstruction, and the clumping litters absorb moisture, which, in a dog's intestinal tract, can be deadly. Teach your dog to leave the cat box alone, but to safeguard your dog, be sure the litter box is inaccessible to him, too.

You can add other obedience exercises to fit your household and lifestyle. Just look at your normal routine, figure out when and where you'd like your Yorkie to behave a little bit better, and begin training. As you practice, you'll find many different ways to use these skills in your household and daily routines.

Cooperation, Not Confrontation

Yorkshire Terriers are very small dogs, and although they have a feisty terrier attitude at times, especially at this point in life, they can also be easily intimidated. It's important that you learn to strike the right balance. Although your tiny terrier might try to challenge you and push all your buttons—barking, chasing the cat, or destroying a roll of toilet paper—don't turn his attitude into a confrontational one with your response to this behavior.

Think cooperation rather than confrontation. In the dog's world, a confrontational attitude can work one of two ways: It can cause more aggression from the other dog, or it can intimidate the other dog. Neither of these helps your relationship with your Yorkie.

To emphasize cooperation, praise him for good behavior. When he behaves in a way you like, no matter whether he did it on his own or did as you asked, smile at him and praise him. "Yeah! Look at you! Thank you!" Behaviors that are rewarded will happen again.

If he does something you don't want to happen again, interrupt it and show him what to do instead. For example, if your Yorkie comes dashing down the hall with one of your socks, distract him or stop him without turning it into a chase game, and take away the sock, saying "No, this is mine!" Then walk him to his toys, encourage him to pick up a toy, and praise him for doing so.

When, in the future, he picks up a toy, praise him and play with him. "Good to have a toy! Yeah!"

Never ask him to do anything on his own he doesn't yet understand. You can help him do it and then reward him, but don't expect compliance until he's done it on his own with your supervision several times.

This can be a challenging month; if you feel yourself getting angry or frustrated, put your Yorkie in his crate for a while and take a break. Deal with his antics later.

Climbing, Tunneling, and Jumping

Your little Yorkie lives in a world that's much bigger than he is. You can get a tiny view of it by lying on the floor. Lift your head until your eyes are at his eye level, and look around at your house. Everything is huge and so much higher than he is!

To make his way around your home and to reach people, he is probably jumping up and down stairs, jumping up onto furniture and then back down, and climbing onto things and then jumping down. A Yorkie has to be somewhat of an athlete just to live with people.

Although Yorkies are quite athletic, puppies are not always as coordinated as they could be and injuries are not uncommon. Teaching your Yorkie to move over, around, and through various obstacles safely can help build his confidence and coordination. Plus, as he practices regularly, he can build some muscle—that will help prevent injuries, too.

You can find obstacles everywhere. An easy one is a cardboard box. Using a cardboard box bigger than your Yorkie, open the bottom and the top and set it on its side so it becomes a cardboard tunnel. Now, using treats as a lure, entice your Yorkie through that cardboard tunnel, telling him, "Sweetie, tunnel!" Praise him and give him the treat as he comes through.

When he's done that several times, partially close one end so he has to wiggle through it. Do this a few times and then partially close both ends and encourage him to work his way through. Make it slightly more challenging each time but encourage both his mental skills—figuring it out—and his physical skills—working his way through.

> ### HAPPY PUPPY
>
> Yorkies love to have fun, and if you're cheering him on and providing treats, he may just try to do too much. So keep the sessions short, have fun with your puppy, and stop before he gets tired.

To help him learn jumping skills and coordination, place a piece of wood—a 2×4 or 4×4—flat on some nonslippery floor such as carpet. Again, use a treat to lure your Yorkie over it. As he jumps and lands, praise him. Then, very gradually, ask him to jump other things that are low in height but look different. A fireplace log, a shoe box, or a brick are all fine. With practice, his jumping skills will get better and he'll be less likely to hurt himself.

When human athletes are building muscles and perfecting their skills, they practice those skills. You can help your Yorkie by providing safe obstacles for him to climb on, go through, or jump over. Just keep your training sessions short so he doesn't get overtired, and always make them fun. Be your puppy's cheerleader, praise him, and use some really good treats to motivate and reward him.

You and Your Puppy

You and your Yorkie puppy are already well bonded—you smile when you look at him, and he perks up when he hears your voice. However, as he moves toward his teenage months, that relationship can become strained, especially when he's getting into trouble.

If you find yourself getting angry or frustrated at your puppy, put him in his crate and allow yourself some puppy-free moments. Sit down, put your feet up, and relax. When you've calmed down and are ready to deal with your tiny hellion again, then you can let him out of his crate.

A Good, Tired Puppy

Yorkshire Terriers love to run and play. Although far too often Yorkies are treated as babies rather than tiny terriers, these dogs are happiest when they're active.

This works to your advantage because a tired puppy is more apt to be a good puppy. Your Yorkie isn't going to be getting into trouble if he's had a chance to run, play, and use up all his excess energy. This is important now, but it'll be even more important as your puppy grows into adolescence in the next few months.

Play retrieving games with him to wear him out and let him have some fun. Toss some appropriately sized balls or toys away from you, and ask him to bring them back. If he wants to play keep-away or won't release the ball, trade the ball for a treat, saying "Sweetie, give. Thank you!"

Arrange play sessions with another puppy who's close to the same age and size, or another bigger puppy who's known to be gentle. Let them run in a fenced-in area until they're both tired.

Go for long walks in different places where your Yorkie puppy can investigate all the strange sights, smells, sounds, and surfaces. This mental exercise combined with physical exercise will wear him out, too.

Ideally, arrange a good exercise session once a day, with several smaller play sessions throughout the day. In between, your puppy will be more likely to nap rather than get into trouble.

Playing Scenting Games

Scenting games give your Yorkie a chance to have fun with you as well as use his good sense of smell to gain some treats. In addition, it's fun to show off to other people exactly how talented your Yorkie is!

To play this game you'll need just a few things:

- ❧ You'll need a handful of really good treats with a strong smell. Tiny bits of turkey hot dog or Swiss cheese will work well.
- ❧ You'll need three to five small paper cups. Use the size often kept in the bathroom.
- ❧ You'll also need a flat place to practice, such as a TV tray top you can set next to you on the sofa.

You'll use the TV tray as a tabletop, so place that beside you with your Yorkie either next to you or on the other side of the TV tray.

Let your Yorkie sniff one of the paper cups. Then place a bit of treat in it and let him lick it out. You want him to think these paper cups produce treats, so do this three or four times.

Now, place a bit of treat on the TV tray and cover it with the paper cup. Tip the cup a little and encourage your Yorkie to get the treat, "Sweetie, find it!" When he noses the cup out of the way to get the treat, praise him and let him have the treat. Practice several times and then quit for this training session.

Review these first steps a couple times on your next training session. Then place the treat under the cup again. When your Yorkie gets the treat easily, it's time to move to the next step.

> ### TIPS AND TAILS
>
> Remember in the old movies when the snake oil salesman would try to fool the country bumpkin by hiding a coin under half a coconut shell and then move the shells around? That's what this game is, except there's no snake oil salesman, there's no country bumpkin, and your Yorkie has a great nose.

Using some tape and a second cup, fasten the second cup to the TV tray. Place the treat under the untaped cup set right next to the taped cup. If he sniffs the new cup, don't do or say anything. Let him figure it out.

As he begins to use his nose to figure out which cup has the treat, add a couple more taped, empty cups to the TV tray. Vary where you place the cup with the treat, too. When your Yorkie is doing well and is finding the treat, untape the cups and continue the game without taping down any of the cups.

Once your Yorkie figures out how to use his nose to find the treat, he's going to be excited about playing this game. You're going to like it, too, not only because your Yorkie will be brilliant doing this trick but you'll also look like an awesome dog trainer.

Month 8 · Creating a Good Canine Citizen

Your Yorkshire Terrier puppy is still in adolescence this month, which includes weeks 29 through 32. She's going to try to push all your buttons and is continuing on the emotional rollercoaster she began a few months ago. She'll be bold and brassy one day and cautious and worried the next.

Yet with all the challenges of adolescence, she's still your Yorkshire Terrier. You have her heart, and she has yours. So deal with her adolescence and her teenage moods, teach her and train her, and have fun with her.

Physical Development

Your Yorkie is getting close to her adult size. In fact, she may have already reached her adult height but still may need to put on a little more weight to reach her adult weight. The AKC breed standard says adult Yorkies may not exceed 7 pounds.

You're still seeing some coat changes now, too, as her puppy coat disappears and her adult coat grows in. This process will continue for many more months. Remember, most Yorkies don't have their adult-length coat until they're 3 years old. But gradually, the last of the soft puppy coat will disappear.

All of your puppy's 42 adult teeth are in now. They're surprisingly large for such a small dog, but this is a reminder that, generations ago, Yorkies were working terriers who hunted vermin.

The differences between males and females are also becoming more apparent this month. Males appear more masculine with a slightly broader skull and heavier bones. Males also often have more coat than females do. Although these gender differences are not as pronounced as with larger-breed dogs, you can still see the differences, especially when a male and a female of the same age stand next to each other.

Health

Many dog owners are interested in more natural ways of caring for their dogs. Some mention the overuse of antibiotics and the long-term problems associated with antibiotic resistance. Some want to feed their pets a more natural, less chemical- and preservative-laden diet. Others simply want some alternatives to traditional dog care.

No matter how deeply you want to participate in your dog's health care, it's important to understand what natural care is and what it can entail. Then you can make a decision you and your veterinarian are both happy with.

Defining Natural Care

For thousands of years, dogs lived with people, slept where their people slept, traveled where their people traveled, and ate the leftover food their people couldn't eat. If a dog was sick, she either recovered on her own or was treated with the same remedies her people used on themselves.

For the last few hundred years, these treatments, which ranged from a hot mustard poultice for a chest cold to oatmeal paste for itching or willow bark tea for pain relief, were called *home remedies*. Different cultures around the world developed their own techniques and home remedies. Often these included the plants found in their particular region.

Today, people often think the terms *natural* and *organic* mean the same thing, especially when relating to food or health care. The terms are very different, though, and misusing them can lead to misunderstandings.

The word *natural* has no legal definition. You might think it means something that grows without assistance, or without pesticides, or without genetic engineering, but none of those definitions have any legal relationship. Manufacturers know people like that word, though, so they link it to many different products, from dog shampoo to dog foods.

The word *organic,* on the other hand, does have a legal definition. And because it does, manufacturers are legally required to use it correctly when describing their products.

As your dog's owner and care provider, you must create your own definition of what you think natural care should be. That could include making educated choices, with your veterinarian's help, regarding vaccinations and a vaccination schedule; feeding a good-quality food made from organic ingredients and minimal processing; keeping your Yorkie at a good weight with adequate exercise to prevent obesity; using better-quality toys, beds, and other care products made from real ingredients rather than chemically created products; or caring for your pet using a *holistic* approach.

> **DOG TALK**

Organic means the food or product is grown or produced using environmentally sound techniques, with no synthetic pesticides, chemicals, or fertilizers. **Holistic** care means the entire pet—all the aspects of the pet's life—must be considered. This includes the pet's physical, mental, and emotional life as well as her relationship with her owner.

Natural care encompasses many different things. For most dog owners, however, it tends to begin with nutrition, including the food that their dogs are fed as well as any nutritional supplements they are given. It also encompasses exercise. For other owners, heath-care techniques are also important.

Alternative Health Care

Conventional or modern veterinary medicine focuses on tests and diagnostics, medication, and surgery. Some veterinarians also stress preventive medicine or preventive health care, such as watching a dog's weight to prevent obesity.

Some veterinarians and dog owners are also interested in alternative health-care practices. Some of these are ancient practices that originated many years before modern medicine—in some cases, thousands of years before.

In many cases, *alternative medicine* for pets has grown out of alternative medicine for people. In other instances, it was developed side by side with human techniques. In any case, no matter what the history, each of these areas has a devoted following.

> ### DOG TALK
>
> **Alternative medicine** is any technique that falls outside the realm of conventional medicine for people or veterinary medicine for animals.

Alternative medicine includes the following:

- ❧ **Acupuncture:** A practitioner places fine needles in specific areas of the pet's body to alleviate symptoms.
- ❧ **Acupressure:** Pressure is applied on specific spots or areas to work with acupuncture or in place of it.
- ❧ **Ayurveda:** The traditional medicine of India includes several techniques, including remedies made from plants.
- ❧ **Chiropractic:** A practitioner manipulates the muscles and joints, as well as the alignment of the skeletal system.
- ❧ **Flower essences:** Diluted formulas that include flowers, leaves, and other parts of flowering plants.
- ❧ **Herbal remedies:** Plants and plant parts used to prevent or treat health issues.
- ❧ **Homeopathy:** Highly diluted preparations used to treat health problems.
- ❧ **Nutrition:** Using foods and supplements to prevent health problems or assist in solving health problems.
- ❧ **Reiki:** Often called "the laying on of hands," this Japanese technique uses the warmth and placement of the hands for treatment.
- ❧ **Traditional Chinese medicine:** This combines herbal remedies, massage, acupuncture, and nutrition as treatment options.

You may find one particular technique is comfortable for you, such as herbal remedies. Or you might want to combine a few techniques, depending on your comfort level with a technique and what your Yorkie needs.

With all alternative techniques, use common sense and caution. If something sounds too good to be true, it probably is. Some techniques—such as acupuncture—have a basis in science and have been tested. However, many alternative techniques—Reiki, for one—have not been scientifically tested.

Conventional and Alternative Care

Conventional, or modern, veterinary care is usually used alone. Most of today's veterinarians were trained to provide this type and level of care, and many dog owners are comfortable with conventional health care for their pets.

However, with more dog owners investigating alternative techniques, many veterinarians are now practicing *integrative care*. By combining modern veterinary care with alternative techniques, dog owners can have the best of both worlds.

> **DOG TALK**
>
> **Integrative care** combines modern veterinary medicine with alternative techniques and also takes into consideration the dog's environment, diet, exercise and activities, and her relationship with her owner.

When looking at different types of care, talk to your veterinarian. What does he think about these alternative techniques? If he's not an expert with a particular technique, can he refer you to someone he trusts?

Nutrition

Yorkies quickly learn that they are well loved. They also figure out how to train their owners. A tilt of the head and a flash of their wide-open eyes quickly gets an, "Oh! Look, she's so cute," followed by a treat. Unfortunately, begging can quickly turn into problem behavior, so you need to either prevent or stop it.

Obesity is a nationwide problem, in pets and their owners. For your Yorkie, too much food can lead to weight gain, as well as begging for and receiving too many treats.

Discouraging Begging

Your Yorkie adolescent may be a funny eater at times, turning up her nose at food she normally eats. Or perhaps she's finicky about training treats. But when you have a plate with a hamburger and french fries, she's at your knee drooling!

It's very easy for simple drooling to turn into begging, which is one bad habit. Begging while you're eating can turn into pushier behavior such as pawing at your leg. Many a smart little Yorkie has learned how to jump up on a dining-room chair and then up onto the table to steal from your plate. Begging and food-stealing can also lead to trash can–raiding.

A dog begs because it's a self-rewarding behavior. The dog begs and then is given tasty foods. It's just like training: The dog does something right and is rewarded.

To prevent begging, first of all, never feed your Yorkie puppy from your plate or from the table. If you have some leftovers you'd like her to have, save them and add them to her bowl later. But don't give them to her as you eat or from where you normally eat.

Also, should she come up, sit, and stare at you with those big, dark eyes while you're eating, stop and move her away from the table or where you're eating. She can go to her crate or exercise pen or, if her down-stay is reliable, she can lie down away from the table.

If she doesn't hold the stay, calmly walk her to her crate, close the door, and leave her there until you're finished with your meal.

> **TIPS AND TAILS**
>
> It's important that everyone in the family agree that begging is not allowed. If one person continually feeds the dog from the table or drops her scraps in the kitchen, your Yorkie will continue to beg.

Obesity: A Growing Problem

No pun intended, obesity is a growing problem among dogs today. Some statistics show that as many as 30 to 40 percent of all adult dogs are overweight.

Not many Yorkie teenagers are overweight—most are too active. However, as we discussed in previous behavior and training sections, habits learned in puppyhood will continue on into adulthood. If your puppy is eating too much and not getting enough exercise now, she could easily become overweight as she grows up.

If you're feeding a commercial food for all life stages or a puppy food, be aware that the feeding guidelines on the package are simply that—guidelines. If you feed the amount recommended and that's too many calories for your individual puppy, she could potentially end up overweight.

TIPS AND TAILS

To evaluate your puppy's weight, take a look at Appendix B. It's hard to actually see a Yorkie's body under the coat, so either use your hands to feel your puppy or take a look at your puppy when she's wet and her hair is flat.

If you think your puppy is gaining too much weight, don't drastically cut the amount of food you give her. If you do, you'll have a hungry teenager who will be very unhappy. She may then decide to eat the cat's food, eat plants outside, or raid the trash can.

Instead, decrease her food very slightly each day and add extra fiber to make her feel full. For example, for the first week of her diet, cut her food slightly and add an equal amount of cooked or steamed chopped green beans. At the end of a couple weeks, reevaluate her body condition. If she's lost some weight, continue without making any additional changes.

HAPPY PUPPY

Green beans, wax beans, grated zucchini, grated squash, puréed pumpkin, and broccoli florets are all high-fiber foods most dogs enjoy. Lightly cook or steam the vegetables so they're more digestible.

During this time, extend your walks, play sessions, or exercise, too. Weight loss for dogs is the same as it is for people, and they need fewer calories in as well as more calories burned.

Grooming

In the past few months, you've gotten a good start on the grooming skills you're going to need to continue over your Yorkie's lifetime. Of course, this applies even if you've decided to keep your Yorkie in a shorter puppy cut rather than in a full-length coat. All Yorkies, no matter how long their coat, need regular grooming.

However, even with good grooming, your puppy may begin scratching and chewing at herself. This will probably drive you wild trying to stop it, and in the process, your puppy can create tangles and matts and turn her skin raw.

Scratching and Chewing

Scratching and chewing have several different causes. Some are related to health issues, while others may be environmental.

Dog clothes: If you have a sweater or other article of clothing on your Yorkie and she appears to be scratching at that, take it off. You can dress your Yorkie before you go outside—especially with cold-weather clothing—but don't leave outfits on her all the time. The clothes will cause the hair to tangle and matt underneath them as well as rub on her skin.

Collar or harness: A tight collar or harness can cause an irritation, too. She needs to wear a collar with identification on it, so choose a small, lightweight collar with an emergency quick-release snap just in case she gets caught on something, and fasten her tags to that. (Cat collars often work well for Yorkies.) Remove all other collars and harnesses when she's in the house.

Fleas: These horrid little pests can cause a great deal of damage to a tiny dog. Not only does each flea drink a drop of your Yorkie's blood each time it bites, but if you see one flea, there are a hundred you don't see. A flea infestation actually can cause a tiny-breed puppy to become anemic. Talk to your veterinarian and find out what products he recommends as safe for your puppy.

Flea bite allergy: When fleas bite, a tiny bit of saliva is transmitted to the dog. After having been bitten, many dogs develop flea bite dermatitis (FBD). This allergic reaction causes the dog to have red, itching skin. FBD can make your Yorkie miserable because every single bite can cause a reaction. Plus, secondary skin infections are also common. Controlling fleas is of utmost importance.

Inhalant and contact allergies: Although Yorkies aren't as prone to allergies as many other breeds, allergies still occur. Some dogs are allergic to grass, others are sensitive to molds and mildew, and still others may be allergic to pollen. Allergies are just as individual to dogs as they are to humans. If your Yorkie is biting, chewing, and scratching and has no fleas, talk to your veterinarian. He may recommend allergy tests.

Food allergies: Yorkies with allergies to a food or a food ingredient tend to lick and chew at their paws and the base of the tail. Some also rub their belly or hips on the carpet. Your veterinarian may recommend an allergy test, but more often he'll recommend a *food elimination test.*

> ### DOG TALK
>
> A **food elimination test** consists of feeding the dog a diet that consists of one protein and one carbohydrate source. When the dog's allergies clear up, you introduce one new food at a time until the allergy reappears. You then know the source of the allergic reaction and you can eliminate it completely.

Itching can drive your dog crazy, and her scratching and chewing will only make the problem worse. Try to determine the cause of the itching, and talk to your veterinarian about a solution and treatment.

Soothing the Itch

Your veterinarian must be a part of the solution to stop the itching, but you can help your Yorkie, too. You should use these alongside the veterinary care, however, not in place of it.

Oatmeal shampoo: Many commercial oatmeal shampoos are available and most are recommended for itchy skin. Follow the directions. Most recommend leaving the shampoo on the skin for a few minutes before rinsing.

Antiseptic wash: A first-aid antiseptic wash is good for cleaning the skin and temporarily relieving the itch. It's not safe for your puppy to lick, though, so be sure to rinse it out of her coat after a few minutes.

Witch hazel: Dampen a cotton ball with witch hazel and pat it on the worst of the itchy spots. Don't let your Yorkie lick those spots until they're dry.

Benadryl: If all else fails, ask your veterinarian if you can give your Yorkie Benadryl to give her some relief. The dosage is normally 1 milligram per pound of body weight, but ask your veterinarian for his recommendation because your puppy is so tiny.

You know how it is when you have an intense itch—when that mosquito bites or the poison oak is breaking out—and how overwhelming it can be. You just *have* to scratch that spot even though you know it doesn't make anything better. In fact, scratching usually makes it worse. Your Yorkie is the same way. If something itches, she's going to want to scratch it. So alleviate that itching as quickly as you can.

Social Skills

The American Kennel Club (AKC) is best known for registering purebred dogs and sponsoring dog shows. However, one of the best programs the AKC runs is the Canine Good Citizen (CGC) program. All Yorkshire Terriers should be Canine Good Citizens.

At this age, your puppy's adolescence brings with it many changes. She's growing up, maturing, and looking more like an adult. She's also going through mental, emotional, and behavioral changes, too. So it shouldn't be a surprise that your Yorkie puppy's social skills are affected by these changes.

A Canine Good Citizen

The AKC began the Canine Good Citizen program more than 20 years ago to recognize responsible dog owners and well-behaved dogs. The exercises required for the title mimic real-life skills—things you and your dog probably do every day. When the dog is able to pass all 10 exercises, she is awarded the title Canine Good Citizen and can have "CGC" listed behind her name. The program is open to all dogs, purebred or mixed breed, registered with the AKC or not.

The exercises include the following:

- The dog, with her owner, allows a friendly yet unknown person to walk up and greet her owner.
- The dog, with her owner, when approached by a friendly person, allows that person to pet her.
- The owner shows responsibility by ensuring the dog is clean, healthy, and well groomed.
- The dog and owner can go for a walk, and the dog is under control.
- The dog and owner can walk through a crowd, and the dog is under control and doesn't pull or wrap the leash around people's legs.
- The dog and owner can demonstrate the dog knows and will do a sit, down, and stay when asked.
- The dog comes when called.
- The dog behaves politely around other dogs and doesn't lunge or bark at another dog.
- The dog does not panic in response to a visual or sound stimulus, such as a jogger or a flapping trash bag.
- The dog can be left with another person for 3 minutes. For example, perhaps you need to use the restroom while out on a walk and your neighbor holds the leash.

The CGC has become so popular, many landlords now require it as a condition of allowing a dog in a rental home. Some insurance companies offer discounts for dogs who have passed the CGC, and many therapy-dog organizations use the CGC as a test for potential therapy dogs. To find a CGC evaluator in your area, go to the AKC's website, akc.org.

When Your Puppy Is Unsocial Toward People

Adolescence is a difficult time for dogs and their owners. You may be discouraged to find your puppy now barks at people when you're out in public. You may feel like all your efforts at socializing your puppy were in vain—after all, you made it a point to take your Yorkie to meet people and other dogs and visit a variety of different places.

When she's unsocial, don't blame yourself. This behavior is more normal than not during adolescence. Her behavior doesn't mean you did a poor job of socializing her; rather, her behavior reflects more of the stage of development she's in right now.

> **TIPS AND TAILS**
>
> To be sure your adolescent remains safe and social to people, continue taking her places. Don't force her to greet strangers, but be sure she continues to go places with you so she continually sees people she doesn't know.

Use her obedience training to help her behave herself. Watch her body language, learn what she does just before she barks, and distract her when you see her about to open her mouth. Turn her away, and redirect her attention to you before she erupts, and praise her when she does pay attention to you.

You also need to protect your puppy from herself. If she's feeling particularly antisocial on any given day, don't force her to visit with people. When you're out on a walk, tell people not to pet her. When guests come to the house, leash your puppy and have her lie down at your feet while you sit and talk to your guests. If people are actively moving around, put your puppy in her crate in a back room. Don't force her into a situation where she may make a stupid mistake.

All the socialization you did with your puppy has not been for nothing. It helped build a good foundation for your puppy, and that foundation is still valuable. When your puppy works her way through adolescence, you'll see those socialization skills reemerge. Plus, without that socialization, adolescence would have been much worse.

When Your Puppy Is Unsocial Toward Dogs

During the turmoil of adolescence, Yorkies can be potentially aggressive toward other dogs. Although friendly with known canine friends, she can be nasty to strange dogs. Your Yorkie may find some dogs to be annoying or threatening, and some dogs may just be too pushy for her taste. Don't expect her to like all other dogs.

This is going to be more evident now, not just because your puppy is an adolescent and her brain is so volatile, but also because she's growing up.

> Dogs follow strict rules of social interactions that communicate clearly what the individual dog's intentions are. Body language—including postures and movements—as well as sounds are uniform through all breeds. These help prevent miscommunications and misunderstandings.

At some point during adolescence, your dog may be a little short-tempered or impatient, and a squabble may break out. This may just be some growling and snarling and never move beyond the verbal. Unfortunately, though, sometimes these squabbles do turn into fights.

Tiny dogs like Yorkies are at an obvious disadvantage in a fight. They are so small that if a larger dog grabs the Yorkie and shakes, the Yorkie might be severely hurt or even killed. Yorkies don't understand this and often challenge—barking and growling at—dogs much larger than themselves.

Dog fights are ugly but tend to have a few predictables:

🐾 Intact males tend to be quicker to fight, especially with other intact males.

🐾 Intact females will fight with other females, intact or not.

🐾 Males rarely start a fight with females, and often won't respond if challenged by females.

If your dog has been in a dog fight with another adolescent dog of the same sex and about the same size and no one needed to go to the veterinarian, don't panic. That means both dogs had good bite inhibition—and during adolescence, that's good news.

However, if your adolescent puppy is challenging many dogs of both sexes, and the size of the dog doesn't matter to her, you might have a problem. This doesn't mean you have a bad dog or that she's now a crazy dog, but you do need some help to figure out what's going on. It's definitely time to call a behaviorist for an evaluation.

While your puppy is going through adolescence—and while her brain isn't working well—limit her playtime with dogs to the dogs she already knows well. Don't go to the dog park and turn her loose with unknown dogs. That's setting her up for failure. If she doesn't start the fight, she may be willing to answer a challenge she would have ignored when she was younger or later when she's older.

TIPS AND TAILS

If a dog fight happens, don't try to grab the dogs' collars. You're likely to get bitten because most dogs try to grab their opponent's neck or face. Instead, ask for help. You and the other person should grab the dogs' back legs, lift the legs, and pull the dogs away from each other. Keep the legs elevated until the dogs stop trying to get to each other. Leash the dogs— don't pick up your Yorkie and hold her because you might get bitten—and walk them away.

Continue taking her places where she'll see leashed, well-behaved dogs. Training classes are a great way to continue her exposure to other dogs. Even if she can't play with the other dogs, she needs to continue to be around them, so don't isolate her.

Behavior

Teenagers—human and canine—get into trouble. Their brain is constantly changing, and often they don't think things through as they should. So how can you deal with a canine adolescent without constantly being angry with her? It's best to be proactive rather than reactive. After all, punishment after the fact never changes anything.

Being Proactive

You know your puppy better than anyone else—probably better than she even knows herself. After all, as an adolescent, she's not thinking well right now.

Use that knowledge to help your puppy behave herself. By being proactive and helping her be good rather than waiting until she's made a mistake, you can maintain a more positive relationship with her.

If you wait until she's made a mistake, you'll be interrupting those mistakes, yelling at her, grabbing her out of harm's way, or taking things away from her that she's chewed. That's not good for either of you.

To be proactive, keep your house and yard puppy-proofed. She's not grown up yet and can't be trusted not to chew, dig, or steal things she shouldn't have. Continue restricting her freedom in the house for the same reasons.

Keep enforcing your household rules, too. If you don't want her to chase the cat, raid the trash can, or jump up on the furniture, don't slack off now. Be sure everyone in the house understands the importance of a united front and enforces the rules with you.

Continue taking her outside to relieve herself. Even if she hasn't had a housetraining accident in a long time, keep taking her out, asking her to relieve herself, and praising her for going. Not only is she a teenager who needs to be reminded, but leg-lifting can begin anytime, and those housetraining skills—and the supervision—are important.

Speaking of leg-lifting—just a reminder that males and females can both do it. To be proactive, when you see your Yorkie assume that sideways position, interrupt her (or him), saying, "No! Knock it off!" or the words most comfortable for you.

Know your Yorkie's body language and behaviors. For example, when you see her stare at another dog, stand tall on her front toes, and stiffen her body, interrupt her and turn her toward you, "Sweetie, leave it! Watch me. Good girl to watch me!"

She knows the phrase "Leave it" means "ignore what you're paying attention to at the moment." She also knows "Watch me" means to look at you. So by asking her to leave it and look at you, you moved her attention from something she was going to bark at and redirected it to you so you could praise her for looking at you. A potentially bad moment became a good one.

Be patient. As the saying goes, "This, too, shall pass." Your Yorkie will grow up, and with your help, she'll be a wonderful dog. Just understand adolescence can be trying, and there's no shortcut to getting through it.

Spoiling Your Yorkie

It's so easy to spoil your Yorkie. She's tiny, she's incredibly cute, and she has won your heart many times over. So is spoiling your Yorkie *bad?* That depends on what you consider spoiling.

If you consider giving your Yorkie good veterinary care spoiling, then no, spoiling isn't bad. Some people might consider good food and regular grooming "extras," but you probably consider them necessities. Taking care of your Yorkie and giving her the best care you can provide shouldn't be considered "spoiling" her.

However, you can consider your Yorkie spoiled if you allow her to show you disrespect and you don't do anything to change it. If she mouths or bites you or urinates on your personal things, that's disrespect. Ignoring you is, to a certain extent, normal during adolescence and shouldn't be considered a sign of being spoiled … unless you allow her to continue doing it.

Feel free to spoil your Yorkie by giving her the best care you can. However, set rules of behavior for your Yorkie, and help her follow those rules. Reinforce the household rules you established months ago, and ensure she behaves nicely with both people and other dogs when out in public. She needs to behave herself with you and other family members, too.

The Yorkie who is carried everywhere in a purse and is dressed like a human baby is not spoiled because those behaviors are not the dog's choice. The dog would prefer not to wear clothes except in inclement weather, and most of the time the Yorkie would prefer to be on the ground.

Just keep in mind, a tiny dog who is a tyrant in her own home and is rude when out in public is not a happy dog. Dogs are happiest with a kind leader who shows them what to do and how to do it. Dogs thrive with a schedule and guidelines. Dogs like cooperating and especially being rewarded and praised for that behavior. These are the makings of happy dogs.

Your Yorkie's View of the World

Not all of your Yorkie's attitude right now is based on her adolescence. Some of it's also because she's discovered that her world is so much bigger than she is and is potentially dangerous.

As a young puppy, she was oblivious to this. She was so tiny, she was carried a lot and protected from things that could harm her. The world revolved around her, and she was perfectly fine with that.

As she's grown up, however, she's probably come to the realization that almost every dog she meets is bigger than she is. Plus, when she plays with other dogs, she's found out they can hurt her, even when playing. A heavy paw across her back hurts! A larger puppy running her over as if she wasn't even there hurts, too. It doesn't take long before the tiny Yorkie puppy becomes a little defensive.

People are huge, too, even young people. The most dangerous part of most people is their feet. A Yorkie who isn't paying attention could be kicked or stepped on. Even hugs can hurt. People like to hug tiny dogs, but if they hug too tightly, it's painful for a small dog.

The homes people live in are proportionately large. The sofa seat is twice the Yorkie's height so she has to jump way up and then way down. The hallway that would require a large dog to take six steps requires a Yorkie to take five times as many steps.

Most Yorkies grow out of this reactionary stage where they become more protective of themselves. But if the dog has been frightened too many times or is just naturally a little timid, she may remain overly cautious.

There's not much you can do about it except be careful of her and be sure other people are just as cautious. Limit rough handling and take care that she isn't hurt. With careful handling, her confidence and natural enthusiasm will return.

Training

During the teenage years, human teenagers test boundaries, challenge authority, and try to gain some independence. Eventually they will gain that freedom.

Canine teenagers do the same thing, but you want your puppy to look to you for guidance rather than strive for independence. Dog owners who don't understand that this challenging stage is a natural part of growing up often get frustrated. They feel that all their efforts at raising a good puppy have been wasted, that they worked so hard to do the right thing and now their puppy is a wild little beast.

Don't fall into this mind-set. The teenage stage of development is natural, and with your help, your Yorkie will grow out of it and become a wonderful pet and companion.

Going Back to Class

As we've mentioned, group training classes are a great idea because they help keep your teenage Yorkie well socialized. Even if your puppy has already attended a basic obedience class, enroll in another one. The exercises will be repeated, but the class will provide you and your teenager a chance to work with distractions in a controlled situation.

Because you learned the basics already, during the second time through you both can concentrate on fine-tuning your skills. You'll be amazed at how much you didn't hear from the instructor the first time through the class!

Let your instructor know your Yorkie is a teenager. He may have some tips for you, especially if he sees some rude behavior during class.

Practicing Your Training

Training works best when it's practiced on a regular basis. You're not trying to turn your little Yorkie into a robot, but you do want your Yorkie to be responsive to you. She should listen when you ask her to do something, and she should be compliant and willingly respond to your requests. It's not too much to ask her to abide by your rules for good behavior at home and when out in public.

Start by refreshing her basic obedience skills when at home, out on walks, and in training class. Some refresher training with praise and treats keeps the training fun and helps the two of you work together.

If your puppy acts as if she's never heard those basic obedience commands before—and this does happen in adolescence—teach them to her again. Start at the first training steps, and remind her how to sit, down, stay, and the other exercises.

After you've reminded your Yorkie what the basic obedience exercises are, use them:

- Have her sit and stay at open doors so she doesn't dash out.
- Have her sit at the gate and garage door for the same reason.
- Have her sit before she jumps into or out of the car to prevent her from hurting herself or getting into trouble.
- Be sure she's lying down and staying away from people while they're eating so she's not begging.

These are just a few ways you can use your Yorkie's training skills. Take a look at your normal routine, think about where you'd like your puppy to have a little more self-control, and use her obedience skills to do that.

The more you use your puppy's training skills, the better they'll become and the more second-nature they'll be. You want your Yorkie to look to you for guidance on how she should behave or react in any given situation, and her training will help with that.

Granting Permission

Another way to teach your teenager to look to you for guidance is to give her permission to do things. You can also deny her permission to keep her out of trouble.

Let's say, for example, your Yorkie puppy needs to go outside to relieve herself and has come to you and gotten your attention. Ask your puppy, "Do you need to go outside?" Walk her to do the door, ask her to sit, and praise her. Then open the door and give her permission, "Okay, go outside."

Just the act of having your puppy sit for a few seconds helps teach her self-control—an important skill right now. If she's sitting and waiting, she's not dashing out the door as soon as it opens. Nor is she running between your feet or tripping you. Plus, by waiting for your permission, she's looking to you for guidance, "Okay, can I go outside now?"

You can do the same thing in other situations:

🐾 Have her sit and wait when she's inside the car as you open the car door. You'll want to hook up her leash before she jumps out. When you hook up her leash, you can lift her down or give her permission to jump.

🐾 Have her be polite and sit and wait when you set down her food bowl. Then give her permission to go to her bowl.

🐾 Have her sit and wait at the gate before you open it. Then give her permission to go through the gate after you've put her leash on her.

We've mentioned these situations before as examples of using the basic obedience exercises. But now, in adolescence, they're also important for teaching self-control as well as reinforcing the habit of looking to you for permission to do things she wants to do.

And just as you give your teenager permission to do things, you can also deny it. Tell her no, she can't go out the front door, she can't jump into the car, and she can't have your leftover sandwich. By either giving or denying permission, you are teaching your puppy that she is to look to you rather than simply do what she wants to do.

The Yorkie Scientist

Your Yorkshire Terrier adolescent is not going to follow your every obedience command or every guideline without making a mistake. Mistakes are normal, and they are going to happen. Many mistakes will be accidents. Others will be experiments.

Kate Abbott, a dog trainer in Vista, California, says dogs are like scientists. When they ask a question (via their behavior) and it's answered by you or through a consequence of their actions, they then ask another question. So when your teenager tries one variance of behavior and you don't like it, she'll try something else to see what you have to say about that. She's experimenting, asking "Is this right? Or how about this?" The brighter, more intelligent the dog, the more questions she might ask.

You need to answer each of your teenager's questions very clearly. If, for example, you ask her to sit and she continues to stand, tell her, "Sweetie, sit," and help her do it. Don't continue to say, "Sit, sit, sit, sit," until she finally does it. Instead, ask her once, using clear communication, and then help her do it, as you taught her in Month 4.

Or if you ask her to sit and she lies down, do the same thing. Tell her sit, and help her do it. After all, you didn't ask her to lie down; you asked her to sit.

Don't get angry when she's experimenting to see where her boundaries are. Just realize that this, too, is a natural part of this stage of her life, and work through it together.

You and Your Puppy

You can have a lot of fun with your puppy this month. Adolescence is challenging, but focusing on that alone isn't healthy for the relationship you have with your puppy. Sometimes you need to forget about adolescence and just have fun together.

Touching Paw to Finger

One of the first tricks many people teach their puppy is to shake hands. This trick is a little different when you have a tiny Yorkie, though. So instead of you reaching out to grab your Yorkie's paw, you can teach her to touch her paw to your fingertip.

Here's how:

🐾 Have your Yorkie on leash so she can't dash away.

🐾 Ask her to sit facing you.

🐾 There's a small indentation behind your Yorkie's front paw, just below her ankle. Reach out with one finger and lightly touch that indentation.

🐾 When she lifts her paw to move it away from your finger, tell her, "Sweetie, finger! Good" (You can use any word you want, of course.)

🐾 Practice several times and then take a break to play something else.

🐾 Come back later, and repeat the training steps. When she begins lifting her paw as you reach toward her, praise her enthusiastically. If she continues to reach toward you, gently touch her paw with your finger and praise her again.

As you practice this, have her reach more with her paw before you touch her and then praise her. Ideally, you want her to reach up with her paw to touch your finger.

Spinning

Although the touch-paw-to-finger trick is cute, it's much too quiet for many young Yorkies. They like active tricks best, and spinning is a good one.

Here's how to get your Yorkie to turn circles:

❧ Have some good treats in your pocket and one in your hand.

❧ With your Yorkie standing in front of you, let her sniff the treat.

❧ Moving the treat slowly to encourage your Yorkie to follow it, make a circle with your hand and treat, from her nose around to her tail. She should move toward her right.

❧ As she moves in a circle, tell her, "Sweetie, spin!"

❧ When she completes the circle, praise her and give her the treat.

❧ After three or four circles, take a break and play something else with her. Later, repeat the training steps.

> **TIPS AND TAILS**

Never ask your Yorkie to do so many spins that she gets dizzy or gets an upset stomach. Trick training should be fun for both of you.

When your Yorkie understands the game, make your hand signal smaller and smaller, until eventually you can use a small, circular hand signal rather than leading your puppy by her nose.

Spinning the Other Way

Once your Yorkie understands to spin to the right with a hand signal and your verbal command, teach her to spin the other direction. This time she'll move to her left.

Your verbal command can be, "Sweetie, spin left," or "Sweetie, spin the other way." The actual words aren't important because she's going to learn as you teach her no matter what the actual words are. But when you show off her tricks, people will be amazed when you tell her to spin to her left and she actually does. They'll think she knows her right from her left.

Teach her to spin this direction using the same training steps as before, but have her move to her left. Emphasize the different verbal command so she learns that each direction has a different command.

Fun with Food-Dispensing Toys

Food-dispensing toys are a fun reward for your Yorkie. These toys have a place that can hold bits of food. When you give the toy to your dog, she then has to work to get the food out of the toy.

One of the first food-dispensing toys, which is still popular, is the Kong. Made of heavy rubber, it looks like a hollow snowman, with three gradually larger round parts. The hollow Kong has a small hole at one end and a larger hole at the bottom where you can tuck kibble or other small foods. The Kong's shape causes it to move and bounce erratically so your Yorkie has to chase it to get the food out of it. Many other food-dispensing toys are available in a variety of sizes for use with toy-breed dogs as well as larger dogs.

If your Yorkie eats too fast and chokes herself, or if she eats so fast she vomits afterward, eating her meals from a food-dispensing toy will slow her down. Because it takes her time to get the food out of the toy, she'll eat slower rather than gulping down his food.

Food-dispensing toys can also keep your puppy amused. If you need to get some work done and your puppy is bored, a food-dispensing toy will keep her occupied.

When you have to leave the house, a food-dispensing toy enables you leave without your Yorkie raising a fuss. She'll be so distracted by her toy, she won't even notice you're gone.

When guests come to your house, give your Yorkie a food-dispensing toy while she's in her exercise pen. She'll be busy with that instead of whining and barking to be released from her pen so she can join the party.

You can feed your puppy one or two of her meals from a food-dispensing toy, especially if she eats kibble. You can also feed her bits of carrots, slices of apple, tiny chunks of cheese, or bits of meat from the toy.

You may have to show your Yorkie how to use a food-dispensing toy. Most puppies figure them out quickly—especially after a bit of food has fallen out—but some puppies aren't bold enough to try. Roll a loaded toy in front of your Yorkie, and encourage her to chase it. Praise her when she does, and then sit back and watch.

After you and your puppy have played with a couple different types of food-dispensing toys, you'll discover which ones she likes best. Some may be too heavy for her or too clumsy. Pass those along to friends with larger dogs. You'll also figure other ways to use the food-dispensing toys to your advantage.

Making Time to Play

We all lead busy lives, and it's easy to get caught up in work responsibilities, household chores, family activities, yard work, home repairs, and all our other day-to-day activities. Then, because you added a Yorkie to your life, you have to remember to socialize her, train her, and keep her groomed. Sometimes it probably feels like you don't have one extra second in the day.

Find a few seconds—or better yet a few minutes—and sit on the floor and play with your Yorkie. Play tug with her, throw her ball and encourage her to bring it back, or just rub her tiny tummy.

There's always enough time to play with your puppy. Not only is it good for the relationship you're developing with her, but it will relax you and make both you and your puppy feel better.

Month 8	Month 9	Month 10
	Socialization in public	
	Adult teeth are in—chewing continues	
	Ready for more advanced training	
	Moderate growth	
	Sexual maturity	

This month, which covers weeks 33 through 36, your puppy is more coordinated, stronger, and more athletic. He's running, jumping, playing, and having a great time. This desire to be active and busy is great right now because exercise and playtime with you help keep him out of trouble. After all, a tired puppy is a good puppy.

Your puppy is still in adolescence, which means he's not going to be cooperative *all* the time, but you'll be seeing less and less challenging behavior as time goes on. This month you'll also see moments—flashes—of the dog he's going to grow up to be.

Physical Development

All Yorkshire Terriers share some characteristics, but as you may have noticed, not all Yorkies are exactly the same. Some Yorkies are larger or smaller than others, some have a longer or shorter coat, and the shades of the blue coat color may be different.

There is a plan, however, and that's the breed standard. Wise breeders use this description of the breed as a means of producing the best Yorkies they can.

The Breed Standard

The Yorkshire Terrier Club of America maintains the breed standard for Yorkies registered with the American Kennel Club. For a pet and companion, the breed standard may not seem to be important. However, the breed standard is the description of the perfect Yorkie and is what keeps a Yorkshire Terrier looking like a Yorkie rather than, say, a Shih Tzu.

The Standard is just a description, however, and it's understood that no one—dog or human—is perfect. Each Yorkshire Terrier has his own variations or individual characteristics that make him unique.

> **TIPS AND TAILS**
>
> The Standard applies to adult dogs, not puppies or adolescents. There are conformation dog-show classes for puppies, but it's understood that puppies are different from adults.

Let's talk about some of the more important portions of the Standard. To read the full American Kennel Club's official standard, go to akc.org/breeds/yorkshire_terrier.

General appearance: The Standard addresses the fact that the Yorkshire Terrier is a toy-breed dog with a terrier heritage. There must be a balance of the tiny elegant dog with the terrier's sturdiness, compactness, and strength. The Yorkie should also express confidence and self-importance.

Head: The head is difficult to see under a full coat, but you certainly can feel it with your fingers. The head should be in proportion to dog's body—small yet not too small. The eyes are medium size, not too prominent, and dark. The ears are upright, small, V shape, and not set too far apart. The nose is black.

Body: The body should demonstrate the breed's terrier heritage and be strong without being overly muscled. The body is compact, and the height is the same at the point of the shoulders and the height of the rump.

Size: Yorkies shall not exceed 7 pounds.

> **TIPS AND TAILS**
>
> There's only one size of Yorkies. Any dogs advertised as teacups, minis, baby dolls, purse puppies, or any other size connotations are not correct. These terms are just marketing ploys.

Coat: The correct coat is of utmost importance. It's what sets Yorkies apart from other long-coated terriers. The coat is parted from the base of the skull to the base of the tail. It falls to each side of the part and drapes to the floor. The coat is silky in texture, glossy, and fine.

The coat on the head is also long and is gathered into a topknot on top of the head or is parted and gathered into two sections. The hair on the muzzle is very long.

Color: An adult Yorkie's distinctive steel-blue coloring begins at the back of the neck and extends to the root of the tail. It's not a silver-blue or a blue interspersed with black hairs; it's a clear, rich, steel-blue that's been compared to the blue of a mountain stream.

The head, chest, and legs are a rich tan. This tan is not pale or washed out but a golden tan.

> **TIPS AND TAILS**
>
> Each registry, including the Canadian Kennel Club and The Kennel Club in Great Britain, has its own breed standard. Although most are very similar, there are differences, one of which is whether the breed's tail should be docked or left natural.

More About Color

The color of the Yorkshire Terrier's coat is important to the breed, as evident by the number of discussions concerning color in magazines, in books, and online. To make things more complicated, colors are difficult to put into words. What's steel-blue to one person might not mean the same thing to someone else.

The AKC breed standard calls for "a dark steel-blue, not a silver-blue and not mingled with fawn, bronzy, or black hairs." This blue has been compared to polished steel and gun-muzzle blue. However, the best comparison is that of cool blue water in a mountain stream.

The tan is also subject to a great deal of debate. The AKC standard calls for a rich, golden tan. Most people can visualize this without difficulty. One conformation judge, when critiquing the dogs in his classes, said that tan really isn't a correct color. He prefers the description of "golden tan" because "tan" can be a variety of shades.

> **TIPS AND TAILS**
>
> Fédération Cynologique Internationale (FCI), an international registry for purebred dogs, calls for similar colors as the AKC: a dark steel-blue on the back with a rich, bright tan.

In October 2007, the Yorkshire Terrier Club of America clarified the standard's description of colors by stating that any Yorkshire Terrier who was a solid color, rather than blue and golden tan, was to be disqualified from conformation competition. In addition, dogs of any colors other than blue and tan, or with white spots other than a tiny (less than 1 inch) one on the forechest, were also to be disqualified.

This clarification was brought about because different-colored Yorkies—including chocolate and tan dogs as well as solid-colored ones—were being registered. Parti-colored dogs, which are white with patches of other colors, have also become popular, and these *can* be registered because the AKC does not deny registration due to color alone. However, the dogs cannot compete in conformation classes because the color is an automatic disqualification.

The Biewer Terrier

The Biewer Terrier originated in Germany from a white, blue, and tan Yorkshire Terrier. Although bred from Yorkshire Terriers and sometimes called Biewer Yorkies, most Yorkie fanciers prefer a separation of the two and would like to see them exclusively called Biewer Terriers. Several clubs, including the Biewer Terrier Club of America, have been formed to guide the formation of a new breed.

The primary characteristic of the Biewer is that the dogs are white with varying amounts of blue (or black) and tan (or gold). There can be more or less white or color, depending on personal preference. The Yorkshire Terrier breed standard only allows a tiny spot of white on the front of the chest that's less than an inch wide, so Biewer Terriers aren't allowed to register with the AKC and complete in conformation shows.

Biewers can also be slightly larger than Yorkies, with a weight up to 8 pounds allowed. In all other ways, the Biewer is similar to the Yorkie.

Health

At this age, your Yorkie has finished his vaccinations and is healthy and strong. Your veterinarian may still have you wait for spaying or neutering, but that will be happening soon.

An added benefit of this age and your Yorkie's growth is that he's probably past the dangers of hypoglycemia. This occurs most often in young puppies and tiny Yorkies, so your strong teenager is less likely to face that threat. However, he should still eat three meals a day, or two good meals and a couple small snacks, to keep up his blood sugar.

However, your Yorkie can still get sick. He may cough and sneeze, have diarrhea, or vomit. (But hopefully not all at once.) In previous months, we discussed potential Yorkie health problems along with instructions for when to call the veterinarian. This month, let's look at how to care for your adolescent at home.

Caring for your Yorkie at home is less stressful for your puppy, but don't hesitate to call your veterinarian. If your puppy doesn't show signs of improving, if he gets worse, or even if you're just worried, make that call.

Recognizing Pain and Discomfort

Your Yorkie is more active now than he has been at any other time in his life. Unfortunately, this means at some point he's going to step wrong and twist a leg, or he's going to jump and land hard and stress his shoulders. Athletes get hurt, and that applies to canine athletes as well as human ones.

Each puppy handles pain differently; some are stoic and show pain only when it reaches an extreme level. Often the owners of stoic dogs aren't aware their dog is in any pain at all because the dog hides it so well. Other puppies cry at the slightest discomfort.

It's important to know your individual puppy and know how he handles pain:

🐾 Does he get quiet and go curl up away from everyone?

🐾 Does he come to you and become very clingy?

🐾 Does he whine, cry, or whimper?

🐾 Does he limp, or does he tough it out?

Know what's normal for your Yorkie so you can quickly recognize subtle cues of an injury. If you learn how your puppy handles minor aches and pains, you'll be better prepared when he really does hurt.

> **TIPS AND TAILS**

If your dog is in pain, muzzle him before you try to determine what hurts. Dogs who hurt might bite, and although your Yorkie is tiny, he can still hurt you. He won't purposely try to hurt you, but biting is a self-defense mechanism triggered by pain or panic.

A small ice pack on the site of the injury can help relieve swelling for your adolescent athlete, just as it can for human athletes. Snuggle your Yorkie close, and put an ice pack wrapped in a dish towel or hand towel on the spot for 5 minutes and then take it off. Let your puppy warm up for 5 to 10 minutes and repeat the ice pack.

Don't give your Yorkie any over-the-counter pain medications without first consulting with your veterinarian. Although buffered or coated aspirin is usually safe for short-term pain relief, it can have significant side effects, including severe gastrointestinal upset and potentially even bleeding. If your veterinarian recommends aspirin, you can give your Yorkie 5 to 10 milligrams per pound of body weight, with food.

Dealing with Common Upsets

Your Yorkie might experience a few bodily function upsets you can care for at home. Each of these could signal a more dangerous condition or disease, so keeping in touch with your veterinarian is important.

Diarrhea: Yorkies can have a sensitive digestive tract. Anxiety, nervousness, excitement, or a new experience can cause diarrhea. Even a change in water can cause it.

You can treat the diarrhea at home as long as no other signs of disease are present. To begin treating it, don't feed your adolescent for the next 24 hours and offer him ice cubes instead of water for a few hours. Then let him drink as much as he wants to avoid dehydration. Every few hours, rub some corn syrup on his gums to keep his blood sugar from dropping.

If your veterinarian has preapproved it, you can give your adolescent antidiarrhea medication; however, get the dosage recommendations from your veterinarian. Pepto-Bismol and plain Kaopectate (without salicylates) are generally considered safe for dogs. Imodium AD, in $\frac{1}{2}$ tablet doses, is generally considered safe, too.

After 24 hours, feed your Yorkie a bland diet over several small meals. This could include boiled chicken, puréed cooked pumpkin, cottage cheese, boiled rice, cooked oatmeal, or soft-boiled eggs.

> **TIPS AND TAILS**
>
> Call your veterinarian if you see any blood in your Yorkie's stools, if his diarrhea persists for more than 24 hours, if foreign objects or parasites are in the stools, or if the diarrhea is accompanied by vomiting.

Vomiting: Vomiting can occur for many reasons, including overeating, eating too fast, eating nonfood items, eating spoiled food, or disease. Your Yorkie may also vomit if he eats some grass. This doesn't mean he has worms, by the way, as is commonly believed.

Withhold food and water from your vomiting Yorkie for the next 12 hours. If your veterinarian recommends it, Pepcid ($\frac{1}{2}$ tablet for a Yorkie) is considered safe and may help settle your pup's stomach. Rub some corn syrup on his gums every few hours to prevent his blood sugar from getting too low during this fast.

If the vomiting and dry heaves stop when his stomach is empty and has rested, you can begin offering him ice cubes every few hours. If he doesn't vomit any more and the water from the ice cubes stays down, you can offer him a $\frac{1}{2}$ cup of water mixed with a $\frac{1}{4}$ cup of pediatric electrolyte solution.

After 12 hours with no vomiting, offer him a bland diet as was recommended for diarrhea. Offer several small meals throughout the day rather than larger meals. Feed him this bland diet for 2 or 3 days before you reintroduce him to normal food.

> **TIPS AND TAILS**

Call your veterinarian if there's blood in the vomit, if the vomiting doesn't stop when his stomach is empty, if the vomiting begins again when you introduce food, or if you see any other signs of illness.

Coughing: Many different things can cause coughing, from allergies to heart disease. However, in puppies and adolescents, the most common cause is a respiratory infection often called kennel cough. Even well-vaccinated puppies can develop kennel cough because there are many different strains.

Home treatment consists of first keeping him quiet. Limit his activities because if he's active, he'll start coughing more. Your veterinarian may recommend an over-the-counter cough syrup to calm his throat.

Use a harness instead of a collar when he's coughing. Don't put a collar back on him until he's fully healed and no longer coughing.

> **TIPS AND TAILS**

Call your veterinarian if your puppy begins to show any symptoms other than coughing, if he develops a fever, or if the coughing doesn't lessen with the cough suppressant.

Allergic reaction: Swelling from bee stings, spider bites, or other allergens that cause your puppy's face or throat to swell can be potentially life-threatening. Call your veterinarian immediately if this happens. She may recommend you give your Yorkie ¼ to ½ a Benadryl (1 milligram per pound of body weight) and bring your puppy to the clinic right away.

Treating Your Puppy

Your veterinarian can diagnose an illness, treat an injury, and prescribe medications. However, you'll need to be able to continue the treatment at home. If you know how to do it, you can save additional trips to the vet clinic.

Giving pills and capsules: To give your puppy a pill or capsule, sit on a chair and have him sit on your lap with his back to you. Reach over his head with one hand, and from above his head, take hold of his top jaw by pressing his lips against his top teeth.

As he opens his mouth, use your other hand to place the pill or capsule in his mouth, as far back as you can. If the pill is too far forward, he'll spit it out, so try to get it on the back of his tongue. Then close his mouth and gently rub his throat to encourage him to swallow. Give him a treat now so he swallows for sure.

Giving pills in food: If the pill can be given with food, it's much easier to hide the pill in a bit of cheese or meat. But the key is to have two pieces. Hide the pill in one, give it to your puppy, and show him the second piece so he swallows the first one quickly. Then give him the second piece. Not all medication can be given with food, however, so always ask your vet first.

> **TIPS AND TAILS**

Don't try to hide the pill in a bowl of your puppy's food. Most Yorkies will eat around the pill or spit it out. It could end up on the floor, and you may not realize he didn't get his medication.

Giving liquid medications: Liquid medications are usually given by eyedropper, syringe, or medicine bottle. Have a seat and have your puppy on your lap facing away from you. Close his mouth and slightly tilt his chin up. Place the tip of the eyedropper or syringe between his lips at his cheek. Be sure the tip is in his mouth facing toward his throat but not in his throat.

Slowly administer the medication, stopping frequently so your puppy can swallow. Don't try to rush it, giving him too much, or he will choke and cough, spraying the medication all over.

Administering suppositories: Sometimes medication is administered via suppositories that must be inserted into the rectum. This is more common when a dog is vomiting and will throw up any oral medication, or if the dog is having bowel problems.

To insert the suppository, lubricate the suppository with petroleum jelly. Hold your Yorkie's tail with one hand and lift it so the anus is visible. With the other hand, insert the suppository so it's completely inside the rectum. Let go of the tail.

Eye drops: Have the dog sit on your lap, with his back to you, and tilt his chin up. Steady the hand with the medication against his head. Then, with the hand not holding the medication, gently pull down his lower lid. Without touching his eye with the bottle, drop the prescribed number of drops in his eye.

You can use the same technique if your veterinarian recommends flushing the eye with saline solution or artificial tears. A towel over your knees can help keep this from turning into a mess.

Eye ointment: Have your dog sitting on your lap with his back toward you. Hold the medication in one hand while steadying his head with the other. Using the hand steadying his head, gently pull down on his lower eyelid. Rest the hand with the medication against his head so you don't poke him with the ointment tip. Place the prescribed amount of medication inside his lower lid, between the lid and the eyeball. Close his eye, and very gently massage the lower lid to spread the medication.

Ear medications: Depending on the problem requiring medication for the ear, the application may vary. Your veterinarian will show you how to apply it. However, the most common treatments require the medication to be inserted into the ear canal.

Your veterinarian may ask you to clean the ear before applying medication. Again, she will provide instructions on how to do this and what to use.

When the ear is clean and dry and you're ready to treat your puppy, have him sit on your lap with his back toward you. Fold the flap of the ear being treated back over his head. Place the tip of the ointment or bottle into the ear canal slightly—only as far as you can see and no farther. Don't push the applicator into the ear, or you could damage the sensitive tissues. Apply the required amount of medication and remove the applicator. Put the ear flap back up, and gently massage the base of the ear.

Nutrition

Nutrition is a complicated subject in its own right. Trying to understand all the parts of nutrition—proteins from meats and from plants, fats, carbohydrates, vitamins, minerals, and water to say nothing of amino acids, enzymes, and the process of digestion and the metabolizing of nutrients …. It's no wonder experts don't agree on what people should eat, never mind what dogs should have.

If your Yorkie is doing well with the diet he's eating right now, don't make any changes. A quality commercial diet for all life stages that's complete and balanced is absolutely fine during adolescence. If you're feeding him a homemade diet, either raw or cooked, and he's healthy, has a shiny coat, and has plenty of energy for play, don't make any changes now.

Giving Your Puppy Treats

It's fun to give your puppy treats. After all, many human cultures equate food with love, and many dog owners give their dogs treats to express their affection. Plus, dogs love extra treats!

When you have a very tiny dog, though, it's much easier for the puppy to get too much. Although obesity is rarely a problem with puppies of this age simply because they're so active, too many calories will catch up, and your Yorkie could later face the health problems associated with obesity.

Training treats are important right now because you and your Yorkie are doing a lot of training. Although your voice and toys are good rewards, treats are the best reward for most puppies. (We talked about training treats in Month 6, so turn back for a quick refresher if you need to.)

> **TIPS AND TAILS**

Keep in mind that anything extra you give your puppy should total less than 10 percent of his daily calories. So if your Yorkie eats about 225 calories per day, he should get no more than 22 calories of treats each day.

Limit the number of "just because" treats you give your puppy. If you have an urge to feed your puppy a treat, do a few quick obedience skills first. Ask your puppy to sit, lie down, and sit again before handing over the treat.

If you use food-dispensing toys to help keep your puppy distracted or amused, put one of your puppy's meals in the toy. Or use healthy, low-calorie treats such as bits of meat or carrots in the toy.

You can give your Yorkie treats; just do so with some thought.

Foods to Avoid

Your Yorkie cannot eat everything you eat because some people foods are potentially toxic to dogs. Even if they're not toxic, they could still cause gastrointestinal distress.

Here are some foods to avoid feeding your Yorkie:

Chocolate: Bitter baker's chocolate is the most toxic to dogs, followed by dark chocolate. But even milk chocolate can be dangerous if a Yorkie consumes enough of it. Be sure no chocolate is left out where your Yorkie can get it—especially around the holidays. Unfortunately, many dogs are just as attracted to it as people are.

Grease: If you trim the fat off a cut of meat or have some grease left in the pan after cooking, don't share it with your Yorkie. Too much grease causes gastrointestinal distress, including horrible diarrhea. In some dogs, too much grease can also trigger an attack of pancreatitis.

Spices: Some mild spices won't hurt your Yorkie, for the most part. If you cook your meat with some black pepper and want to share some of that with your Yorkie in his meal, that's fine. But heavy spices or hot spices aren't good for your puppy and could cause an upset stomach.

Moldy and mildewy foods: If you have some cheese that has developed mold, don't share that with your puppy. Throw it away. Many dogs are just as sensitive to molds and mildew as some people are. It can make your puppy sick or trigger an allergic reaction.

For a more complete list of foods to avoid, see Appendix D. Just remember that although your Yorkie is very much a part of your family, he's very tiny and so his food intake must be limited. Plus, he is a dog, and his nutritional needs are not the same as a human's.

Guarding Food and Treats

Many Yorkie puppies of this age begin showing the tendency to guard things they treasure, such as their meals, treats, and food-dispensing toys. Their wild cousins did this for survival many generations ago when food was scarce, but your puppy isn't in any danger of going hungry in your household, so you can teach him this isn't allowed.

Although this isn't specifically a Yorkie characteristic, Yorkies are known to guard things. This is particularly true in busy households, especially ones with children and other dogs. Perhaps in these situations the Yorkie feels threatened while eating. Many times, however, the guarding behavior will appear with no trigger or apparent cause.

The first signs of food guarding might be a growl if anyone approaches his food or tries to reach for his food-dispensing toy. Some puppies lie on top of the treasured item to guard it as they growl and show their teeth.

To prevent inappropriate food or *resource guarding,* practice the "Leave it" exercise with a variety of different objects he shouldn't have, from the trash can to the family cat. At this point, don't use an object he's guarding. For now, practice the exercise with many different items so he understands that if he's told to leave it, that thing isn't his. Use lots of praise and rewards while practicing so your teenager learns this exercise is an opportunity for lots of praise. You don't want this to turn into a battle.

> **DOG TALK**
>
> **Resource guarding** is a natural behavior that causes a dog to guard things he likes, including his owner, food, toys, and other things important to him. It's an unsafe behavior because the dog who is guarding may bite to defend his prized item.

Then begin teaching him the exercise "Drop it" so he'll spit out items you don't want him to have. Start by trading him something he has in his mouth for something even better.

Say, for example, he picks up one of your socks:

- Pick up his treasured stuffed rabbit toy, for example, and tell him, "Sweetie, bunny!" and show it to him.
- If he still has the sock, walk toward him as you show him the toy. Don't say anything about the sock.
- When you approach him, hold out the toy.
- If he spits out the sock, let him have the toy as you tell him, "Sweetie, drop it! Good boy."

When he understands the exercise and the words "Drop it," begin using it, trading one thing for another.

If your Yorkie begins guarding things seriously, growling, and snarling, and you're concerned about this behavior, call a dog trainer or behaviorist right away. Don't hesitate and hope the behavior will resolve itself because it won't. Invariably, without intervention, it will get worse.

> **TIPS AND TAILS**
>
> Once something is in your Yorkie's mouth, it's too late to teach him not to grab it. That's when you trade him something he likes better.

Grooming

Your puppy will need a bath from time to time. Giving your Yorkie a bath isn't difficult if he still has a short coat or if you have it trimmed short. However, as the coat lengthens, bathing it can be more of a challenge.

Fixing up the famous Yorkie topknot requires some practice. But there are also a few techniques to make it easier.

One of the downfalls to the Yorkie's coat is that it attracts all kinds of stuff. Wrapping your puppy in bubble wrap to keep him clean and safe isn't practical, so you need to be able to deal with all kinds of grooming challenges.

Giving Your Yorkie a Bath

The first step in bathing your Yorkie actually has nothing to do with getting him wet. You need to thoroughly and completely brush and comb him and get any and all tangles out of his coat before you get him wet. Hair expands when it gets wet, and if there are any tangles in his coat, they'll only get worse when they're wet. Wet matts turn into a solid mass and are almost impossible to detangle.

Brush him first with a pin brush and follow that with a comb. Be sure no burrs, grass seeds, or dirt remain in his coat, and remove everything you've put in it, such as rubber bands, barrettes, or bows.

Put a cotton ball in each ear to keep most of the water out. Don't push the cotton ball down into the ear canal; just place it in the ear so it catches the water.

Then place your Yorkie in the sink and begin to bathe him:

🐾 Using water that's a comfortable temperature for you—warm but not hot—get your Yorkie wet. Start at the back of his head or neck, and work down his back to his tail and down to his paws. Lift the hair as you go down his body so he's wet all the way to his skin.

🐾 Get your hands lathered with shampoo and begin working it into his coat.

🐾 Work the shampoo into his coat down to his skin, but be careful not to create any tangles as you do this. It might take a few baths before you get the hang of this technique.

🐾 Use a tearless shampoo on your puppy's face, but still be careful not to get any in his eyes.

🐾 Rinse his face first and then the rest of his body, beginning at his neck and working down and back. Rinse him until all the shampoo is completely out.

🐾 Now use a conditioner and follow the same process, beginning at the back of his head or neck and moving down and back. Be sure to work the conditioner into all of his coat.

🐾 Rinse again to be sure all the conditioner is out.

🐾 Using your hands, gently squeeze all the water from his coat.

🐾 Now wrap him in a towel and hug your Yorkie gently. Pat the towel up against him so it absorbs as much water as possible.

> **TIPS AND TAILS**

Do not rub your Yorkie with the towel. This will cause the coat to tangle and matt. Instead, just wrap your Yorkie in the towel or pat him with it.

After you've absorbed most of the water with the towel, you can blow-dry his hair using the low setting on the blow dryer. Use your fingers to separate his hair at first, followed by a wide-toothed comb. Be careful not to use the dryer on one spot for too long because it can burn his skin. Instead, move it around and dry the coat gradually all over.

Doing the Yorkie Topknot

It takes some practice to do the Yorkie topknot so it looks nice but doesn't pull on your Yorkie's skin. Most groomers suggest starting to do the topknot before the hair on the head gets very long so you get to practice and your puppy gets used to it.

Here's how:

- After you've thoroughly brushed and combed your Yorkie, comb the hair on his head so it falls in the direction it grows.
- Then, using a rat-tail comb, part the hair from the outer corner of one eye to the inner corner of the ear on that side of the head. Comb that hair up and back between the ears.
- Do the same thing on the other side of the head.
- Gather up the hair you combed back between the ears. Comb it again to straighten and neaten it.
- Place a rubber band at the base of this hair, making sure it doesn't pull on the hair. If it pulls, your puppy will rub it and scratch at it.
- You can add a bow over the rubber band if you like.

Take the hair out of the rubber band each time you brush and comb your puppy—which should be at least once a day. If you leave the rubber band in any longer, the hair may tangle and matt. To remove the rubber band, carefully snip it with scissors.

Removing Burrs, Foxtails, and Seeds

In the spring and summer, grass and weed seeds are the bane of dog owners. Although your Yorkie's coat doesn't pick up the grass and weed seeds like dogs with fluffier coats, the seeds still stick and grab on to even your Yorkie's silky coat. Most seeds have barbs or hooks that latch onto the coat. As the dog moves, the hooks and barbs grab more hairs, and soon a tangle forms. If seeds get into your Yorkie's paw between the pads, those barbs and hooks hurt and can work into the skin.

You can pick out many grass and weed seeds from your Yorkie's coat. Just be careful you don't get a barb in your fingertips. If the seeds won't pull out, you may be able to brush or comb them out. Or use a little hair conditioner—a good, thick slippery kind—to work out the tangle and seed. Then rinse out the conditioner.

If you still have a tangle with the seed in it and a matt has formed around the seed, you may have to trim it out. Place a metal comb between the matt and your Yorkie's skin, and using scissors, trim on the matt side of the comb so you don't cut your puppy's skin by accident.

Getting Out Gum and Sticky Stuff

How many times have you gone for a walk and stepped in gum someone has spit out on the sidewalk? It's tough to get off the bottom of your shoes. Unfortunately, it can be just as hard to get it out of your Yorkie's coat.

Many groomers recommend applying ice to the gum or sticky stuff. Place your hand or something else between the gum and your Yorkie's skin to keep the ice off his skin while you freeze the gum. When the gum or sticky stuff is very cold or frozen, try to break it out of the coat. You may have to reapply the ice several times as you're working at it.

You may also be able to use a small amount of vegetable oil on the gum. Massage the oil into the coat around the gum with your fingers. Then see if the gum will slide out. Of course, now you'll need to give your Yorkie a bath to get the oil out of his coat.

Sometimes the only thing you can do is trim the sticky stuff out of your puppy's coat. If you need to do this, do so carefully so you don't cut his skin. Slide a comb between the sticky stuff and his skin, without pulling up on the skin. Then trim on the outside of the comb, away from the skin. Snip very slowly and in tiny cuts so you don't make a mistake.

Cleaning Out Oil and Grease

Your Yorkie's coat can pick up spots of oil or grease anywhere. Perhaps you spilled something in the kitchen or the garage, or you went for a walk in the neighborhood and someone was working on his car.

Oils and greases of various kinds can be tough to get out of the coat because many dog shampoos won't break up the oil and grease so it can wash out. The oil and grease can also cause the coat to clump and matt.

A bigger problem is that your Yorkie may try to groom himself to remove the foreign substance, and many oils and greases can cause health problems. Cooking oils and meat greases aren't toxic but can certainly lead to vomiting and a horrible case of diarrhea. Motor oils and greases made from petroleum products can be toxic and need to be removed from the coat right away.

If you believe your puppy has tried to groom himself and has ingested any oil or grease, forget about bathing him and instead get him to the veterinary clinic right away. Treatment for the ingestion can begin first, and he can be bathed at the clinic while he's being treated.

> **TIPS AND TAILS**
>
> Symptoms of petroleum-product poisoning include difficulty breathing, vomiting, tremors, and convulsions. It can be fatal for your puppy, so get veterinary care immediately.

Many professional groomers use the dishwashing soap Joy to remove oil and grease. In fact, it works so well, wildlife rehabilitation specialists who try to save birds covered in oil after disasters also use Dawn.

Start by getting your Yorkie wet down to his skin. Then beginning at his head, start working the soap into his coat and working down his neck to his shoulders and then the rest of his body. If he has any oil or grease on his face, suds that up last, avoiding his eyes. Be sure to work soap into each paw, rubbing the soap in between each pad and around each toenail. Any oil or grease left between his pads will cause him to lick. Massage his skin and coat for a full 5 minutes, giving the soap time to work. Then rinse thoroughly and repeat.

After the second soaping and rinse, work a mixture of 2 cups white vinegar to 1 gallon warm water into his coat, and rinse again. This helps remove anything left in the coat, including any soap residue.

Removing Paint

If your puppy gets nontoxic paint on himself, you don't have to worry too much about it. Many times, it will fall off the hair when it has dried. Or when you brush your dog, the brushing action will cause the paint to fall off. But if you don't want to wait, you can remove it.

If the paint is a latex or acrylic, it may wash out just fine. Use some Dawn and try to work out the paint. Then rinse well and follow up with a vinegar rinse.

If the paint isn't one made for water cleanup, do not use paint solvents on your puppy. They are toxic. Instead, try to get the paint out with mineral oil and then wash well with Dawn. Rinse and follow up with a vinegar rinse.

If the paint doesn't come out, trim it out using the same technique as was described for gum and other sticky stuff.

Ungluing Glue

If your dog gets glue, hot glue, or other adhesives into his coat, they are not going to come out easily. Glue is glue; it will stick to his hair, and it'll cause more hair to stick together until the glue dries. His coat will have a big clump of glue and hair.

Wearing rubber gloves so you don't end up stuck to your dog, try to wash out as much as you can. Use Dawn, rinse well, and then rinse with vinegar, as for gum and sticky stuff.

Next, trim out any remaining glue. After you've trimmed his coat, you might want to wash that spot again just in case any glue remains.

Removing Porcupine Quills and Cactus Spines

Terriers, even toy terriers such as Yorkies, can be curious and pushy and stick their noses where they shouldn't. As a result, they may end up with porcupine quills or cactus spines stuck in their skin.

Porcupine quills are different sizes and forms depending on the species of porcupine. When touched by another animal, the quill releases from the porcupine's skin and embeds itself in the skin of the dog or predator.

Cactus spines don't always detach from the plant, depending on the species, but many are barbed. Once they make contact with skin, they don't pull out but rather work deeper into the skin.

If your pup gets stuck with porcupine quills or cactus spines, get him to the vet right away. Don't try to pull out the spines or quills on your own. Both are very painful, and most veterinarians recommend sedating the dog for removal. This is especially true if the dog got them in his face or paws or has a lot of them.

Smelling Like a Wet Dog

The wet-dog smell your Yorkie adolescent occasionally has is usually caused by oils from his skin as well as bacteria that can build up on his skin. Intact males sometimes also have an odor. Some dogs are more prone to odor than others. This is sometimes caused by the food your dog eats, but other times it is simply an individual characteristic. Humidity can also cause this smell. If it's been raining recently or is more humid than normal, your dog may be smellier.

Although giving your dog a thorough bath can get rid of the bacteria on his skin as well as the skin oils, it doesn't always get rid of the odor and no one really knows why. Perhaps the hairs absorb some of the odor.

Some of the waterless shampoos can help by cleaning the dog and his coat without using water. Ask for a recommendation from your breeder or a groomer as to which products to use because some leave an unwanted residue on the hair that dulls the wonderful shine of your Yorkie's coat.

If an odor persists, have your puppy examined by the veterinarian first to be sure he doesn't have a health problem. If your puppy's healthy, make an appointment with a professional groomer and have her take a look (and sniff) and get her opinion.

Social Skills

There's so much to remember when raising a puppy. You owners concentrate on making sure your puppy is well housetrained, you've begun obedience training, and your puppy is well socialized. Sometimes it's hard to remember to have fun and enjoy your puppy, too!

That should be your goal this month. Continue taking your puppy places, but instead of focusing on introducing him to new things, focus on having fun.

Sharing the Experience

One of the joys of sharing your life with a dog is his companionship. So enjoy spending time with him as you go for a walk, and watch his reactions. What does he do when the motorcycle goes by? Does he ignore it? Or does he turn and watch it drive past? You don't have to say anything. Just look at the world from his point of view. You'll find it fascinating.

Here are some other ideas for having fun with your Yorkie:

😸 Go to a park and sit in the grass. Hold on to his leash, but let him sniff and investigate. Then cuddle with him as you both enjoy the sunshine.

😸 Walk by the local elementary school while the kids are out on the playground. Let him watch and listen to the kids.

😸 Sit on the bench at the waterfront and listen to the seagulls and the waves crashing. Smell the ocean breeze, and watch your puppy's reactions to it all.

😸 Go downtown one Friday or Saturday evening, and from a safe place, watch the evening parade of people.

😸 Take your puppy to an outdoor café. Have him do a down stay under your chair or the table as you enjoy your lunch.

The difference between enjoying your puppy's company now and the socialization you did months ago is that now your puppy is already comfortable with the world around him. You can share these experiences without worrying about his reactions.

Showing Off Your Yorkie

Some people only enjoy big dogs—real dogs, they say—but others are tickled with tiny dogs. When you meet someone who is attracted to your Yorkie, stop and chat with her.

People who have never lived with a tiny-breed dog may have some questions about the experience. Are tiny puppies fragile? Are they dolls instead of real dogs? How much does he eat? Now that you've had your puppy several months, you're an old hand at this, so feel free to answer their questions.

Keep in mind, too, many of the tiny dogs (of many breeds) people see are misbehaving or not representing other little dogs well. The dog might be lunging and growling at other dogs or kids, might be carried in a shoulder carrier, or might be frightened of his own shadow. Seeing your well-behaved, well-socialized Yorkshire Terrier might be a different experience for them. You and your Yorkie are good ambassadors for the potential of the breed. Enjoy the spotlight!

Sharing Your Yorkie

Many adult Yorkshire Terriers are excellent *therapy dogs*. If you find that your Yorkie likes people and is willing to have people he doesn't know pet him, you might want to consider this very rewarding volunteer activity.

> **DOG TALK**
>
> **Therapy dogs** are privately owned dogs who, with their owner, visit other people to provide affection, hugs, and a break in the daily routine. Service dogs, by comparison, work for their owner by performing a variety of trained tasks.

Although most therapy-dog organizations require dogs be at least 1 year old for certification, the training often takes a few months. So if you begin now, he can be certified when he's a year old.

Therapy dogs need to be …

🐾 Social toward people and obviously like people. A dog who isn't happy about being petted or turns away isn't going to be a good therapy dog—or a happy one.

- ❧ Well socialized to people of all ages, sizes, and ethnic backgrounds.
- ❧ Well trained. A therapy dog's obedience skills need to be very good to be a therapy dog. Although your Yorkie might be carried a lot on visits and may sit in people's laps, he still needs to be well trained. This helps keep him safe, and therapy-dog organizations and their insurance companies require this.
- ❧ Comfortable around medical equipment such as walkers, wheelchairs, canes, machines that make noise, and those that smell funny. He also needs to be okay with trash bags opening and sheets flapping.

If you think therapy-dog volunteer work is something you'd like to do, ask your dog trainer if she offers therapy-dog training. Many do, and in a class situation, your dog can get used to quite a few things before going to a facility. See Month 12 for more information on therapy dogs.

Behavior

Your Yorkie is quickly becoming a great friend, and you should definitely enjoy the time you spend with him. After all, that's why you have a dog. However, he's still in adolescence, and at this time in his life, he still needs a parent who is a good leader.

You can learn a lot about leadership by watching an adult dog who is good with puppies. Your puppy's mom taught him a lot. Plus, if you have an older adult dog at home, you've probably seen how your older dog has taught your puppy. Take some time and watch their interactions.

Learning from Mom

Your puppy's mother instinctively knew how to teach her puppies. If the puppies bit her too hard as their puppy teeth were coming in, she would nose them and perhaps roll them over. She wasn't rough but was, in fact, very gentle. But she did interrupt the behavior she didn't like.

When the puppies got a little older, were more active, and were playing with each other, she would interrupt their play when one puppy would get too rough or would bite too hard. Her harshest correction would be a deep growl, and perhaps, with the rowdiest puppy, she would pin him with one of her paws.

By emulating how an adult dog teaches, you can become a better leader yourself:

🐾 When behavior happens that she wants to stop, such as a puppy biting her paw with sharp puppy teeth, she did something about it immediately. She will not wait for the puppy to stop on his own but instead will react immediately as the puppy does it.

🐾 She didn't carry on a conversation about the biting; she didn't bark for 5 minutes or growl for 10. Instead, she interrupted the problem behavior quickly and sharply.

🐾 Her communication with the puppy is very clear. If a puppy bit her, she growled and moved away from the teeth to interrupt the behavior.

🐾 She did not hold a grudge. After the behavior was interrupted, it was all over.

Adult dogs communicate very well with puppies and adolescents. When all is going well, the adult is warm and affectionate, plays with the younger dog, and snuggles with the younger puppy when sleeping. It's wonderful to watch their relationship.

Yet should the puppy or adolescent push the adult too far, the result is very clear as well. The adult will get very still, and if standing, will be up on her toes, getting taller. Her body will be turned toward the adolescent so her increasing size is obvious. The adult's head will be up and a lip may lift over one canine, baring it. She'll also emit a deep rumble.

If the teenager wilts and shrinks, accepting the correction, the adult will hold the pose for a few moments longer to be sure the communication is seen and understood. Then it's all over. The adult doesn't walk around grumbling for hours and doesn't hold a grudge. The communication is clear and concise.

Being a Good Leader

Both human and canine teenagers need good *leaders*. Not just because the teenage brain isn't working well right now but also so the teenager has a guide about how to grow up.

> **DOG TALK**

A **leader** is one who guides or commands, who serves as a guiding force as part of a team. A leader is one who is looked up to.

As a human leader for your Yorkie teenager, you can use some of the adult dog's examples. Use eye contact, for example. When your puppy is thinking about misbehaving or is getting too rowdy, make eye contact with him when you can. Don't smile when you do it, no matter how cute he is.

Use your voice. When he's beginning to make a mistake, use a deep voice, "That's enough!"

At times, silence is golden. When your puppy isn't necessarily making a mistake but is acting out or just being obnoxious, sometimes eye contact and silence are the most effective way of communicating. After all, your puppy is used to either praise or a verbal interruption, so silence can be unsettling.

Don't hold a grudge. When your teenager accepts your guidance, it's over. That doesn't mean you have to love on your puppy right now; in fact, it's better if you don't. Let him think about what happened.

Enforce your rules. Don't let the hassles of adolescence cause you to slack off on household and social rules that have already been established.

Praise him when he does something right or when he makes a good choice.

It's important that you continue to be warm and affectionate with your puppy during his adolescence. A good leader is. Just don't praise and pet your puppy immediately after you've had to interrupt bad behavior or a teenage challenge.

Continue to prevent bad behaviors when possible and help your puppy do what you want him to do. But when an adolescent challenge arises, think of how your puppy's mother would have handled it.

Love Isn't Enough

It would be nice if all you had to do was love your dog. Unfortunately, love is not enough. You may be providing your Yorkie with the best food, lots of toys, and veterinary care because you love him, but that doesn't mean he's automatically going to be a good dog.

Use your leadership skills to help your dog. He is, over the coming months, going be a better friend, but during adolescence, he needs your leadership as much as, if not more than, your friendship.

Don't accept a challenge. If your teenager growls at you for any reason, don't turn that challenge into a fight. Not only might you get bitten, but you don't want him to think fighting you is allowed. Stay calm, pick him up or use his leash to move him away from the situation, and quietly put him in his crate until he calms down.

Nothing in Life Is Free

One of the easiest ways to ensure your Yorkie teenage doesn't go through life with a sense of entitlement is to teach him that nothing in life is free. This means he needs to do something for everything he wants.

You already started this several months ago when you taught him to sit for everything he wants. Continue that. If he wants a treat, he needs to sit first. If he brings you a toy to throw, he can sit first. He can sit for his meals and sit to have the leash hooked up to his collar so you both can go for a walk.

As he matures, though, a single sit may not be enough. He may need to sit, lie down, and then come back up to a sit. He can do one or some of his tricks, too.

Use lots of praise during these sessions, and finish by giving him what he wants if it's appropriate. If it's not the right time for his meal or a walk, for example, don't give it to him. Just praise him for his efforts.

Surviving Temper Tantrums

Teenagers, both human and canine, tend to think the world revolves around them. Teenage humans want the best things money can buy, including a car as soon as they're old enough. At this age, many teenagers tend to feel their plans are more important than the family's.

Canine teenagers can't put their thoughts into words, obviously, but their actions convey their thoughts. Your Yorkie puppy wants to play when he wants to play, and if you're busy, that has no meaning for him. He wants to eat when he's hungry, and if he needs to go outside, he needs to go outside *right now!*

> Teenager puppies tend to throw temper tantrums if these behaviors worked
> well for them in puppyhood. They also throw tantrums when they feel they
> deserve something and it's not appearing as desired.

Some canine teenagers will throw a temper tantrum when things don't go their
way, barking, jumping up and down, and otherwise acting like a spoiled puppy. Some
temper tantrums can escalate into mouthing and biting.

If your teenager has a temper tantrum, don't scream at him, fight with him, or try
to make him behave at that moment. During a temper tantrum, his brain isn't thinking; he's simply reacting.

Instead, be quiet, and either take hold of his collar or pick him up. Walk him to
his crate, quietly put him in it, close the door, and walk away. If you're not at home
and a crate isn't available, walk him away from the scene of the temper tantrum, have
him sit and then lie down, and stay. Then be sure he does it and have him remain in
the down stay until he calms down.

After the tantrum is over and your puppy has calmed down, don't try to apologize
to him or pet him and love him. You also shouldn't hold a grudge and mutter threats
at him. Instead, keep calm and be matter of fact. The temper tantrum is over and so is
your reaction to it.

Training

Training continues to be important this month as your teenager moves through adolescence. You can help keep the household and social rules in his mind during a time
he's apt to forget them. Plus, training can keep his mind challenged.

Don't forget to have fun with your training, though. The two of you have been
working on the basic obedience exercises for a few months and the both of you might
be getting a little bored. If you make a point of having fun with the exercises, though,
you can stave off that boredom.

Finding Your Own Way

Every teenager is different, every Yorkshire Terrier is unique, and every dog-and-
owner relationship has its own quirks. Therefore, when you train your Yorkie during
adolescence, you are going to have to find the approach that works best for the two of
you right now.

The training approach you've used up to this point might still be working well, and if so, don't change anything. But if your Yorkie is rebelling or fighting you, or if neither of you is having fun, it might be time to make a change. Sometimes even a minor change is enough to make things fun again.

There are many ways you can do this:

🐾 Keep the training sessions very short, sometimes even just a couple minutes at a time.

🐾 Incorporate the training sessions into your life. Ask him to do some of his basic obedience exercises in different rooms of the house throughout the day.

🐾 Mix up training and play. Do a couple sits and downs and then play ball. Call him to come when he's bringing a ball back.

🐾 Be a cheerleader. Have him perform an exercise or two or three, and cheer him on. Don't praise him just for the sake of praising; dogs know when something's fake. But praise him well when he's doing something right.

🐾 Incorporate trick training into your obedience-training sessions. Have him sit, stay, roll over, or weave through your legs. Have him lie down, stay, and then spin. Trick training is fun, but it's still training and he's still cooperating with you.

🐾 Be sure he gets enough exercise. A tired puppy is more apt to be a good puppy.

The best training advice there is for surviving canine adolescence is never let your Yorkie turn training sessions into a war zone. He may be tiny but he's a terrier with a very smart little brain. So keep your training sessions short, positive, and fun, and be smarter than he is.

Continuing the Crate

Don't stop using the crate or exercise pen yet. Your puppy is still immature, and he's not ready for unrestricted access to his world. In fact, most Yorkies aren't mentally ready for full freedom of the house until they're closer to 2 years old.

> **TIPS AND TAILS**
>
> If you think 2 years is a long time for your Yorkie to grow up, set that thought aside. Many larger-breed puppies aren't mentally mature until they're 3 or 4 years old.

You may be tempted to give him more freedom because he hasn't had a house-training accident in a long time. He also may be good about playing with his toys instead of chewing on things he shouldn't chew on. With no problem behaviors, it's easy to think your puppy is ready for more freedom.

It's important to remember there haven't been any problems because you're doing things right. You're keeping him safe and setting him up to succeed. If you took away that guidance, he might continue to be good for a little while, but his immaturity would pop up soon. Then he'd be tempted by something or distracted and he'd get into trouble.

So continue to limit his freedom, supervise him when he's out of his crate or exercise pen, and be sure he's doing what you want him to do. He will grow up, and by doing things this way, those good behaviors will turn into habits.

You and Your Puppy

You can have a lot of fun with your puppy this month as long as you don't let his adolescence get to you. If you get angry when he ignores you or challenges you, you need to take a step back, take a deep breath, and tell yourself, *This is not a personal attack on me!* Repeat this as often as you need to.

Adolescence is natural; it's the preparation of a young animal for adulthood. The parents of human teenagers often question their sanity, too, so you're in good company. This stage of life is easier to get through if you constantly remind yourself not to take it personally.

Playing Inside Games

Little dogs have a distinct advantage over their larger cousins when it comes time to play. It's tough to play games with a German Shepherd or Golden Retriever inside the house. A Golden dashing after a thrown ball can knock over half the furniture in the living room in one dash.

Your Yorkie, though, can have fun playing games in the house without causing any damage. This makes it easier to have fun with your puppy while he gets the exercise he needs.

> **HAPPY PUPPY**
>
> Games played in the house can be great fun and easier to play, but don't forget your puppy does need to get outside to play, too. Just like you, he also needs some fresh air and a chance to enjoy the world outside.

Run and jump: Throwing a ball or toy down the hall for your Yorkie to retrieve is a fun game, but you can change it up a little to make it more fun. Place a few 2×4 boards on the floor of the hall crosswise so they reach from wall to wall. Spread them out so your Yorkie has room to take a few leaps between each board.

Now when you throw the ball down the hall, your puppy will run and jump, run and jump, and run and jump. The height of the 2×4 is low enough it won't stress his growing bones or joints but will still give him some good exercise.

Find it in a box: This game requires a couple cardboard boxes that are bigger than your Yorkie. Close the tops of the boxes but leave a hole in each one that's big enough for your Yorkie to climb through. Put one box on the floor, toss a treat or toy inside, and encourage your Yorkie to find the treat.

You may have to help him initially, and praise him when he's brave. Do this several times and then bring out the second box. Introduce that one the same way.

When you've played the game a few times and he's pretty bold about finding his toy or treat in either one of the boxes, put out both boxes. Have him sit and stay, and place a toy or treat in only one of the boxes. Release him from the stay, and encourage him to find the treat. Cheer him on as he hunts for it.

Cardboard tubes: Lots of different things can be turned into dog toys. The cardboard tubes that hold toilet paper, paper towels, and gift-wrapping paper are great toys.

Use one as a makeshift bugle. Blow through it to make funny noises, and let your Yorkie investigate the far end to see where the noise is coming from.

Or fold one end over, put a treat inside, and let him discover how to get it out. After he's gotten the treat, let him shred and rip the tube to pieces. Yes, you'll have to clean up the mess, but there's no harm in letting him have fun doing it.

Don't Forget …

When people get wrapped up in a tough situation, it's easy to forget things. Don't let your puppy's adolescence get you so distracted that you forget to enjoy him.

Make it a priority to massage him daily, to keep an eye on his health and his grooming, and also because it's a great way to maintain that loving relationship you have with him. It only takes minutes to give your tiny dog a massage, but stretch it out. As you do this, you'll calm yourself, your blood pressure will drop, and he'll relax, too.

Most of all, have fun with him. Play games, do some trick training, and laugh with him. It'll do you both loads of good.

Month 9   Month 10   Month 11
Socialization in public
Adult teeth are in—chewing continues
Ready for more advanced training
Moderate growth

This month your Yorkshire Terrier puppy is ready for anything the two of you can do together. She's still in adolescence, but she's through with the worst of it. She's bright, intelligent, and a wonderful companion. With you by her side, she can conquer the world!—or so she thinks. The two of you can have some great fun this month, but continuing your training is also important. Her mind is busy now, and training can help keep her out of trouble.

The importance of grooming continues, as it will throughout your puppy's lifetime. Working with a groomer who can help you and your Yorkie is also important.

Grooming

As your puppy is growing up, you're seeing more and more of her adult coat. The color is changing now, and the coat is getting longer. If you're allowing the coat to grow longer, you're also fixing her topknot, brushing, and combing her every day. If you chose to keep her coat shorter, you still need to brush, comb, and check her for tangles every day.

Some grooming chores you should do on a regular basis all year around, of course, including wiping the sleep from her eyes, cleaning her ears, cleaning her teeth, and brushing her coat. You may need to clean under her tail once in a while and perhaps trim the hair back there. This is especially important for long-coated Yorkies. And when your Yorkie gets dirty, a bath may be in order.

However, there are a few things to keep in mind as the seasons change. These will vary according to where you and your dog live. Obviously, winter grooming needs in San Diego are very different from those in Chicago.

Spring Grooming

After a winter inside a heated house, your Yorkie puppy's coat is apt to be dry. Be sure she's eating a good diet with natural fats, such as from meat, to help her grow in a healthy coat.

The first thing to be ready for come spring is the shedding. Yorkies don't have much undercoat, so shedding is minimal. Plus, because you've been keeping her coat brushed and combed every day, this reduces shedding even more. But if your Yorkie is going to shed, the worst of it is usually in the spring. Daily brushing is extra important right now to keep this to a minimum.

In many parts of the country, the first ticks show up in the spring as soon as weather warms up. Don't forget to examine your puppy often, especially after walks in tall grass or brushy areas.

Spring is also the time to start your dog on flea, tick, and heartworm medications if you took her off those treatments during the winter. Your veterinarian may want to do a heartworm check before prescribing new medications.

Summer Grooming

Parasites are one of the biggest challenges during the summer months. Your Yorkie should remain on the flea, tick, and heartworm medications, depending on where you live and the pests in your area. Talk to your veterinarian about whether you need to be concerned about any of these.

Protect your puppy from mosquitoes during the summer, too. Citronella spray or a natural pest repellent often works well. Pay particular attention to her face, paws, and ears, but know a mosquito can get to the skin anywhere if the coat is parted because of her position as she's relaxing.

One of the common complaints of Yorkie owners during the summer is fly bites on the puppy's ears. Flies will bite the tips of the ears and, with repeated bites, draw blood. This attracts more flies, and pretty soon, the ears are in bad shape.

Some Yorkie owners use repellent sprays to keep the flies away, but most Yorkies hate sprays in the face. The most recommended, effective, and easy-to-use product is SWAT, a pyrethrin-based ointment that both repels and kills flies. It's made for use on horses but is safe for dogs. To apply, rub the ointment on your Yorkie's ears, and anywhere else flies are biting. It helps heal wounds as well as repel the flies.

Hot spots can also develop during the summer. These are usually caused by allergies or a wound the dog won't stop scratching. They require veterinary care and medications to heal.

As grasses and weeds dry out in the summer heat, watch for foxtails, burrs, and grass and weed seeds that stick in your Yorkie's fur. When they get caught in your Yorkie's coat, they can work into her skin, create matts in her coat, and lodge between the pads of her feet. Just as you check her for fleas and ticks, also check her for grass and weed seeds.

Fall Grooming

Depending on where you live, fall grooming needs can be a continuation of summer, with grass seeds and pests continuing to be a problem. Keep an eye on your puppy's coat, watching for fleas, ticks, and grass and weed seeds. Watch for fly bites on her ears, too, because they can still be a problem, especially during a fall heat wave.

Fall is also a prelude to winter, and it will become obvious this is happening when your Yorkie begins shedding again. She's not shedding nearly as much as most other breeds, and in fact, depending on her coat, you might not see much at all. But those Yorkies who have some undercoat will shed now in preparation for winter.

Winter Grooming

In many parts of the United States, fleas and ticks disappear during most of the winter months when the weather is cooler, as do mosquitoes and flies. That relieves some grooming chores, but winter brings with it some additional concerns.

If your community puts down salt or other products to melt ice or keep sidewalks and streets safe during winter weather, always wash off your Yorkie's paws when you get back home. Don't let her lick her paws before you wash them because many of these products can be harmful when ingested.

Look into dog boots for your Yorkie. These protect her paws in the winter from both the ice and the products used to melt the ice on streets and sidewalks. Use lots of treats, praise, and patience to teach your puppy to wear these boots.

When your Yorkie puppy comes in from walking or playing in the snow, check her paws for balls of snow and ice stuck between her pads. These can form quickly and hurt. If she's licking her paws after she comes inside, this might be what's going on.

If your Yorkie's coat appears to be drying out because of the dry air in your home, add some flaxseed oil to her food. This nutritious oil will help keep her coat healthy. If you find your skin drying out, too, you may want to use a humidifier; this will add moisture to the air and will help both you and your dog.

Working with a Groomer

We've discussed using the services of a professional groomer several times in previous months. A groomer can provide guidance on how to maintain your Yorkie's coat, help you keep her coat nicely trimmed, and help you keep your puppy's paws and under-the-tail area neat and clean.

A local groomer also knows what needs to be done each season in your area. Every region has unique weather-related concerns; certain insect pests; and burrs, seeds, and other dangers for your Yorkie.

Just as your veterinarian is your partner in your Yorkie's health care, a groomer is your partner in your Yorkie's coat care. Keep in touch with your groomer. Talk to him when you bring your Yorkie in and ask him how your dog looks, if there's anything else you should be doing in between visits, and whether or not he saw a problem with your dog's skin and coat. Then bring him flowers or a plate of home-baked cookies once in a while. He'll be thrilled.

Physical Development

Your Yorkie is growing up and looks less like a puppy and more like an adult each month. Larger-breed puppies of this age are growing up, too, but they still look immature. It's amazing how fast your Yorkie is maturing.

Improving Bowel and Bladder Control

Your Yorkie should be sleeping through the night with little trouble now. Her bowel and bladder control is more mature, and as long as you aren't asking her to hold it for more than 7 or 8 hours at night, she should be fine.

Females tend to get better control earlier, so if your young male Yorkie is a little slower, don't worry. He'll get this control soon, too.

Don't ask her to have the same control during the day, however. It's not healthy for her to go 8 hours at night without relieving herself and then go 8 hours during the day, too. As a general rule, when she's awake and active, she'll need to go outside about every 3 hours. In addition, she should go outside after eating, after exercise or play, and when waking up. Just think about when you need to relieve yourself. She probably needs to go at the same times.

Understanding Sexual Behaviors

If your Yorkie hasn't been spayed or neutered yet, you may be seeing some behaviors that are related to sexual maturity this month. These are natural behaviors, but just because they're natural doesn't mean you should let them go on.

If you're planning on spaying or neutering your Yorkie but your veterinarian prefers to wait a little while, perhaps until she's through growing, just be careful. At this age, your female can come into season, and if a male dog finds her, she could have an unwanted litter of puppies. Plus, a male dog of this age is mature sexually, and it's amazing how quickly he can escape from the yard if he smells a female dog in season in the neighborhood.

Mounting: Both male and female dogs will mount other dogs, the family cat, and perhaps even your leg. Interrupt your puppy, tell her to knock it off, and have her do something else that will distract her. Have her sit, down, and sit again and then praise her.

Marking: Marking, or leg-lifting to urinate to claim ownership of something, is more common in males but females often do it, too. Leg-lifting often occurs outside, but some dogs urinate on furniture in the house—or in some situations, even on the owner's leg.

If your Yorkie begins marking, keep him on leash inside and out for a while, and keep him in his crate or exercise pen when you're inside. When he starts to sidle sideways in preparation to mark, interrupt him and move him out of position. Praise him when he relieves himself correctly.

Fighting: Both males and females fight, but they do so for different reasons. Males tend to fight over a female in season or when another male trespasses into their territory. Females tend to fight when another dog is disrespectful.

Many dogs go an entire lifetime without participating in a fight. You know your Yorkie best, so if you know there are some things that tend to set her off, protect her in those situations.

Escaping: When the sexual hormones are streaming through your Yorkie's body, all your Yorkie's common sense disappears. Your Yorkie may have never tried to escape from the yard, but when a female's in season or a male can smell a neighborhood female in season, that Yorkie will do anything to satisfy that need.

Some Yorkies have climbed fences, others have raced out doors as they're opened, and others have dug under fences. Just be careful and never assume your Yorkie won't try something. That instinct to reproduce is strong.

Health

By this age, your Yorkie is through with her vaccinations and may be going in to be spayed or neutered soon. Hopefully, she hasn't faced any illnesses or injuries and is enjoying a strong body and good health.

This is a good time to share some canine health trivia and some information—and misinformation—veterinarians wish their clients knew. It would be easy to blame the internet for all the urban legends and false information that's been spread about dogs, dog health, and behavior, but that would be wrong. Some of this misinformation has been around for a long time.

A wet nose means good health: Many healthy dogs do have a cold, wet nose, but a dry nose doesn't mean the dog is sick. A hot nose may mean the dog has a fever, but taking the dog's temperature gives a much more accurate reading.

> **HAPPY PUPPY**
>
> A happy, healthy adult Yorkshire Terrier has a temperature between 100°F and 102°F.

A wagging tail means the dog is happy: This isn't true at all. Although happy dogs do wag their tails, a dog's tail moves with many different emotions. In fact, the best guideline for deciphering a wagging tail is if the tail is moving at all, the dog is feeling an emotion.

Licking helps heal wounds: The urban legend usually says a dog should be allowed to lick her wound to help it heal. It's not a bad idea to let her lick it initially, especially if there's some dirt or debris in the wound because she can lick it out. But then you or your veterinarian need to clean the wound and treat it, and you should discourage your Yorkie from licking it. Some medications make her sick if she licks and ingests them, and if she licks too much, she could prevent the wound from healing.

A dog's mouth is clean: The saying (myth) is that a dog's mouth is cleaner than a cat's or a human's. Not necessarily. Does the dog have sparkly clean teeth? If so, her mouth might be clean. But if she has tartar and plaque buildup, then no, her mouth isn't clean—and in all reality is probably loaded with bacteria. If she just licked her genitalia, her mouth isn't particularly clean at the moment, either. All mouths, no matter whether they be canine, feline, or human, tend to have flourishing colonies of bacteria.

Take every urban legend, trivia, or tidbit of information with a grain of salt. If you have any doubt about the legitimacy of the claim—especially for those things that might affect your Yorkie's health—ask your veterinarian.

Nutrition

The best nutritional advice this month is to maintain. Your Yorkie is still going to need a balanced and complete food labeled for all life stages. If your puppy is healthy, growing well, and maturing nicely, keep doing what you're doing. If her coat is shiny and healthy and her eyes are bright and sparkling, don't make any changes.

If the two of you have been very active—perhaps with training, exercise, and play—she may need more calories to keep up with that level of activity. However, just feeding more food isn't always the answer because Yorkies are rarely gluttons. Your Yorkie has a very tiny tummy, remember. She may stop eating when she feels full even if she hasn't eaten enough to satisfy her energy needs.

In addition, more food than normal can cause soft stools or even diarrhea. Your dog will then lose the benefit of that food because it will be moving through her system too quickly. So satisfying your adolescent's nutritional needs can be tough.

Fats Can Be the Answer

If your dog hasn't lost any weight but just doesn't have all the energy she needs for her increased activities, sometimes just adding some extra fat to her diet is the answer. Calories from fats are the most easily metabolized, and the blood sugar remains more stable with fats than with other sources of energy.

The downside to fats is that if your Yorkie isn't using that energy every day, her body will store the fats. This is okay if she's thin, as most adolescent Yorkies tend to be. But this isn't okay if she tends to gain weight, as she may as she grows up.

To increase the fat in your Yorkie's diet, you can add one of the following to her normal daily diet:

🐾 1 tablespoon ground beef or bison, cooked

🐾 1 teaspoon goat's milk cheese

🐾 1 teaspoon full-fat yogurt

🐾 1 teaspoon full-fat cottage cheese

If your Yorkie's digestive system is used to one or more of these foods in these lesser amounts, you should be able to increase the food prior to a hard training session, performance sports competition, or just a really busy day without the risk of diarrhea.

Feeding Home-Cooked Foods

You can also add some home-cooked foods to your Yorkie's diet to boost her nutrition. You can add to her normal diet as a supplement, give her a small amount on a normal basis, and increase the amount you give her when she's more active than normal.

On a daily basis, never give her more than 10 percent of her daily diet. That way, the nutritional balance of her food will be maintained.

However, if you and your dog will be having a busy weekend, training or exercising, for example, beginning on Thursday you can increase what you give her to 15 percent of her diet. Then on Sunday, go back to the normal amount.

Here are some good foods you could include in your Yorkie's diet:

- 🐾 ½ hard-boiled egg, yolk and whites
- 🐾 1 tablespoon scrambled eggs, with cheese mixed in
- 🐾 1 tablespoon cooked fish, such as mackerel or albacore
- 🐾 1 tablespoon macaroni and cheese

Ideally, any supplemental food you give your puppy should be high in protein with a reasonable amount of fat. Never add spicy or greasy foods to her meals.

Using Common Sense

Your Yorkie's diet is one of the keys to her good health. Frequent changes aren't good for her and are apt to upset her digestive tract.

What is most important is to feed her a good-quality food or a well-balanced homemade diet—and stick to that food or diet as long as your adolescent is thriving on it. Make changes if she's not doing well, has itchy skin and a dull coat and doesn't seem to be doing well.

That good food will probably be perfectly adequate for most of your teenager's activities. However, if you feel that she is losing energy, is losing weight, or in some other way could use some nutritional help, gradually add some healthy calories to her diet. If she continues to look or act less than perfect even with those extra calories, it's time to call your veterinarian. You need to be sure something else isn't going on with your puppy.

Social Skills

Not everyone is going to like your Yorkie. Some people don't like toy-breed dogs; they prefer large dogs. Other people may have met too many little dogs who were yappy and rude.

Likewise, your Yorkie isn't going to like everyone she meets. But that's okay.

When People Don't Like Your Dog

You and your Yorkie have spent countless hours together, training, socializing, and working on her good social skills, and she is a well-loved member of your family. Even with all this, though, some people won't like your little dog.

You aren't going to be able to change the opinions of everyone who dislikes your dog. You can, however, help your dog be the best Yorkie around. Show the world she's well trained, isn't rude, and doesn't bark at other dogs or people walking past. By setting a good example, you might even change some people's opinion of toy-breed dogs and Yorkies in particular.

You can also protect your dog from people who don't like her. If someone is negative, is being loud, or worse, acts threatening to your dog, get her away. Pick her up and walk away. Don't let someone scare her or potentially hurt her.

When Your Dog Doesn't Like Someone

Your Yorkie won't like everyone. Usually it's because she can feel when someone doesn't like her. She may react by ignoring that person or, especially when she's still young, she may be uneasy and growl.

Your adolescent may also react to someone who looks or acts different. If she meets someone who dresses differently than you do, she might bark or growl. If she's not used to toddlers or young children, she might react when one toddles by laughing or crying.

As an adolescent, your puppy isn't always going to make good decisions about who she should be worried about and who is fine. She's mentally immature and also lacks confidence at times—especially in strange or, in her mind, potentially threatening situations.

Redirect her attention from the person who concerns her back to you, and praise her for paying attention to you. But don't hesitate to get her out of a bad situation, too.

When your Yorkie is all grown up and mentally mature, pay more attention to her reactions. When she's an adult, she'll be more perceptive, and when she chooses to dislike someone, there's probably a reason why.

When Your Yorkie Misbehaves in Public

There will be moments when your Yorkie misbehaves in public. Even a well-trained, well-socialized adolescent is going to make a mistake once in a while.

Your response to her mistake is important. If you overreact or get angry, you can make matters worse. Your puppy could believe that your overreaction is due to the same thing she reacted to. For example, perhaps your neighbor and her dog are walking toward you and your dog. The neighbor's dog begins jumping up and down in eagerness to play with your Yorkie. But your Yorkie isn't happy about the other dog's exuberance and begins barking angrily, her hackles up and teeth bared. If you get mad at your puppy and yell at her, she could think you're angry at that exuberant dog, too. You're her backup!

Instead, simply remove your puppy from the situation. Tell your neighbor, "Sorry! I lost track of time and need to get home!" Then turn away and take your Yorkie away from the dog who has her worried.

Yelling, screaming, and getting angry at your dog for misbehavior never makes anything better. The better option is to remove her from the situation.

Also think about what happened:

🐾 What exactly did your Yorkie do?

🐾 What caused her to act like that?

🐾 Was she justified to act like that?

🐾 What did you do in response?

🐾 Could you have done some different or better?

🐾 Will some training or socialization help your Yorkie react differently in the future?

Considering the answers to these questions, you can help your Yorkie the next time a similar situation comes up. Or perhaps you can prevent the reaction altogether.

Behavior

Thankfully, your Yorkie is through the worst of adolescence now, but that doesn't mean she's completely done with it. Growing out of adolescence is a slow, months-long process. She won't be mentally mature until she's about 2 years old, so just because she's through with the worst of it doesn't mean you're free and clear.

In the last few years, a number of new toys have come on the market that challenge a dog's brain. These new, smart toys make the dog to think to solve a puzzle. They're wonderful for your intelligent Yorkie.

Working Through Adolescent Regression

One of the most common complaints from owners of Yorkie adolescents is about their puppy's behavior regression. They question why their puppy is ignoring them, why she's not listening to even basic commands, and why she's doing things she hasn't done since she was a young puppy.

This regression is so normal in adolescents that it's more normal for the teenager to hit this stage than not. It's not unusual to ask your Yorkie to do something she knows well, such as stay, and watch her walk away from you. She won't even act like it's a problem.

She's not defying you; it's even more basic than that. She has selective hearing right now, and what you're saying isn't even registering with her. However, just because this is a normal stage of adolescence doesn't mean she's allowed to ignore you.

Set her up to succeed. Use her leash a lot during this time. The leash isn't just to take her for a walk; it can also help you teach her to listen to you again. She can drag the leash around the house, as long as you're there to supervise so she doesn't get it tangled.

> **TIPS AND TAILS**
>
> Continue to refresh her lessons often when she's ignoring you or not listening. Repetition is good. It can help her refocus her wandering brain right now.

Some of your Yorkie adolescent's behaviors aren't even a regression; they're a *reversion* to puppyhood. Your teenager may have been quite well behaved, showing you what she's going to be like as an adult, and then when she's in a mood, she'll come dashing toward you with one of your dirty socks in her mouth. When you try to get it back, she runs away.

Take a deep breath. Again, this is just adolescence, and this, too, shall pass. Use the leash, and let her drag it. When she comes dashing past, step on the leash to stop her from running away, and take the sock from her. Hand her one of her toys, and praise her for playing with the toy instead.

Smart Dog Toys

Nina Ottosson was one of the first makers of "smart toys" for dogs. In 1990, she began designing interactive toys to keep her dogs occupied when she couldn't take them out for exercise. She knew a bored dog would find ways to amuse herself, and she wanted to avoid that—especially because she had two young children at the time who also needed her attention.

The toys she designed have knobs to move, pieces to slide, drawers to pull out, and other parts to manipulate so dogs can find hidden treats. The toys are not for the dog to use alone, like food-dispensing toys, but instead are for dog and owner to do together.

Since their introduction, other dog trainers and manufacturers have designed more smart toys. All have the same idea that using challenging toys and mental stimulation can keep a dog's mind occupied and alleviate boredom.

These toys also teach problem-solving skills. Some dogs, especially puppies and adolescents, give up if they can't solve a problem right away. Some even give up on food-dispensing toys if they don't get an immediate reward. But when you and your dog play with a smart toy together, and you cheer on your dog's efforts, she can learn to persevere long enough to get the treat.

Training

This month, training continues to be an excellent way to channel your Yorkie's adolescent brain. She needs to think about things, about what to do and what not to do, and the best way to do that right now is by continuing to learn.

You might find, though, that you need to vary how you train your adolescent. What worked when she was a baby puppy might not be effective any more. You might need to find new ways to motivate her. You might also find that different things distract her.

Training is one of those things that's constantly changing and evolving. Pay attention to her and her responses to you as you work together. And be willing to change and to try new things.

Finding What Motivates Her

It's time to reevaluate the motivators you're using for getting and keeping your Yorkie's attention. When she was a young puppy, it was probably quite easy to get her to focus on you by using food treats. But she's changed a lot over the past few months, and what motivates her might have changed, too.

Ideally, your voice as you praise her should be a good motivator. If you can say, "Sweetie, good job! Thank you!" and her head comes up, she looks at you, and her tail wags wildly, that's a good motivator.

You're going to need more than just your voice for those adolescent times when she's more distracted than normal. Try some different food treats so you have a few choices. The ideal treats are small and have a good smell, and your dog can eat them quickly.

Think outside the box when you try some treats. You've probably been using some bits of meat and cubes of cheese. But what about pieces of apple slices, slices of baby carrots, or bits of cooked sweet potato? Try some dry kibble cat food, too. Your Yorkie will probably like a fish flavor.

> **HAPPY PUPPY**
>
> Vary the treats you use from day to day and training session to training session. Your dog will be more excited when she has no idea what treat you have until you begin your training session.

Your Yorkie may also be motivated more by toys than food. A squeaky toy often works well because it triggers those ancient terrier hunting instincts. Toss a squeaky toy in the air for your dog to catch to create some great enthusiasm. A tug toy is also good for building excitement.

Try some different things to see what excites your dog. Then mix up a few of those things as rewards during your training sessions.

Enrolling in Class Again

You and your dog have probably attended a kindergarten puppy class as well as a basic obedience class. Hopefully, the two of you were successful in these classes and learned a lot.

Talk to your dog trainer about the next level of classes. Maybe an intermediate obedience class or even something fun, such as a trick-training class, would be good for you and your Yorkie. A group class of any kind will keep your Yorkie socialized to a variety of other dogs.

Plus, a class is good for both of you. Your training skills can benefit from the instructor's attention during class, and it might help you to watch how other dogs' owners teach their dogs. Your Yorkie will continue to learn how to ignore distractions and get better at paying attention to you.

Training for Life

Your training should not be limited to just training class and practice sessions. Some dogs learn the lesson that training means those skills apply only at certain times and in certain places. That's a bad lesson for your dog to learn because then she'll assume all other times are open for other behaviors.

To prevent this, practice anytime and anywhere, especially those times and places where you want your adolescent to behave herself:

- ❖ When you're waiting for your tea water to heat, ask your dog to sit, down, sit, down, and stay.
- ❖ When you take out the trash, ask her to sit at the door and stay.
- ❖ Ask your dog to come across the living room and sit in front of you.
- ❖ Have her come to you down the hall and sit in front of you.
- ❖ When you're out on a walk, ask her to sit and stay at each curb. Then give her permission to walk with you.
- ❖ When you go down the block to talk to your neighbor, ask your teenager to sit while your neighbor pets her.
- ❖ While talking to your neighbor, have your Yorkie show off her tricks.

When you practice these skills often and in different places, they become second nature for your Yorkie. Plus, when you continually ask her to do different exercises, she'll be less apt to challenge you.

Teaching "Heel"

In Month 4, you learned how to introduce your puppy to walking on a leash without pulling. Constant pulling is annoying. Plus, due to her *oppositional reflex*, pulling leads to more pulling. Your Yorkie adolescent doesn't have to pull. There's no reason why she can't learn to walk nicely on the leash. It just requires some training, practice, and self-control on her part.

This exercise is called "*Heel.*" When your Yorkie heels, she maintains her position by your left side no matter where and how you walk. That means if you get caught out in the rain and need to jog back to the house, your puppy jogs right next to you.

> ### DOG TALK
>
> **Oppositional reflex** causes your dog to push against force. If you pull on your dog, she pulls back. If you push her, she pushes against you. "**Heel**" is the command that means "Walk by my side with your shoulder next to my left leg." Your Yorkie needs to maintain that position no matter what the distractions.

The difference between the no-pull exercise in Month 4 and the heel this month is the level of self-control. In her fourth month, your puppy had enough concentration to keep some slack in the leash. However, asking her to do more than that at that age would have been too much. Even so, at that age you still had to remind her several times on every walk about the tightness of the leash.

At 4 months, your puppy was too mentally immature to learn and perform the heel. Plus, even if she did learn it—and some owners do teach the heel at a younger age—it would have been difficult for her to concentrate for long. However, at 10 months, there's no reason why your puppy doesn't have enough concentration to heel with you.

Here's how to teach "Heel":

🐾 Leash your teenager, and have her sit by your left side. Have a pocketful of high-value treats.

🐾 Let your left hand hang naturally by your side. Gather up the leash so most of the slack is taken up but it's not too tight. If the clip of the leash is hanging loose, that's good.

🐾 Hold a treat in your right hand, let your puppy smell the treat, and tell her, "Sweetie, watch me!"

🐾 When you have her attention, tell her, "Sweetie, heel," and begin walking forward.

🐾 When she's walking with you, doing the watch me, praise her, "Good! Yeah!"

🐾 If she gets distracted, use that treat to get her attention again.

🐾 After about 10 steps, stop and have her sit. Praise her.

🐾 Repeat these steps several times and then stop and take a break. Play with your puppy for a few minutes before you repeat the steps.

> ## TIPS AND TAILS
>
> Your voice is a training tool you use to tell your puppy what to do, to praise her, and to interrupt bad behaviors. Treats are also training tools you can use to lure her and reward her. Another training tool is the leash to help her stay close to you.

Don't get into a pulling war with your puppy; that will cause her to fight you even more. Instead, focus on helping her succeed by using these steps.

If she's determined to pull, simply turn and walk the other direction. When she pulls forward, for example, without any warning to her simply turn around and walk the other direction. When she catches up with you, dashes past, and tries to pull again, turn around. It may take a few repetitions before she decides to pay more attention to you. When she does, praise her.

Gradually, over several weeks, extend the distance you ask her to heel before giving her a break. If she gets distracted, can't seem to maintain focus, and is having trouble with the heel, back up a few training steps. Vary your treats, making sure you have a high-value treat for the lure and reward and maybe even use a squeaky toy instead of food treats. Give her plenty of verbal praise to motivate her.

Also, don't be in a hurry to stop using the treats or toys. Consider them a training tool just like your voice and the leash. You won't have to use treats forever, but they are an important part of the training process now and through adolescence.

Making Heel Fun

Heeling in a straight line all the time can be boring for you and your teenager, especially one with a short attention span. So when she understands the heel, add some variation to it:

🐾 Heel 10 feet at a fast pace, turn around 180 degrees, heel 10 feet, stop, and have your dog sit. Be a cheerleader, "Yeah! Good girl! Look at you!"

🐾 With your dog heeling, jog, then walk a normal speed, then walk slowly, and jog again.

🐾 Place two outside trash cans about 10 feet apart, and heel in a figure-eight pattern around the cans. Stop and sit your dog when you're between the two cans.

🐾 Have your dog heel, stop and have her sit, go forward again at the heel, stop, and have her down. Heel forward, stop, and have her sit.

You can come up with some variations of your own. Just mix it up so you and your dog stay focused, stay entertained, and enjoy your training sessions.

Preparing for Off Leash

Although most communities have leash laws requiring all dogs to be on leash, accidents can happen. A collar can become unbuckled, a collar can slip over the dog's head, or a leash can break.

Teaching your dog to respond to you all the time, every time, no matter what the distraction, and whether or not she's on leash is essential. The idea that a dog can work without a leash is exciting, but unfortunately, most owners try to train their dog off leash too soon, when the adolescent isn't ready, and the training backfires.

Teaching your Yorkie to work for you without a leash is two-pronged. You want to instill in her the desire to work for you, and you want to teach her she has no choice. To build that desire to work for you, you have to work on motivation. Find those treats or toys or tugs that really get your Yorkie excited. Learn to use your voice to get her amped up to do something for you.

> **HAPPY PUPPY**
>
> To practice your verbal praise, start talking to your dog using a happy voice. Your goal is to have her wag her tail, wiggle, dance, and bounce all over. The power of your voice is amazing, but you have to know how to use it.

Keep that motivation high as you train with her. Keep her on her tiptoes, watching you, with her tongue out, her eyes bright, and her tail wagging. If she's getting bored and distracted, either you lost your motivation or your training session was too long. Right now, short and sweet is best.

To teach your adolescent she has no choice but to listen to you, continue training with the leash throughout adolescence. Make working for you a habit so she's no longer challenging or testing you. Vary leashes, too, so one particular leash doesn't come to mean cooperation. Use a 6-foot leash, a 4-foot one, a fabric one, and one made for cats rather than dogs. Have a leather one, a nylon one, and perhaps even a makeshift rope leash. The idea is that she cooperates with you no matter what.

Don't try training your dog without a leash for at least 6 to 8 more months—or longer if, at a year and a half, she's still mentally immature. If you try too soon, she may decide to dash away from you and then you'll have to refresh her training from the very beginning to get that idea out of her head.

Off-leash control requires your Yorkie to cooperate. She has to *want* to do this, and she needs to be able to ignore distractions. That requires a great deal of training as well as mental maturity.

You and Your Puppy

This month is a great time to find new things to do with your puppy. Continuing her training is obviously one thing. Going for walks in different places is another, as is introducing smart dog toys. Doing some more trick training is also great; it's fun, yet it's still more training.

Getting the Newspaper

A good job for your Yorkie could be bringing you the newspaper in the morning. If the delivery person drops it at the end of the driveway, send your dog after it. You can stand in the doorway in your robe and slippers without offending your neighbors.

Here's how to teach this trick:

🐾 Have a rolled-up section of an older newspaper. Use some tape to tape the roll fairly snugly.

🐾 In the living room, when you and your dog are both relaxed, show her the paper. Shake it in her face a little to get her excited. If she touches it, praise her, "Good girl!" Do this several times and then take a break.

🐾 Play with her with it again, but now wait for her to touch it with her mouth and then praise her. Again, do it several times and then take a break.

🐾 Now you'll introduce the command, "Sweetie, get it!" When she reaches for it and grabs it, praise her.

🐾 Toss the newspaper a couple feet away, encourage her to get it, and praise her when she does.

🐾 Gradually increase the distance until she's getting it no matter where you're throwing it in the house.

Now reteach the same training steps outside. Have a leash on her, and begin again at the first training step. You want to repeat the training steps because she's going to be more distracted outside. However, she'll move through the steps faster because she's already learned them once.

When she's retrieving the newspaper from various places in the front yard, begin placing the newspaper down the driveway rather than throwing it. Have a long leash on your Yorkie, and let her drag the leash as she goes after the paper. Praise her enthusiastically when she brings it back.

When your Yorkie is willingly retrieving the newspaper from the end of the driveway after you've placed it there, give her a chance to help you after the next newspaper delivery. Put on her long leash and ask her to get the newspaper that was just delivered. If she's hesitant, point to the newspaper and encourage her. And be sure to praise her when he does it. "Yah! Good dog!"

> **TIPS AND TAILS**

You can use this technique to teach your Yorkie other tricks, such as getting your slippers from the bedroom. Use the same training steps, but do it in the house and using one slipper at a time.

Varying Her Toys

So many toys are available specifically for dogs. You may be tempted to buy lots of toys in hopes that they'll keep your Yorkie occupied and out of trouble.

Toys can help keep your puppy busy, but too many toys can also be a problem. If your puppy is always surrounded by toys, she may begin to think *everything* is a toy—and that could include your shoes, the TV remote, your cell phone, and anything else she finds attractive.

If you like to see your puppy play with toys and want to buy her lots of toys, that's fine. Just don't give them all to her at once. Give her three or four each day, and put away the others. Tomorrow, put away today's toys, and bring out three or four different ones. By rotating the toys, you can keep them fresh and exciting and, therefore, more appealing to her.

Varying the Walking Speed

You can even do something as easy as varying the speed you take your walks. Walking faster is good exercise, and it challenges your puppy because she has to do it while she's heeling next to you.

How fast you walk depends on your physical condition as well as your puppy's. She has short legs, and although she's an excellent athlete, she has to take many steps for every one of yours.

If you're not quite ready for a long walk at a fast pace, you can work up to it gradually. Begin the walk at a quick pace that's comfortable for both of you. When you begin to feel uncomfortable or your puppy begins lagging behind, slow down to a normal or slower walking pace. When you've both rested, you can pick up the pace again. Alternate normal pace with fast pace for as long as you can. Over time, as your fitness level improves and so does your puppy's, you can extend the time you're walking fast.

While you're walking, have your Yorkie heel. This is especially important while you're walking fast because you don't want her to step in front of you and trip you.

> **HAPPY PUPPY**

If your Yorkie isn't used to sustained fast walking, either, build up to it gradually. Not only do you want her muscles to toughen gradually, but her paw pads also. Her pads can get scuffed or torn if you do too much before they get a chance to toughen.

As you and your puppy walk together, no matter whether it's for training, for exercise, for socialization, or to use up some excess energy, enjoy it. Watch your puppy's reactions to the world around her. What is she looking at? What is she sniffing? How is her view of the world different from yours?

Share things you see with your puppy. Point out a bird's feather on the ground. Chase after a butterfly. If your Yorkie is startled when a sea lion at the beach barks, redirect her attention with a happy comment, like "What was that? Wow!"

Pay attention to your puppy during your time together—no texting or phone calls! Enjoy her as well as the world around you both.

Adolescence Wanes

Socialization in public

Adult teeth are in—chewing continues

Ready for more advanced training

Slow growth—reaches adult size

When you look at your Yorkshire Terrier this month, you'll see less and less of that small, fuzzy, black-and-tan puppy and more of the adult dog he is going to become. This is sad, in a way, because puppyhood—like childhood—is so fleeting. It's also exciting because this adult dog will be a part of your life for many years to come.

At this age, your puppy isn't fully out of adolescence, and he's still going to get into trouble once in a while. He is, however, going to be showing more signs of brilliance, and you're going to love that!

Physical Development

You won't see many changes occurring in your puppy this month. Instead, you'll see a continuation of the maturation that began a couple months ago. Gradually, your Yorkie puppy has transitioned into an adolescent and is now changing into an adult.

Changes to Anticipate

Most of the changes to adulthood are very gradual—so gradual you may not notice them. People who only see your puppy every other month or so may notice them, though, or you may see them if you take photos of him and look back at earlier ones.

As he heads into adulthood, here are some of the physical changes you'll see:

Strength: As he changes, his muscles are getting stronger. He's never going to be a really muscular dog—that's not what Yorkies are. But he is a tiny athlete, and proportionately, he is strong.

Speed: Hunting terriers have to be quick. Rats, mice, and voles have to be fast to survive, so your Yorkie's ancestors had to be just as fast in order to be successful. Your Yorkie's speed may surprise you.

Agility: Again, this is a trait provided by his hunting ancestors. Your Yorkie is quite agile and nimble, especially as he grows out of his puppy clumsiness.

Substance: As your puppy matures physically, he'll develop a little more chest than he had as a puppy and he'll be a little broader though the hips. This is all relative, of course. Your Yorkie will never be as heavy or broad as larger dogs, and he isn't supposed to be. He won't even have as much substance as some heavier terriers. However, in comparison to himself in puppyhood, he will have more chest and hips than he did.

With most breeds, attitude usually isn't discussed in the same conversation as physical development, but with Yorkies it is. As your Yorkie grows up and gains confidence, you'll see a change in him physically. He'll be carrying his head higher, and he'll be more apt to make direct eye contact. Yorkshire Terriers are known for having attitude, and your dog will show it with his every posture and movement.

Longevity

As your Yorkie becomes an adult, your thoughts might drift toward the future. How many years can you expect to share with your furry companion? Thankfully, Yorkies tend to live many years, as long as they can avoid some of the health problems associated with the breed.

The age span varies depending on the source, but most experts say Yorkies usually live between 12 to 16 years. This is a wide gap—4 years—but many variables are at play, including disease, accidents, quality of care, nutrition, and heritage. How long did your Yorkie's parents live? How about his grandparents?

> ### TIPS AND TAILS
>
> Contrary to popular belief, 1 human year does not equal 7 dog years. This doesn't take into account size and breed differences—most small dogs tend to live longer than large ones. Plus, the first couple years—from puppyhood to adulthood—are more equal to a human reaching early adulthood.

In 2010, two Yorkshire Terriers were celebrated as having reached 22 years of age. Lucy, from the Netherlands, was quite gray but still going strong. Billy, from the United Kingdom, was not only 22 at the time but going for walks twice a day and still playing tug games. He was blind in one eye and didn't have many teeth left, but he was otherwise healthy.

Your veterinarian probably won't even consider your Yorkie a geriatric dog until he reaches 10 or 11 years old. With good care and genetics, your Yorkie can also look forward to a long life with you.

Health

One of the best ways to help your Yorkie grow into a healthy adulthood, and later into a healthy geriatric, is to be sure he gets the best health care you can provide. Hopefully, you've found a veterinarian you can trust.

Unfortunately, the price of veterinary care can be expensive. Accidents and illnesses never announce themselves ahead of time so you can save money to cover those costs. For this reason, you might want to look into veterinary health insurance.

Disasters are something else you should plan ahead for. Granted, we usually get warnings about hurricanes and blizzards, but tornados, earthquakes, and wildfires arrive unannounced. Making some preparations ahead of time can help keep you and your Yorkie safe—or as safe as possible—in the face of a disaster of any kind.

Health Insurance for Your Yorkie

The concept of pet health-care insurance may be a new idea for many people. But in fact, the first insurance company for pets originated about 30 years ago. Veterinary Pet Insurance (VPI) was the first company to offer this service and remains the largest pet health-insurance company today, with more than half a million policy-holders.

Pet health insurance may cover tests you might not otherwise pay for. It's much like your own health-care insurance—it's there so you can have the care you need when you need it.

One of the primary differences between health care for people and pets is that with pet insurance, you pay the bill first and then you submit the bill for reimbursement. You still need the money upfront to pay for your pet's care but you will be reimbursed. Some dog owners keep one credit card set aside for this purpose.

Many companies also offer wellness-care coverage, or preventative medicine. When these costs are covered, more people can focus on keeping their dog healthy rather than simply responding when the dog is ill or injured.

The most common reasons for dogs visiting the veterinarian were these, as reported by Veterinary Pet Insurance:

- 🐾 Ear infections
- 🐾 Skin allergies
- 🐾 Skin infections
- 🐾 Noncancerous growths
- 🐾 Upset stomach and/or vomiting

- 🐾 Intestinal upset and/or diarrhea
- 🐾 Arthritis
- 🐾 Bladder infection or urinary tract infection
- 🐾 Bruise or contusion
- 🐾 Underactive thyroid

Other health issues normally covered include these, in order of frequency of coverage:

- 🐾 Allergic reactions
- 🐾 Skin cancer
- 🐾 Sprains and strains
- 🐾 Torn toenails
- 🐾 Fungal skin disease
- 🐾 Eye injuries and/or infections
- 🐾 Abrasions
- 🐾 Seizure disorders
- 🐾 Kidney disease
- 🐾 Liver disease
- 🐾 Heart failure
- 🐾 Tooth removal
- 🐾 Addison's disease
- 🐾 Foreign body in the stomach
- 🐾 Lyme disease

Many more health problems are covered, including diabetes, bronchitis, urinary incontinence, and torn knee ligaments. The list of covered problems is long, and most health-care companies post on their website what's covered and what's not.

Embrace Pet Insurance lists the following as some of the problems Yorkshire Terriers face:

- 🐾 Patellar luxation
- 🐾 Portosystemic shunts
- 🐾 Legg-Calve-Perthes disease
- 🐾 Hydrocephalus

Before you invest your money in a pet health-insurance policy, take a look at several different companies and policies. A good website where you can do that is Pet Insurance Review, petinsurancereview.com/dog.asp.

Planning for Disasters

Natural disasters can hit anywhere. Liz and her dogs have been evacuated due to natural disasters several times. Where she lives in southern California, the disaster is often wildfires. Thankfully, their home has been spared, but unfortunately, many others were not. In the 2003 wildfires in San Diego County, more than 2,000 homes were destroyed.

Disasters happen anywhere and anytime. With some disasters, you may have to hunker down at home and see them through while at other times, you may need to evacuate. In any case, you need to be prepared.

> **TIPS AND TAILS**

One way to help your Yorkie deal with changes that occur during his lifetime, disasters or otherwise, is to introduce him to changes first. Every once in a while, have him spend a night in a hotel with you, visit your relatives, or go camping. Always come home afterward to the normal routine. He'll learn that changes are okay and that as long as he's with you, everything is fine.

A disaster preparedness kit can be a lifesaver as well as make life more livable immediately after a disaster. When evacuated because of one wildfire, Liz lived at the local beach for 3 days with her dogs. Her husband was helping fight the fire. So Liz and the dogs, as well as their cat, rabbit, and ferret, lived out of their truck camper because it was impossible to get a motel room with all the animals. Without her disaster kit, Liz and her animals would have been miserable.

Liz uses a plastic trash can with wheels to store and carry her disaster kit. She keeps it just inside the side garage door so that even if the garage is damaged, she can reach it and wheel it out. If you opt for a trash can, be sure it fits in the trunk of your car.

The San Diego County Office of Emergency Services recommends that every person have immediate access to several important documents, including their Social Security card (or number) as well as a driver's license for identification. You also need to have your medical information and medical coverage contacts. Have your personal banking information but also have some cash on hand.

The following is a list of other items you should have in your combined disaster kit for dogs and people:

Dog medical information: The first items to get for your disaster kit include your pet's medical information, including vaccination information and dates, and copies of any prescriptions. Update this regularly. Have your veterinarian's name, address, and phone number, too, as well as the local emergency veterinary hospital.

Family medical information: You should also have the same medical information for yourself and everyone in your family. That includes doctor's names and contact information, health-care coverage, prescription information, eye glass or contact prescriptions, and vaccination information.

First-aid kit: In Month 6, we included a list of items that should be in your first-aid kit. Be sure everything is updated or replaced regularly. Replace items that have been used or have expired. Plus, you should have a first-aid kit in your home, in your car, and with your disaster supplies.

Nonperishable dog food: Pack enough food for at least 7 days. Before Hurricane Katrina, the recommendation was 2 days, but in the aftermath of Katrina, Hurricane Rita, and several other disasters, 7 days is now recommended. Nonperishable food can be canned dog food or dehydrated food. Every 6 months, when you check your first-aid kit, pull out the stored food, use it, and replace it with fresh food in your disaster kit.

Nonperishable food for people: You need 7 days' worth of food, too. Just as with your dog's food, rotate yours.

Food-preparation implements: You need dog bowls, paper plates, glasses or paper cups, spoons, plastic wear, storage containers, plastic bags, and garbage bags. If you have any camping gear, store that near your disaster kit. Have some aluminum foil, too. It can come in handy.

Water: Store more water than you think you'll need. In your disaster kit, a case of bottled water is a good start. However, you may want to keep a couple of 5-gallon jugs stored near your disaster kit. The bare minimum limit of water per day per adult human and adult Yorkie is 2 quarts. However, when active or in times of stress or hot weather, you'll need more.

Yorkie supplies: Be sure you have a collar with identification tags, an extra leash, a crate, and photos of your pet should he get separated from you. Also have some basic grooming tools, including nail clippers.

Emergency shelters must make provisions for pets. However, they generally require you to crate your pet. So be sure a crate is easily accessible.

Sanitary supplies: For people, have toilet paper, paper towels, feminine products, sanitary wipes, tooth brushes and toothpaste, and liquid soap. For your Yorkie, have plastic bags for picking up after him as well as a couple of towels and a bottle of waterless shampoo. Be sure to include an extra comb and brush in the kit, too.

Tools and supplies: To hear information from the emergency broadcast system, you need a battery-operated radio and extra batteries. You'll also need a couple of flashlights and extra batteries. A manual can opener, a pocketknife, a pair of heavy-duty scissors, and matches are good to have, too. It's a good idea to have a small toolbox with a Phillips screwdriver, a straight-edge screwdriver, pliers, and a hammer.

Electronics: Do you have an extra battery for your cell phone and laptop? Can you find them easily in an emergency? Have an extra charger, too, including a car charger.

Clothes and shoes: Plan on appropriate clothing for at least 7 days. Include a couple of blankets and sleeping bags in your safety supplies, too.

It's also important to know what you'll do in a disaster because having a plan of action can help prevent panic. This plan should take into account the type of disaster that occurs in your region. Where Liz lives, wildfires and earthquakes are the biggest threat. Wildfires require evacuation—sometimes a distance away from home—and that must be planned for. Earthquakes don't give any warning so they're weathered at home. However, afterward there may be disruptions in electricity, natural gas, and transportation if roads are damaged. Stores may not have their supplies replenished, so having supplies at home is important.

HAPPY PUPPY

The last thing you may think about during an emergency is playing with your puppy. But stress relief is good for you, your family, and your Yorkie. A couple dog toys stashed in the emergency kit can provide amusement for your puppy and your family when laughter is greatly needed.

Plan for disasters that happen in your locale, for both staying at home and leaving. If you're stuck at home, you have all of your supplies with you, but you may be without power. Can you still cook, or would you need to eat cold foods? What if you don't have any water? What if the water system is contaminated? Water decontamination tablets are good, as is a big-enough pot to boil water. Bottled water can keep you supplied for a few days.

If you need to evacuate, where can you go with your Yorkie? Would relatives be willing to take you in, or would you need to go to a shelter or a motel? Make plans ahead of time and call those relatives or check for local pet-friendly motels.

Have a point of contact who lives far enough away that he wouldn't be affected by a local disaster. Give that person's contact info to everyone in your family so they can check in should a natural disaster occur.

Planning and preparing for an emergency ahead of time is essential. You'll still be worried and scared, but with this preparation, you'll have less to worry about.

Nutrition

Last month we recommended your not making any changes in your Yorkie's nutrition, especially if he's doing well. That advice continues to apply this month—unless, of course, you have some concerns. If your Yorkie has some health challenges or if you've heard of some dog-food recalls that include the food you're feeding, then a change might be in order.

Dog-Food Recalls

Dog-food recalls happen for a variety of reasons. Perhaps the manufacturer has tested a batch of food and found it lacking in a certain vitamin or containing too much of another. In 2011, a dog-food company found that the plant machinery was adding too much vitamin D to the food. Unfortunately, several dogs had already become very ill before they discovered this.

Consumer complaints lead to most of the investigations into pet food and the resulting recalls. The sad thing is, those complaints are caused by the illness or death of a beloved pet.

In 2006 and 2007, food manufactured at the Menu pet-food plant in Canada triggered a widespread recall. Ingredients from China had been tainted with melamine so when tested, the food would show higher protein levels than it really contained. Thousands of pets were affected, and far too many died.

In 2012, the Diamond pet-food manufacturing plant in South Carolina was found to have salmonella contamination. This plant manufactured more than 14 pet-food brands, so there were a huge number of recalls, including for some high-priced brands. Unfortunately, a few months later, Diamond's Missouri plant was also found to have problems, and it announced more recalls.

If you feed your Yorkie a commercial dog food, it's important to pay attention to dog-food recalls. Several blogs pay attention to these recalls and regularly post them online. One of these is HonestDog.com. Several writers post to this blog, including Gina Spadafori and Christie Keith, both of whom were instrumental in publicizing the 2006 and 2007 pet-food disaster. Bookmark this site, and check it often.

Evaluating Your Yorkie

It can be difficult to know whether your dog's food is the best for him. If he's eating it and he's alive, does that mean it's okay? That's simplifying things tremendously, of course, but it is the first question to ask because tainted foods have killed so many dogs.

To evaluate your Yorkie's food—commercial or homemade—grab a pen and sheet of paper. Make two columns, and at the top of the first column write "Good Health" and at the top of the second column, write "Could Be Better."

Then go through the following list. If your Yorkie is great, mark the "Good Health" column. If your Yorkie has a problem, list the problem in the "Could Be Better" column. For example, the first item is eyes. If your Yorkie's eyes are bright, clear, and only have matter in the corners when he wakes up, put "great" or "healthy" in the first column.

However, if your Yorkie's eyes always have goop in them or water constantly, and he rubs at them, list those problems in the second column.

Here are the categories to evaluate:

Eyes: Your Yorkie's eyes should be bright, alert, and clear with few tears running down the face. He shouldn't be rubbing at his eyes. His eyelids should not be swollen, and his eyelashes shouldn't be rubbing on the eyes.

Ears: His ears should be clean, dry, and skin-colored. They shouldn't be itchy, red, dirty, or inflamed, and he shouldn't be scratching at them or shaking his head.

Teeth: These should be clean with little to no tartar buildup. The gums should be pink, not red or inflamed. Missing teeth can indicate a potential problem such as gum disease.

Mouth: His mouth should be clean, and he should have good breath.

Paws: His paws should be clean and dry, with no red spots and no staining of the hair due to excessive licking. His paws shouldn't be itchy, either.

Skin: His skin should be clear, dry, supple, and elastic. No red spots, no hot spots, and no itching should appear.

Hair coat: His hair should be glossy and shiny, with rich color. He should have no bald spots or chewed spots, and little to no broken coat.

Weight: Your Yorkie should be of a good weight, neither skinny nor heavy. See Appendix B for help in doing a body-mass assessment.

Energy: Yorkies are active little dogs. Your Yorkie should be willing to run, jump, and play at any time.

If you've marked several things in the second column, make an appointment with your veterinarian. Some health problems—thyroid disease, for example—can have multiple symptoms. While you're there, ask your veterinarian if your Yorkie's food could be causing these issues. Bring the food label with you.

If you decide to change foods, read labels carefully. Then go back to the nutrition sections of this book for assistance in choosing a better food or diet for your pup.

Grooming

When several Yorkie owners get together, they often complain about dog groomers. If you're unhappy with your Yorkie's groomer, be proactive. You can do something about it, and should—after all, this is *your* Yorkie and he depends on you for his care and safety. Talk to the groomer, voice your concerns, and listen to his answers.

Be sure you're keeping up on your end of the grooming equation, too. Groomers complain about dog owners as much as owners complain about groomers.

The Grooming Appointment

A professional groomer can be your partner in keeping your Yorkie looking spectacular, just as your veterinarian is your partner in keeping your dog healthy. Many Yorkie owners like to do the grooming themselves, and if you enjoy that, super. If you'd like some help, that's fine, too.

When you make an appointment with a professional groomer, she'll ask you to bring in your Yorkie at a specific time. Please keep that appointment, including the time, because most groomers have their time strictly scheduled. If you bring your dog in late, the groomer's schedule for the day is disrupted. If you don't show up at all, she loses business.

When you bring your dog in for the grooming appointment, let the groomer know what you'd like done. If you don't want your dog to get a haircut and just want a bath and blow-dry, tell her. If you'd like a specific cut, ask her if she can do it with your dog's coat.

Don't be surprised if the groomer has recommendations for you. If you want to keep a certain length of coat, the groomer may advise something different. Perhaps in her experience, that type of cut is difficult to do or it may not look right on your dog. Ideally, there should be some give and take. You know what you like, and the groomer knows what will work and what won't.

In a typical grooming session, a groomer will …

🐾 Brush and comb your Yorkie. She will be sure there are no tangles, matts, or debris in the coat, and if there are, she'll take care of them before bathing your pup.

🐾 Bathe, condition, and blow-dry your Yorkie.

🐾 Give your Yorkie a haircut, depending on your request. If you want your Yorkie to grow out a long coat, the groomer will just trim under the tail, slightly around the genitalia, and on the bottom of the paws. If you like to keep your Yorkie in a shorter cut, she can do that, too.

🐾 Check your dog's ears, plucking out excess hair, trimming around the ears, and cleaning the insides.

🐾 Do the topknot and usually finish it with a bow.

🐾 Trim your pup's toenails.

> **HAPPY PUPPY**

Take your Yorkie for a nice long walk or a play session before the grooming appointment. Be sure he has relieved himself before the appointment, too. He'll be more comfortable and happier.

Usually you drop off your dog at the groomer and return later to pick him up. When you come back, take a good look at your Yorkie before you take him home. If you see any problems or something isn't as you requested, ask the groomer about it before leaving. The groomer should fix it or to explain why it's different.

Leaving your Yorkie at the groomer's shop for several hours is usually harder on you than it is on your puppy. You'll be without your puppy, but the process is pretty exciting for your Yorkie. He'll be watching the activity in the shop, the people, and the other dogs—and smelling new things, too. Plus, your Yorkie will be getting a lot of attention throughout the grooming process.

Finding a New Groomer

If you need to find a groomer, or a new groomer, go to nationaldoggroomers.com, the website for the National Dog Groomers Association, a professional organization for groomers. Click on "Find a Groomer" on the home page.

You can also ask your veterinarian for a referral. Or if you see a handsome, well-groomed Yorkie out on a walk, ask his owner where they go for grooming.

Pay the grooming shop a visit before you schedule an appointment. Is the shop clean? There probably will be dog hair everywhere, even if they vacuum throughout the day, and the shop will smell like wet dogs. But it shouldn't smell bad.

Are dogs left standing on grooming tables unattended? A dog leashed on a table unattended could jump off and choke or hurt himself.

Are dogs left in dryer cages with no supervision? Although cages with a dryer that blows warm air onto the dog are common, the dogs still should be supervised. The air could get too warm, or a dog could overheat.

The dogs shouldn't be handled too harshly, either. Most groomers are firm with the dogs, and that's fine. After all, if the dog is wiggling, hasn't been taught to stand nicely on a grooming table, or is fighting the groomer, she won't be able to do her job. But there's a difference between being firm with the dog—letting the dog know he needs to cooperate—and being too rough, scaring the dog, or hurting him.

When you make an appointment with the groomer, give her all the details about your dog's coat. If you tried to trim it and it's now raggedy, tell the groomer. If you haven't brushed and combed your dog in 3 weeks, tell her that, too, so she can be sure to schedule enough time.

Be prepared to pay for the groomer's services. If you want your Yorkie to have a long coat but you bring him to the groomer's shop full of matts, you'll pay for that time above the groomer's normal time.

Tipping isn't always necessary, but the groomer will appreciate it, especially if you're asking for something special. Tipping is also nice if you know your dog isn't always cooperative on the table.

Social Skills

You've been working hard the last several months to ensure your Yorkie is well social-ized to people, dogs, new sights, sounds, and in general to the world around him. As adolescence hit, you've had to deal with his sometimes-unsocial attitude. Continuing to take him out and about is of utmost importance now. Don't isolate him, even if he's sometimes rude in public. Isolation only makes things worse.

Choosing a Carrier

When you take your Yorkie out and about, most of the time he needs to walk on his own four paws. As we've discussed in previous months, he's tiny, but he's still a dog and will be much happier on his own paws. He can get some exercise, sniff the grass, look for lizards, be petted by people, and just be a happy dog.

However, there will be times when you need to carry him. Scoop him up if you're going to be in a crowd where he might be stepped on or so crowded he'll be worried. You may also want to carry him if he's going to be vulnerable in a large group of chil-dren or larger dogs. If the weather is hot and the asphalt or concrete underfoot could burn his paws, pick him up.

Although some owners of tiny dogs simply put the dogs in a purse or tote bag, that isn't always the best choice. Sometimes a carrier is better. The best carrier has …

- 🐾 A solid bottom to give the dog some stability. If the bottom is soft, the carrier or purse could fold up around the dog.
- 🐾 Screened sides or opening for ventilation.
- 🐾 Zipper or hook-and-loop closures so you can fasten your dog inside to prevent him from jumping out or escaping.
- 🐾 Wide, padded straps so it's comfortable for you to carry.

When your Yorkie is in the carrier, don't let him bark or growl at other dogs. He may feel extra special in the carrier and be braver than he ordinarily might be. But if he's rude and issues a challenge, a large dog could jump up and grab the carrier—and him—from you. Although the larger dog would be at fault for attacking your little dog, your little dog would have to share that fault for instigating it. Don't let your tiny dog bark and growl at other people, either. It's rude.

Protect your tiny dog while he's in the carrier. After all, he's stuck in there. He can't get away from people, he can't hide, and he can't protect herself. Don't let people reach in to pet him, grab at him, hug him, or kiss his face. Instead, keep the carrier fastened and ask people to ignore him. If they won't leave him alone, simply move him away. Don't worry about hurting people's feelings. Remember, your first responsibility is to your Yorkie.

Selecting a Stroller

A stroller is an alternative to a carrier if you're going to be in a situation where your Yorkie shouldn't walk. Strollers are also good when you're going to be out all day and your Yorkie might run out of steam. In a stroller, your Yorkie can rest, relax, or even fall asleep.

Strollers made specifically for small dogs are better than the ones made for human babies. The dog strollers usually have a screen top that can be fastened securely so the dog can't jump out. If you already have one for a human baby, be sure you fasten your Yorkie's leash to the stroller in some manner. That way, if he decides to jump out, he won't get away from you. You must be sure, though, that he won't hang himself with the leash should he jump.

The rules of behavior in a stroller are the same as in a carrier. Most especially, don't let your Yorkie growl at other dogs. He's even more vulnerable in a stroller than he is in a carrier.

Behavior

Dog behavior, like human behavior, never stays the same. You might think you know your Yorkie very well, but one day he'll do something to surprise you. That's okay, though. Although the hope is that his surprise is a fun one rather than a shocking one, these changes keep life interesting.

Misunderstood Behaviors

Dogs have lived with people for thousands of years, but your Yorkie will still confuse you at times. He may react in a way you don't understand, or he may do something unexpected. In this section, let's take a look at some of the things that have flummoxed more puppy owners than just you.

Jealousy: Yorkies love their owners, and when they choose one special person, they will love that one person all their life. They can be jealous when someone else gets close to "their" special person.

When hugging their significant other, many Yorkie owners will find a tiny little dog trying to wiggle in between the two people. Jealousy isn't a problem as long as your dog will back off when you ask him. However, if he barks, or gets protective or nasty, ask him to do a down stay at a distance or give him a time-out in his crate.

If he gets jealous of your attention toward another dog, the family cat, or another pet, the same rules apply. If he won't stop when you ask, have him do a down stay or put him in his crate.

Panting: Dogs pant to lose heat; the only place they sweat is on the pads of their feet. By panting—blowing air over that big tongue—the dog can get rid of a lot of heat.

Dogs also pant for behavioral reasons. When stressed or worried, dogs tend to pant. So even if your Yorkie is cool, he might pant in the veterinarian's office or in a strange situation.

Shivering: Toy-breed dogs such as Yorkies often shiver even when the surrounding environment is just slightly cool. They don't have much body fat, especially young puppies, so they shiver to raise their body temperature.

Some dogs also shiver when they're stressed. You might notice that when you're in the veterinarian's office, your Yorkie might be sitting on your lap shivering and panting.

Yawning: Dogs yawn when they're tired, just as people do. But they also yawn to try to calm a situation. For example, if your puppy is having trouble in a training situation—perhaps when he doesn't understand what you want—he may yawn while facing you. Or if he's in class and another dog is making a fuss, your puppy may yawn toward that puppy.

The yawn is a means of communication asking for calm. Other calming signals include eye blinking and looking away from the person or dog causing the stress.

Tail wagging: Most dog owners assume that if a dog is wagging his tail, he's happy. Most of the time that's true, especially if you have a dog with a happy disposition.

However, a wagging tail really means the dog is feeling emotion. A happy Yorkie's tail wags faster than normal. The happier he is, the faster it wags. An excited Yorkie's tail wags back and forth, but it will be lower than when he's happy. The friendly Yorkie swishes the end of his tail back and forth, but it won't wag as much as the excited or happy dog's tail. A puppy who's feeling worried or anxious wags his tail very low, even tucked down to his hips. The Yorkie who is feeling too big for his britches—who's ready to take on the world—lifts his tail high and wags it slowly back and forth.

The tail's motions are a means of communication, just like all his other postures. The tail alone doesn't convey the message; it's his entire body language.

Rolling in bad stuff: A Yorkie owner asked, "My Yorkie rolled on top of a dead squirrel, rolling back and forth. Why did he do that?" Experts really don't know why dogs do this, but rest assured, your Yorkie isn't the only one who has. It's really more common than unusual.

Some behaviorists feel that predators—and that includes the canine species—roll in stinky stuff to camouflage their natural smell. Other experts disagree with this idea. No one really knows why dogs do this.

> **HAPPY PUPPY**
>
> We may not know why dogs roll in smelly stuff, but we do know many dogs have preferred smells, like a personal cologne. Some like dead animals, some like cat odors, and some like garbage. It seems to be a personal preference.

Mounting other dogs: The owner of a spayed Yorkie asked why her female adolescent mounts (humps) other dogs—males and females—while playing. She assumed only male dogs did that and was confused why her dog was mounting both males and females.

Intact males and female adolescents often mount other dogs because their systems are flooded with hormones. They feel this action is what they should do, so they do it. Plus, the intact dog probably finds that this behavior feels good.

By mounting other dogs, the intact dog is also performing what comes naturally when hormones are raging. This is a behavioral rehearsal for reproduction. Although spayed and neutered dogs won't reproduce, spaying a female dog (and neutering a male) doesn't remove all of the dog's hormones. Some behaviors will continue, although at a lower rate.

Many dogs mount during play sessions with other dogs because they get excited—not necessarily sexually excited, but just overstimulated. All the dogs were running and playing, and your dog was so happy and, well, he couldn't help it if the dog in front of him was just standing still.

Mounting can also be an attention-getting behavior. If the group of dogs is playing, and your dog wants to be the center of attention, mounting another dog certainly gets their attention. Your dog doesn't care if the attention is a spin in place, growl, and snapping jaws. It is still attention.

When your dog is playing with other dogs and begins to mount one, interrupt him immediately. Most adult dogs dislike this behavior, and it's a sure way to start a dog fight.

> ### TIPS AND TAILS

A dog who mounts another dog of the same sex isn't necessarily gay. Your dog is simply taking advantage of the fact that the dog near him is available.

Humping people: Adolescent dogs hump people for the same reasons they mount other dogs. They may have excess hormones, and with their brain missing in action much of the time, humping your leg might seem like a good idea. Your puppy may have also discovered that when he humped someone's leg, he got a reaction. Sometimes any reaction is a good one, according to puppies, anyway.

Stop the behavior immediately. Don't wait for the hip action to begin, but instead, when he tries to grab your leg with his front legs, interrupt him, saying, "Hey!" and knock him off your leg. Have him lie down and stay until he calms down. If he won't hold a down stay, put him in his crate.

Eating cat food and feces: Many dogs, especially puppies, are attracted to cat food. The reason is simple: Puppies are always hungry, and cat food is higher in fat than puppy food. It smells good and tastes even better, so once the puppy gets a mouthful of cat food, he's always going to want more.

Cats have a short intestinal tract and don't digest commercial cat foods well, especially those containing cereal grains. In addition, fat is sprayed on the cat food so the cat will eat it. When the cat doesn't fully digest the food, the feces are more attractive to dogs. To your Yorkie, this is just another snack.

To ensure this doesn't happen, keep the cat food and the litterbox in a place inaccessible to your Yorkie. Never trust your adolescent to ignore the food or the litterbox.

Burying bones: Many dogs like to bury bones and special toys. Some bury them and then stand in front of the buried bone as if to say, "Go away. There is no bone here!"

Burying bones and leftover food probably has its roots in hunting behaviors. For most of the canine race's history, food equaled survival. Canines would eat as much as they could and then try to hide what was left over so scavengers won't steal it.

Although hopefully your Yorkie will never go hungry, that instinct is still there. If he's picking the wrong places to bury stuff, teach him where he can bury it. Turn over some dirt so it's soft, and give him a head start by half-burying a few of his chew toys. Encourage him with praise to dig there.

Making a bed: Many Yorkies really appreciate their comfort and will circle and circle before lying down. Some even like to scratch at their blankets to arrange everything just so before getting comfortable.

Although throughout history, wild canines didn't have blankets and dog beds for their comfort, many did and still do scratch up a nest of grasses or other vegetation for a bed. Domesticated dogs' habit of circling comes from that old instinct to create a comfortable bed.

Housetraining Check-Up

One of the most common complaints Yorkshire Terrier owners have is that the breed is difficult to housetrain. This is due more to owner problems than actual breed or physical issues with the dog.

Granted, Yorkies are tiny, and like many small dogs, they take longer to housetrain than larger breeds. But with patience and consistency from their owner, Yorkies can be well housetrained.

Here are some tips for helping to housetrain your Yorkie:

- 🐾 Maintain the schedule you established months ago. Take your Yorkie out on a regular basis.

- 🐾 Go out with him, ask him to go, and praise him for going. If you simply let him outside and don't go with him, you have no idea if he's relieved himself or not.

- 🐾 If you don't go out with him, you've also lost that teaching moment where you could praise him for going in the spot where you want him to go.

🐾 Limit his freedom in the house. If he has free run of the house, he could easily relieve himself in an out-of-the-way place and you wouldn't know it.

If housetraining accidents continue, make an appointment with your veterinarian. Have your puppy checked for a medical issue that could potentially cause housetraining accidents. If he gets a clean bill of health, you know it's a training problem rather than a health issue.

Training

Environmental enrichment is a technique many boarding and shelter facilities use to keep their animals from becoming bored. By hiding treats and things to play with in the animal's enclosure, the animal is more mentally and physically active. Although you certainly don't consider your Yorkie a captive animal, you can use this science to keep him mentally stimulated and less apt to get into trouble.

> **DOG TALK**
>
> **Environmental enrichment** is the process of creating a more interesting living area, as well as a more interesting life, for animals.

Training is an ongoing process that you should continue during this month and as your Yorkie grows up. Not only does training help prevent problem behaviors, but it also helps to strengthen the relationship you two have.

Environmental Enrichment

At the San Diego Zoological Society's Safari Park in northern San Diego County, and at the main zoo in San Diego, many of the animals are benefiting from environmental enrichment. For example, in the elephant enclosure, the elephants are fed in the food-serving areas but also in other places, including food-dispensing toys. One toy looks like a 50-gallon plastic drum with two holes at the top, which is suspended high in a tree. The elephant has to reach up to the drum, tilt it, and get her trunk inside to get the food. This is a challenge for an intelligent animal who needs mental stimulation.

Your Yorkie is also an intelligent animal who needs mental challenges. We've talked about food-dispensing toys several times in this book, and we encourage you to use these with your Yorkie, both now and on into adulthood. But there are other ways to amuse him.

Have him do a down stay in another room, and hide some treats in the living room. Then release him and let him search for the treats. Initially, until he understands the game, you might have to point to the hiding spots. But when he understands, he'll do it on his own.

When hiding in just the living room becomes too easy, expand the hiding places all over the house. Again, in the beginning, help him search for them.

You can play the same game in the backyard. Invert buckets in different places around the backyard, and place a treat under each one. Every time you do this, change the location of the buckets so your dog has to search for them.

If you keep your Yorkie's coat trimmed short to avoid tangles and matts, you can give him a wading pool in the summer. Fill a shallow child's plastic wading pool with a couple inches of water, and drop in some carrot slices, apple slices, and ice cubes. Encourage him to get in and get the treats.

Once you start experimenting with environmental enrichment, you'll find out what gets your teenager excited and what doesn't. Then you can design some activities specifically for him.

Polishing His Training Skills

Your brilliant adolescent's brain is capable of learning anything you can teach him right now. He still doesn't have the concentration he'll have as an adult, but he has the learning ability. Keep your training sessions short and active.

You can tell when he's getting distracted. He won't focus on you, or he'll only pay attention for half a second. Then his eyes will wander, and he'll be looking at the birds and the butterfly flittering by.

Use this month to polish your adolescent's training skills. Take a look at the exercises he already knows, and make them better. When he works with you during training sessions or when you're asking him to do something for you in the house, how does he respond? Is he slow, waiting to do things on his own time? Does he ignore you, waiting for a second or third request? Or is he just sloppy? Work on having him cooperate a little better.

To do this, have a vision of what you want. In your training classes, if you're envious of how your dog works with the trainer, what is it you like so much? Does a neighbor's dog work with his owner as if the two are a real team? Decide what you'd like from your teenager and also your future adult dog. Having this vision of what you would like from your Yorkie can give your training a focus you can then work toward.

Working on Leash Skills

The most important leash skill for your Yorkie is ensuring he doesn't pull on the leash. Although he can't pull hard enough to hurt you, he can pull hard enough to hurt himself. A little self-control is definitely required.

In Month 4, we introduced teaching your Yorkie puppy to walk nicely on leash. If he's pulling on the leash, refreshing those skills is never a bad idea.

🐾 Put the leash on your adolescent, and go outside. Don't ask him to do anything, and don't give him any directions. Just start walking.

🐾 If he walks with you, keeping the leash loose, praise him.

🐾 If he starts sniffing, turn and walk away from him. If he immediately moves toward you, praise him.

🐾 If he moves ahead of you and tightens the leash, pulling, turn around and walk the other direction.

If, after a few about turns, he decides to keep an eye on you, praise him enthusiastically, "Sweetie, good! Awesome!"

> **HAPPY PUPPY**

When he's doing this fairly well, make a game of it. Walk in zigzags, turning quickly, and going in different directions. Challenge him to keep up with you, and praise him when he does.

The heel is also a good leash skill to reinforce. You introduced this last month, so your teenager might still need some work on it. That's fine. You can still make it better.

🐾 During some of your training sessions, hold a high-value treat in your right hand.

🐾 If he gets distracted, dip that hand down to his nose as you tell him, "Sweetie, watch me!"

🐾 Bring your hand up. When his eyes follow the movement upward and he looks at you, praise him.

Keep the heel sessions short and sweet because it requires a lot of concentration. Heel for 20 feet, stop, and sit your puppy. Heel 20 more feet, turn around, and sit your puppy. Heel 10 feet one direction, turn around, heel 10 feet the other direction, stop, and sit your puppy. Quick and snappy training is important right now to help keep your puppy focused.

Teaching Faster Comes

There are few things better than watching your Yorkie in a flat-out run, with his hair streaming behind him, covering ground as fast as if he's flying. Most adolescents tend to use that speed when they're doing something they want to do, such as chasing a rabbit. Coming when called isn't always that exciting. But there are a couple ways to increase the speed of the come, and both are exciting enough your teenager ought to be very happy to cooperate.

If your Yorkie is fairly reliable and comes to you when called rather than dashing away, he can be off leash. However, if your puppy is apt to head the opposite direction when you call him, fasten a 20- to 30-foot length of lightweight rope to his collar.

- Let your puppy sniff the grass and get distracted. If he's on a regular leash, let him drag it. If he's on a long leash, hold the end of it.
- When he's not paying any attention to you, turn and run away from him. You don't need to run fast; you just want him to chase after you.
- As you turn and run away, call him, "Sweetie, come!"
- When he catches up to you, praise him enthusiastically, "Sweetie, good! Awesome! You are the smartest puppy in the world!"
- If he doesn't immediately come to you, use the leash to help him come. Be gentle—remember, he's a tiny dog. In this case, praise him when he gets to you but not nearly as much as you would have if he had come with no help—or with no reminder from the leash.

Another technique is particularly effective for Yorkies who are toy crazy. If your teenager loves a special toy, he'll love this game.

- Ask your dog to sit but not stay.
- Step away from him. If you can go 10 feet without him moving, that's great. If you can go 20 feet away, that's even better.
- If he moves from the sit when you're a distance away, that's fine. You're not practicing the stay right now.
- Call his name without saying the word "Come," and as he begins moving toward you, hold out the toy, let him see it, and throw it behind you.

- As he picks up speed, praise him.
- When he brings the toy to you, praise him again.

With this technique, he really isn't coming to you, but rather is running after the toy. However, he did respond to his name, and using this technique, you can speed up his response. Later, when you add "Come," he'll really run to you rather than dawdle.

You can mix up all the come techniques you've learned and do them in one training session. Not only is this good training because you're keeping your puppy thinking, but it also keeps the training exciting.

You and Your Puppy

The all-encompassing puppy-raising days are over. Do you remember when you brought your new Yorkie puppy home? He was so tiny and fragile; you thought you'd hurt him just picking him up and holding him close. Several months later, he's still small, but now he's a strong, capable, athletic terrier who wears bows in his topknot while hunting lizards in the woodpile.

The Here and Now

Early puppyhood is often filled with worry, especially when you have such a tiny puppy. At that time, owners also get stressed because they're trying so hard to do everything right. Then when adolescence comes barreling into their lives, worry is sometimes displaced by frustration.

Right now, though, as puppyhood is gradually disappearing and adolescence begins to wane, you can sit back, take a deep breath, and learn how to enjoy your Yorkshire Terrier.

Do you remember why you wanted a dog?

Walking exercise: Did you want to get more exercise and you thought walking a dog was a good excuse? That's a great reason and one your Yorkie can certainly help you with. Hopefully you've been walking with your Yorkie on a regular basis, but if you haven't been going for walks as much as you'd like or think you should, now is a good time to add it to your daily calendar. Your Yorkie will enjoy it, too.

Now that your Yorkie is maturing, you can also pick up the pace on your walks, as we mentioned last month. It takes time to build his muscles and toughen his paw pads, but as you know, your tiny terrier is an athlete and can certainly do this with you. Plus, the exercise is good for him.

A companion: Many new dog owners get a dog for the companionship, and Yorkies excel in this. Although they do enjoy trips outside to chase butterflies and hunt small critters, Yorkies love to spend time with their owners, and that's what companionship is all about.

You may also find, especially as your Yorkie grows up, that he's a mental mirror for you. If you're sad, he may be extra quiet. If you're excited, he may become excited, too. Many Yorkie owners have said that they have become more aware of their own moods by watching their tiny companions.

Social interaction: As you've learned over the past few months, it's almost impossible to go for a walk without someone stopping you to talk about your Yorkie. Although this can be annoying when it happens too often—especially if you're trying to get some exercise—it's also wonderful.

Everyone needs social interaction. People need to talk, laugh, cry, hug, and share experiences with other people. When people have something in common, such as the love of dogs, that can be a great icebreaker. Yorkies are great conversation starters.

Hobby: Some people add a dog to the family as a means of becoming involved in dog activities. Perhaps you saw agility on television or have read about therapy-dog volunteer work. As your Yorkie continues to grow up, you can look into these hobbies and get involved in one or two. (We talk about them more in next month's chapter.)

Dog sports also can be great social activities. Many friendships begin when dog owners who participate in the same dog activities or sports get to know each other. Dog activities are also good exercise for dogs—and their owners. Then, too, all require training of some kind, and continuing your Yorkie's training as he grows up is going to be important.

Security: Many people add a dog to the household for security. A Yorkie cannot defend you should someone break into your home. Although he might try, he doesn't have the size or brawn to defend you. He does, however, have a superb sense of hearing and a watchful temperament. He will bark to let you know when something is out of the ordinary, and sometimes that's all that's needed to help you feel more secure. He'll bark to alert you, and you can handle the situation from there.

The Most Important Thing

The best thing about owning a Yorkshire Terrier—the most important thing—is that your Yorkie is going to constantly make you laugh. It may be when he wakes you up one morning by standing on your chest and licking your nose, or maybe it will be when he disembowels a stuffed toy, growling and shaking it to death.

Laughter is important to your well-being, both your mental and physical health. Numerous studies have shown this to be true, and it's so important that in many places, meetings or classes are organized so people can laugh together. Look at the popularity of comedy clubs, for example.

With a Yorkie, though, you have your personal laugh generator. He's going to make you laugh each and every day. And that's a wonderful thing.

The Joys of Yorkies

Socialization in public

Ready for more advanced training

Slow growth—reaches adult size

Annual vaccinations and checkup

Do you remember several months ago when you brought home your new Yorkshire Terrier puppy? What a tiny little bit of dog she was. If you remember back, you probably were pretty worried, too, because she was so tiny. But she thrived, and the two of you have become close friends.

Now, as your Yorkie approaches her first birthday, she's still not quite grown up. Yorkies are generally considered physically and mentally mature by about 2 years of age, so although your puppy has been through the worst of puppyhood, she's still in adolescence. Gradually, though, the trying behaviors of adolescence will disappear.

Physical Development

Your puppy's body is continuing to change as she grows up, and this is most evident in her coat. Even if you keep her coat trimmed, you'll be seeing some differences in it this month.

Your Yorkie is also going to be approaching her adult size. Although this isn't as noticeable in a tiny dog as in a larger-breed dog, she is getting larger. Most of the changes are small and gradual. One day you'll look at her and realize she's an adult, and you'll wonder where your puppy went.

The Adult Coat

The Yorkshire Terrier's coat is her crowning glory. The luscious colors, the long, flowing hair, and adorable topknot all create a rich, attractive appearance.

If you don't trim your puppy's coat, by the time she's an adult, her coat is beginning to lengthen but it doesn't yet reach the floor. That takes time. Many Yorkies don't have their full-length coat until they're 3 years old.

If you keep her coat trimmed, it won't be so obvious when her adult coat comes in, but you'll still see a change in her coat color. As a puppy, your Yorkie's body color—not the rust-colored markings—was black. As she matures, that black turns to the characteristic Yorkie steel-blue, and you're seeing the beginnings of that change now. Each dog is an individual, so what color coat eventually appears is always a mystery and something to look forward to.

The Adult Size

The Yorkshire Terrier Club of America breed standard states that adult Yorkies shall not weigh more than 7 pounds. Most Yorkies shown in conformation dog shows tend to weigh between 4 and 7 pounds, and adult Yorkies of this weight are strong, active, and healthy.

Some pet Yorkies may weigh a little more than 7 pounds, and that's okay. A larger Yorkie cannot be shown in conformation dog shows and shouldn't be bred because she doesn't meet the breed standard. But being a little bit bigger also means the dog may be a little sturdier than her smaller cousins. In a pet home, especially one with active children, being a little sturdier is not a bad thing.

Tiny adults less than 4 pounds are fragile and prone to a number of potentially serious health problems. If you have a tiny Yorkie, maintain good communication with your veterinarian. Annual exams are a good idea, but if you notice anything out of the ordinary with your Yorkie's health, call your veterinarian.

> ### TIPS AND TAILS
>
> Be aware that size descriptions such as *teacup, micro, mini, baby doll, purse puppy, teddy bear,* and other similar terms for smaller-than-normal Yorkshire Terriers are simply marketing ploys for Yorkies who don't fit the breed standard.

Health

Your Yorkie's continued good health depends on several factors. First is, of course, her genetics. If her parents and other close ancestors were healthy, that increases the odds of her remaining healthy. Her breeder's care continued that good health, and yours does, too. The food she eats also affects her health, as does her exercise, the veterinary care she gets, and her weight. Other factors include her environment and the health of her home. A smoker, for example, could expose her to secondhand smoke.

All these things together can either help create her good health or damage it.

Getting Her Adult Vaccinations

Your Yorkshire Terrier isn't quite ready for her next round of vaccinations, but she will be within a few months. The first distemper (or distemper combination) boosters are normally given a year from her last puppy vaccinations.

Your puppy's veterinarian may have already sent a reminder card or email to let you know your Yorkie's vaccinations are due soon. On this reminder, he may suggest the vaccines she needs, depending on where you live. For example, in some parts of the country, a Lyme disease vaccination is very important because ticks that spread the disease may be prevalent. In other regions, this might not be important. Talk to your veterinarian and find out what he recommends.

After the one-year vaccinations, the schedule may change. For many years, veterinarians recommended all dogs be vaccinated on an annual basis. Recently this has changed.

The American Veterinary Medical Association (AVMA) now says, "Dogs and cats at a low risk of disease exposure may not need to be boostered yearly for most diseases. Consult with your veterinarian to determine the appropriate vaccination schedule for your dog or cat. Remember, recommendations vary depending upon the age, breed, and health status of your pet; the potential of your pet being exposed to disease; the type of disease; the type of vaccine; whether the pet is used for breeding; and the geographical area where the pet lives."

When talking to your veterinarian about vaccinations, some discussion points might include the following:

- Does your Yorkie see other dogs on a regular basis?
- What would be the risks should your Yorkie get sick?
- Are you concerned about a specific vaccine? Or disease?
- Should your puppy get sick, is there a risk to people in the household?
- Is there a risk to other pets in the house should your puppy get sick?
- What is your Yorkie's general state of health?
- What reaction may occur after a vaccination?
- Could the vaccination potentially cause more harm than good?

Once you and your veterinarian discuss the vaccinations, you can make a decision in the best interests of your Yorkie. Hopefully, it's one you and your veterinarian both can live with.

Testing Titers

Every dog's immune system is different, so how each dog reacts to a vaccination can vary. Some dogs develop a strong immunity after one or two vaccinations, while others may not.

Many dog owners are questioning the wisdom of giving booster vaccinations on a yearly basis. Thankfully, it's relatively easy to see if the dog still has antibodies to a particular disease. The vet can draw blood and test for antibody *titers*.

For example, if you want to know if your Yorkie retains distemper antibodies and might not need a booster vaccination this year, your veterinarian can draw blood and send it to a laboratory to run a distemper titer test. But as with so many things, although this alternative sounds wonderful, it's not yet perfect.

Antibody tests aren't available for all canine diseases. Plus, standardized levels of antibodies haven't yet been established. If your Yorkie shows distemper antibodies, for example, does she have enough? At what point does she need a vaccination, and when does she not? More research is needed to determine what minimum titer levels indicate when a dog is safe from disease.

Vaccinosis

Vaccinations have saved thousands and thousands of dogs' lives since their introduction. It wasn't too many years ago that parvovirus was the deadliest scourge puppies could face and would go through a breeder's kennel, killing every puppy. Parvo is still a deadly killer, but the vaccination has saved innumerable puppies' lives by preventing the disease.

This doesn't mean vaccinations are 100 percent safe, however. Many dog owners and veterinarians are concerned about *vaccinosis* because some long-term illnesses have been linked to vaccinations.

> ### DOG TALK

Vaccinosis is a chronic illness that results from vaccinations. It may include immune system diseases, lupus, or cancer.

Vaccinations have been the target of many researchers looking into both human and animal health because vaccinations work by targeting the immune system. Many of the diseases being investigated are also immune system diseases, including lupus, immune system suppression, and bone marrow suppression.

Investigations have shown that many of the dogs who have developed vaccinosis later in life are the same dogs who suffered some kind of a reaction after having received a vaccination. The reaction may have been mild, perhaps just a fever later on the day of the vaccination, or could have been as serious as a seizure or anaphylactic shock.

Report any reaction at all your dog has to a vaccination to your veterinarian. He may recommend you bring your Yorkie back into the clinic for observation or treatment. Even if she needs no treatment, the vet should make a note in your puppy's health records that she had a reaction.

To try to prevent a future reaction, only vaccinate your Yorkie when she's healthy. If she's under the weather—even the least bit sick—wait to vaccinate her. If she's sick or has a compromised immune system, the vaccination will cause even more stress.

Talk to your veterinarian about giving single disease vaccinations rather than combination vaccines. For example, rather than giving a vaccination that has five to seven diseases included in it, your dog could receive a vaccination with only one or perhaps two diseases. This would mean you'd have to make more trips to the vet clinic for vaccinations until your Yorkie is adequately covered, but it could also mean significantly less stress on your Yorkie's immune system.

Vaccinations are important, and they do save lives. However, they're not innocuous. Be a wise dog owner: Talk to your veterinarian, and decide what's best for your tiny dog.

Adult Yorkie Health Issues

Yorkshire Terriers tend to be strong little dogs and generally are healthy. However, there are some health issues you should be aware of just in case your Yorkie becomes ill. The more you know, the better you can respond should something happen.

Some of these health issues are more common in the very small Yorkies. If that's the case, we mention it in the text.

Take a look back at Month 6, and review those health challenges as well. Those health problems are ones that can show up in puppyhood, but some, like patella problems, can also appear during the adult years.

Other health issues that can appear during adolescence or adulthood include the following:

Allergies: If your Yorkie is biting at the base of her tail, chewing on her paws, or constantly scratching, she may have allergies. Dogs can be allergic to a variety of substances, just as people can. Common allergens include foods or food ingredients, pollens, molds, mildews, dust, dirt, or dander. A friend of Liz's had a dog who was allergic to human dander. Thankfully, shots helped the dog cope.

If you think your Yorkie may have allergies, talk to your veterinarian. Tests can sometimes determine what your puppy is allergic to so you can, if possible, avoid those triggers. There's no cure for allergies, but they can be managed.

Bladder stones: Bacteria and urinary sediment can form stones in your dog's bladder. The stones can remain in the bladder, growing larger, or they can move into the urethra, causing pain and potentially blocking urine from leaving the bladder. In Yorkies, bladder stones are most commonly formed from calcium oxalate.

Vets have thought that there's a genetic component to Yorkies developing bladder stones, but they also suspect a nutritional relationship to stones. If the stones are surgically removed, they can be analyzed to determine their content so the vet can prescribe a correct treatment—which may include a change in diet.

The primary symptoms of bladder stones include frequent urination, an urge to urinate without passing urine, and bladder or urinary tract infections. Housetraining accidents are common, too, as is blood in the urine.

Cataracts: If your dog has cataracts, the lens of her eye is no longer transparent. There are several types of cataracts. Juvenile cataracts appear when the dog is young and are inherited. Many older dogs develop senile cataracts as they age, and dogs can develop acquired cataracts after an injury to the eye or illness.

Cataracts are diagnosed through an eye examination, and the vet determines the type of cataract through a case history as well as an examination. Surgery can remove the affected lens, and although the dog can see without the lens, her vision will be blurry. Replacement with an artificial lens is sometimes an option.

> **TIPS AND TAILS**

The Canine Eye Registry Foundation (CERF) maintains a registry to identify dogs carrying the gene for cataracts. Dogs with this disorder, or carrying the gene for the disorder, should not be bred.

Cryptorchidism: This disorder is the failure of one or both testicles to descend into the scrotum. The testicles normally descend by 6 to 8 weeks, but it isn't unusual for them to drop as late as 5 or 6 months. If your dog's testicle hasn't descended by 6 months, it probably won't.

Cryptorchidism is an inherited condition, and those dogs with this problem, or carrying the genes for it, should not be bred. In addition, these dogs should be neutered. A retained testicle carries a high risk of becoming cancerous. Because of this, the dog must be neutered. Talk to your veterinarian as to what age the surgery should be performed.

Dental disease: Dental disease is common in Yorkshire Terriers. Your puppy's teeth are relatively large for her tiny mouth—she has a predator's teeth. If you keep in mind that many years ago Yorkies were mousers and ratters, you can understand why she has such large teeth. Unfortunately, many toy-breed dogs, including Yorkies, have low bone density in their jaws. The combination of large teeth, small jaws, and low bone density leads to problems.

Diet can also lead to dental problems. Your Yorkie needs a good-quality food. Junk foods high in sugar and other artificial ingredients can lead to tartar and plaque buildup. It's important that you clean her teeth at home and also have them checked by her veterinarian. Although your Yorkie can live a long time without teeth, she'll enjoy life more if she retains them.

Dental disease is not just about her appearance or her breath. If her teeth aren't well cared for, she could develop periodontal disease, which can lead to heart disease and many other problems throughout her body.

Distichiasis: Dogs with this inherited condition have extra eyelashes, often an extra row of them. The eyelashes are directed inward rather than outward and rub against the cornea. This is painful, and owners usually notice it when the puppy rubs her eyes and her eyes water a lot.

Although you can pluck the problematic eyelashes by hand, they continue to grow back and the problem continues. Surgery is usually needed to permanently remove the extra row of lashes.

Eclampsia: This condition is caused by low serum calcium while mother dogs are nursing. Nursing growing puppies creates a heavy drain on the mother's calcium levels. Yorkies, like other small and toy-breed dogs, are more prone to this than larger breeds. Symptoms include anxiety, restlessness, pacing, uncoordination, rapid breathing, and seizures. An elevated temperature may reach 106°F.

This is a potentially life-threatening emergency, and the dog needs veterinary care right away. Treatment consists of intravenous calcium gluconate as well as treatment for shock.

Hepatic lipidosis: This condition, also known as fatty liver disease, occurs when fat cells accumulate in the liver. This can inhibit blood and bile flow in the liver and can eventually lead to liver failure. Obesity is one cause of this condition, but anorexia, starvation, cancer, pancreatitis, and other diseases can also cause it. There's also a tendency for it to be inherited.

> ### HAPPY PUPPY
>
> The numbers of obese dogs are rising dramatically, with veterinarians seeing more each year. Although many dog owners feel that food, specifically treats, equals love, dogs are happier when they're lean, active, and healthy. So monitor your Yorkie's weight, and keep her happy and lean.

Symptoms include loss of appetite, weight loss, vomiting, constipation, excessive salivation, and jaundice. Mental depression is also a primary symptom.

Treatment is usually through nutritional management, feeding a specific high-calorie diet. Because there's often a genetic connection, dogs who have suffered from this condition should not be bred.

Hydrocephalus: This congenital disorder is caused by too much cerebrospinal fluid in the brain. The fluid collects in the ventricles, which grow larger with the additional fluid, and in doing so, begin to put pressure on the brain itself. Symptoms include seizures, blindness, and dementia or mental disabilities. Affected dogs often have trouble learning.

Hydrocephalus is diagnosed through x-rays of the skull, MRIs, or CT scans. Treatment consists of reducing the cerebrospinal fluid produced; your vet can determine the best solution. These dogs should not be bred.

Hypoglycemia: This is more common in very young Yorkie puppies or very tiny Yorkies, but it can occur in any Yorkie. If your puppy plays hard, is under a great deal of stress, or isn't eating well, her blood sugar can drop to dangerous levels.

If she gets sleepy unexpectedly, shivers, is uncoordinated, or appears weak, offer her some Nutri-Cal or another nutritional supplement, or rub some corn syrup on her gums. Untreated, she can have a seizure and die.

Keratoconjunctivis sicca: This is a problem with the tear glands in the eyes. In this disorder, the tear glands don't produce enough tears, so the eyes become dry and dull looking. Symptoms may include the Yorkie pawing or rubbing her eyes, a thick discharge from the eyes, or ulcers on the cornea. Untreated, the dog can go blind. This can have a genetic cause. Injuries to the nerves or tear glands or the removal of the third eyelid can also cause it.

Treatment consists of drops applied to the affected eyes either daily or several times a day depending on the medication. Treatment will have to continue for the life of the dog.

TIPS AND TAILS

If your Yorkie needs regular medication in her eyes, it's important to gently touch and rub her head in between treatments. Touch her slowly, be calm, and praise her gently so she learns your touching her head does not always mean medication is being administered.

Legg-Calve-Perthes disease: This disease, which we talked about more in Month 6, occurs in puppyhood, most often between 4 and 11 months. Diagnosis is made by x-ray. The Orthopedic Foundation for Animals (OFA) maintains a registry for this disorder.

Patella luxation: This disorder of the kneecap generally shows up by about 6 months of age. Turn back to Month 6 for more information. The OFA maintains a registry for this orthopedic problem.

Paten ductus arteriosis: During fetal development, a blood vessel connects the aorta to the pulmonary artery and serves to direct blood away from the developing and nonfunctioning lungs. This normally closes at birth. If it doesn't close, and if it's not treated, more than half of the puppies born with this defect will die before 1 year of age. Surgery can usually correct this defect.

This is an inherited condition. The OFA maintains a registry of heart defects, and dogs should be screened for defects prior to being used for breeding.

Portosystemic shunt: Also called liver shunt, this is a condition in which the blood vessel that brings the blood past the liver during fetal development fails to close when the puppy is born. The liver is essential for cleansing the blood of toxins, so with this condition, the puppy's health gradually begins to fail. Symptoms don't always appear in puppyhood and may not be evident until adulthood and even middle age. A vet can make a diagnosis through a bile acid test or through x-rays with contrast dyes injected into the liver circulatory system.

This is an inherited condition that's far too common in Yorkshire Terriers. Treatment may consist of surgery to close off the shunts, but this isn't always possible. In these cases, the vet will recommend medical management, a care regime that includes veterinary supervision, a controlled diet, and perhaps medication.

Progressive retinal atrophy (PRA): This is a degeneration of the cells in the retina of the eye leading to blindness. The first symptom is usually a lack of vision in lower-light situations. Your Yorkie might not want to walk down stairs at night or go outside after dark. Eventually, the puppy will completely lose his vision and go blind.

This is an inherited disease, so dogs should be tested prior to being used in a breeding program. When a canine ophthalmologist has tested the dog's eyes, the results should then be registered with the Canine Eye Registry Foundation (CERF). Yorkies should have evaluations of their eyes at 1, 3, and 6 years of age.

Protein-losing enteropathy: This is a disorder in which the intestines don't process proteins correctly and the kidneys don't remove the proteins from the bloodstream. As a result, the body loses protein, which is essential for good health. Symptoms include diarrhea, weight loss, lethargy, breathing problems, and water retention. Many factors can cause this disorder, including parasite infestations in the intestinal tract, infections in the digestive tract, cancer, food allergies, congestive heart failure, and more.

Your veterinarian will diagnose this through a case history, stool sample, and blood work. He may also suggest x-rays or ultrasounds of the abdomen and chest to look for water retention as well as ulcers or other potential problems. Treatment often begins with a carefully controlled diet. Other treatment options depend on what caused the disorder in the first place.

Thyroid disease: There are many forms of thyroid disease, also called lymphocytic thyroiditis, but the one most likely to affect Yorkshire Terriers is autoimmune thyroiditis. Symptoms can vary; you might see hair loss, digestive disorders, eye problems such as inflamed eyelids (blepharitis), and infertility, to name just a few. Behavioral problems are also common and may include difficulty with training, lack of an attention span, irritability, fearfulness, and anxiety. Owners of dogs suffering from this disorder also mention an erratic temperament in their Yorkies.

This disease tends to be inherited, and because of this, the OFA maintains a registry for it. A blood test will confirm the problem. Dogs should be tested at 1, 3, and 6 years of age.

Tracheal collapse: We discussed this in detail in Month 6, so turn back there for a refresher.

If you see a problem with your Yorkie, or even if you just have a feeling something isn't quite right, call your veterinarian. Early treatment is important with many health issues because beginning medical intervention early can lessen the damage the disease can cause. Ideally, however, your Yorkie will live a long, healthy life without developing any of these health problems.

Nutrition

Nutrition will continue to be important as your Yorkshire Terrier grows up. Good food is necessary not just for puppy growth but also for healthy skin and coat, energy for life and activities, and good overall health. Nutrition touches every aspect of your Yorkie's physical and mental health.

Your Growing Yorkie

As your Yorkie grows up, she'll continue to need a high-protein and moderate- to high-fat food. If she's eating a puppy food, you can change her to a food created for all life stages this month. If she's already on an all-life-stages food, continue without making any changes.

If you find that your Yorkie is gaining weight, continue to feed her three meals a day, but cut back on the amount you give her each time. Also increase her exercise a little. Weight gain and loss in dogs is very much the same as it is for people—fewer calories consumed and more calories burned through exercise and daily activities equals weight loss.

If your Yorkie is thin, increase the total amount of food a little. Don't stop or slow down the exercise because it's important to keep your Yorkie strong and fit. But you can increase her food a little.

> ### TIPS AND TAILS
>
> You don't have to feed exactly the same measured amount of food each day. If the weather is nasty and both you and your Yorkie are quiet and not very active, cut back on the food a little that day. Then increase it a little on the days when your dog is busier.

Food and Health Issues

The food your Yorkie eats has a direct relationship with several different health issues. Obviously, it can affect her weight, but it also can lead to other health problems.

Food allergies: Many dogs, including Yorkies, develop allergies to specific foods or ingredients. Wheat, corn, rice, and beef are commonly linked to allergies, but some dogs also develop allergies to chicken or turkey. Yorkies with food allergies tend to do better when they eat a food with one unique (different) protein, such as bison, elk, or salmon. The food should also have one unique carbohydrate, such as sweet potato.

By feeding your Yorkie one protein and one carbohydrate, you can monitor how she does, allergy-wise. If her allergies disappear, you know your puppy can eat this food with no problem. However, if the itching and scratching continue, switch to another food with a different protein and carbohydrate.

Dental disease: Many experts feel dry kibble foods high in cereal grains and other simple sugars can cause dental problems. Bits of the kibble can lodge between the gums and teeth, causing inflammation and leading to a buildup of tartar and plaque.

Yorkies have no nutritional need for cereal grains and usually do better eating foods with carbohydrates from other sources. In addition, to maintain good dental health, brush your Yorkie's teeth often.

Ear infections: Ear infections have a strong link to food allergies because many dogs with known food allergies also have ear infections. Allergic dogs tend to develop ear infections when eating foods with ingredients they don't tolerate well.

Although each dog's allergies are individual, sugar is a big culprit in ear infections. It could be sugar from cereal grains or sugar from sugar beets. Sugar added to foods or treats to enhance taste or to serve as a preservative can also cause problems.

Gastrointestinal upsets: Vomiting can be caused by a food allergy or a rancid or otherwise spoiled food. Grease can cause diarrhea and intestinal cramps, too. Spices also can cause gastrointestinal upsets. Dogs with a sensitive digestive tract shouldn't eat foods that contain artificial colorings, flavors, or preservatives.

The food your Yorkshire Terrier eats does more than simply nourish her; it can also cause some problems. Pay attention to what your Yorkie eats, and if you're seeing some health problems you feel might be caused by food, stop feeding that particular food and talk to your veterinarian.

Grooming

You started introducing your Yorkie puppy to grooming when you first brought her home, and it has been a regular part of your lives since then. Combing your puppy, arranging her topknot, cleaning her ears and teeth, trimming her toenails, and keeping her clean and neat are part of your lives together. Grooming and Yorkshire Terriers go together.

Over the past few months, you've learned how to avoid tangles and matts as well as how to deal with them should they occur. You also learned how to remove sticky stuff and other problems, such as burrs and foxtails, from your puppy's coat. You've also been bathing and drying her.

There are still a few things you should know, including dealing with a skunk-sprayed pup. If you think your tiny Yorkie is too civilized to chase skunks, think again. Yorkies are tiny, but they are terriers and they love to chase critters.

The Scent of Skunks

There are several species of skunks, and they all can spray. Skunks spray from the anal glands on either side of the anus when they feel threatened. It's amazing how far the skunk can spray and how accurate they can be. A dog who has been sprayed is miserable primarily because the skunk aims for the dog's eyes or face.

> **TIPS AND TAILS**
>
> If your Yorkie has been sprayed by a skunk, don't waste your time with a tomato sauce rinse or bath. Even though this has been recommended for years, it doesn't work and just makes a big mess.

To clean up your Yorkie after a skunk encounter …

- If at all possible, bathe your Yorkie outside. Don't bring her inside until you get some of the smell off her; otherwise, it will permeate your home.

- Mix together 1 quart of 3 percent hydrogen peroxide, ½ cup baking soda, and 2 teaspoons liquid dish soap with grease-cutting properties, such as Dawn or Joy.

- Wet your Yorkie thoroughly and, using your fingers, work the solution into her coat, making sure to get all of her soaped down to the skin.

- Continue to work the soap into your puppy's coat for 5 minutes so the solution can work on the oil from the spray.

- Rinse and then repeat the process.

Don't save any of the mixture if some is left over. The chemical reaction can cause an explosion in an airtight container.

If your Yorkie still smells, you might want to have a professional groomer give your Yorkie a haircut. When it's short, less of the sprayed coat remains on your dog.

Establishing a Grooming Schedule

We've talked about setting up a schedule for grooming chores earlier in the book, but as your puppy moves toward adulthood, it's important enough to mention again. Grooming is going to be a part of both of your lives for many years to come.

The schedule you established for your puppy can change as she grows up. In puppyhood, a large part of what you're doing is not just keeping her neat and clean but also introducing her to the grooming practices she's going to need to get used to. In adulthood, your emphasis is on keeping her neat, clean, and healthy.

Here's a suggested schedule for your adult Yorkshire Terrier:

Combing a long coat: You should do this daily because the long coat can easily pick up debris and tangle. It will also tangle under the legs or under a collar.

Combing a short coat: Every other day is great, but don't go any longer than 3 days without combing her. Even the short coat can develop tangles.

Cleaning under the tail: Clean under her tail daily, checking for bits of fecal matter and removing it. You may want to trim this area regularly to help maintain cleanliness.

Wiping her eyes: At least once each day, wipe her eyes clean of any matter that's accumulated at the inside corner of each eye as well as any tears on the coat.

Brushing her teeth: Yorkies can have dental problems, so spend some time every day working on your Yorkie's teeth. With your help, she may be able to keep them longer than if they were ignored.

Cleaning her ears: Wipe out her ears at least once a week, if not every time you comb her coat. At least once a week, take a good look at her ears to be sure no dirt or debris is inside.

Trimming her toenails: Trim her nails every 2 or 3 weeks. If you and your Yorkie walk on concrete sidewalks every day, that might help grind down her nails so you might be able to go 3 weeks between trimmings. However, if your Yorkie is on carpet and grass only, you'll need to trim her nails every 2 weeks.

Bathing: Bathe your Yorkie when she needs it. Bathing her too often can dry out her skin, so don't do it on any set schedule. When she's dirty and smelly, bathe her.

Professional grooming for a long coat: A long coat requires some maintenance to keep it looking spectacular, so a monthly appointment is usually a good idea.

Professional grooming for a short coat: This depends on how short you like to keep your Yorkie's coat. If you like it really short, it will need to be trimmed more often—perhaps every 4 to 6 weeks. If you don't mind keeping it well combed out while it's growing, you can wait 6 to 8 weeks between appointments.

Maintain communication with your groomer. He may prefer to see your Yorkie every so many weeks because her coat grows fast. Or perhaps you don't keep it thoroughly combed and it matts underneath. Just as your veterinarian is your partner in your Yorkie's health care, your groomer is your partner in her grooming care.

Outfitting Your Yorkie

Yorkies are some of the most dressed-up dogs. They're so tiny and cute that they're easy to dress up. The Yorkie's coat provides some protection from the elements, but because she doesn't have a lot of body fat, maintaining warmth in cold weather can be hard.

Sweaters: Sweaters can help your Yorkie maintain body temperature. A sweater that covers her chest, perhaps partway up her neck, and most of the back is great. Be sure the sweater is snug enough not to allow her legs to get tangled up yet not so snug that it restricts her movement.

To introduce the sweater, put it on her and make a big fuss over her. Then take it off. Do this a few times and then put it on her before a walk. She'll be distracted for the walk and won't pay any attention to the sweater.

Don't leave the sweater on all the time, though. When she's in the house, take it off. The sweater causes her coat to tangle and matt underneath, and she can get overheated.

> **HAPPY PUPPY**
>
> Please don't dress your Yorkie as a baby with outfits that cover her entire body. Although many Yorkies willingly accept a sweater that keeps them warm, very few enjoy being dressed as dolls or babies.

Boots: Tiny dog boots can protect your Yorkie's paws in inclement weather. Boots are great for walks outside in the winter when the weather is very cold or when chemicals have been put down to melt snow and ice. They can also protect in the summer if you walk on hot asphalt or sand.

To introduce the boots, have some pieces of high-value treats in hand. Introduce two boots at a time, either both front boots or both back boots. If you introduce just one boot at a time, she'll lift that paw off the floor and won't put it down. If you introduce all four, she'll freeze and refuse to move. Two is a good middle ground.

Put two boots on her feet, and praise her. Tempt her to walk a step toward you with the treat. Praise her and give her the treat. After a few steps, take the boots off and love her up. Gradually, over a week or two, encourage her to walk more with the boots on. When she accepts two books fairly well and is walking normally after a few short sessions, you can try all four boots.

Other clothes: A life jacket is another good item of clothing for your Yorkie. If you swim or go out on a boat with your Yorkie, she'll need a life jacket. Yorkies can swim, and some are excellent swimmers, but a long-coated Yorkie can get tired quickly because of the extra weight her wet coat adds. Plus, if the water is cold, a tiny dog will get chilled and hypothermic. Life jackets also have a handle on the back so you can reach down, grab the handle, and yank the dog out of the water if necessary.

If you and your Yorkie often walk at night, you might want to invest in a reflective vest. These vests reflect light so your dog is more easily seen in low-light conditions.

If you and your Yorkie plan on doing therapy-dog volunteer work, introduce her to costumes, bandannas, and other cute accessories. Many therapy-dog groups make a big deal over holidays and have the dogs wear fun items so the residents of senior centers, nursing homes, and other facilities get a chance to laugh.

No matter what you decide to get for your Yorkie, be sure it fits well and doesn't restrict her movements or breathing. Most important, make it fun for her. And take it off sooner rather than later. Don't keep any clothing on her for hours at a time.

Social Skills

Your Yorkshire Terrier is probably through the worst of her adolescent behavior by now. However, that doesn't mean she's all grown up. Remember, that won't happen for another 6 to 12 months, depending on the individual dog.

Although she's well on her way toward adulthood, that doesn't mean you can stop her socialization. She still needs to go for walks, meet people, see other dogs, and be a part of the world she lives in.

Combining Adults and Adolescents

Adult dogs are patient with puppies. Most well-socialized adult dogs allow puppies to maul them, chew on them, and sometimes even steal their toys. Adult dogs put up with a lot, but they teach puppies, too. They correct biting with body language, as well as a growl and snarl. They let a puppy steal a toy or treat, but the puppy cannot barge in on their dinner. Adult dogs are patient but do set limits. As your Yorkie adolescent grows up, you will find that adult dogs will be less patient with her when she misbehaves.

If an adult dog does correct your puppy's bad behavior, don't yell at the other dog. Instead, support the adult dog by praising him, leash your Yorkie if she's continuing to be rude, and walk her away. She gets to play and interact when she behaves nicely. If she's rude, she doesn't get to play.

> **TIPS AND TAILS**

Only allow your puppy to play with playmates who are known to be safe and are well socialized. At a dog park, don't allow her to play with unknown dogs. Your dog is tiny and vulnerable, and you don't know what might happen.

Dogs who have been raised with other polite adult dogs are expected to follow certain dog social rules. Although you can teach and train your Yorkie and socialize her, a well-trained, well-socialized adult dog can teach her even more.

Social Conundrums

Out in public, your dog is are on leash and should be on leash unless in a fenced-in area. Being on leash is also the safest for your dogs because no matter how well trained she is, your Yorkie is still a puppy and can get distracted, decide to chase a squirrel, or run off after something else that catches her attention. But being on leash can hamper natural canine communications.

Basically, three things can happen when dogs greet each other on leash:

They ignore each other: If you walk past another dog and owner and the two dogs ignore each other, that's fine. By ignoring each other, both dogs are controlled, both self-controlled and under owner control. Your Yorkie doesn't have to greet every dog you come across while walking. After all, you go for walks without interacting with every person you see.

They play: Should your Yorkie puppy go up to the dog you meet on the walk and greet her nicely, the two dogs might want to play. This is fine and shows your puppy is well socialized.

There's a down side to this, though. After she plays with one dog, she may anticipate a play session with every dog she sees on a walk and may try to pull you toward other dogs. If the next dog plays, her pulling behavior has been rewarded and she'll try to pull even harder to the third dog. So even though the play is good, it's also a problem.

She can meet a few dogs while on the walk, but if she pulls, you need to turn around and walk away. Pulling should never become a self-rewarding behavior. If she pulls, she never gets to play. She gets to play when you give her permission.

They get ugly: If your Yorkie puppy goes up to greet a dog who isn't social, or if she rushes up to greet an adult dog who thinks your puppy is being rude by charging into her face, a fight could ensue. Obviously, that isn't an outcome you want.

Not only could this result in one or both dogs being injured, but now your puppy could think other dogs are a threat. She may avoid other dogs in the future, or she may try to charge other dogs to begin a fight.

> **TIPS AND TAILS**
>
> Avoid all dogs who charge toward you, dragging their owners behind them. This is especially true if the owner is shouting, "It's okay! My dog is friendly!" The dog might be friendly, but she might not be. Plus, she's rude if she's charging toward you and your dog.

No matter what the scenario, it's important for you to teach your Yorkie adolescent to ignore other dogs while on leash unless you give her permission to interact with the other dog. By paying attention to you, your Yorkie will be safe and won't be causing a problem.

Practice the "Leave it " exercise (remember, "Leave it" means "Ignore it") you worked on several months ago. Refresh it by practicing with a treat as you did initially, and when you're out on walks, tell your dog to ignore neighbors' dogs behind their fences. When you see a dog out on a walk, tell your puppy to ignore that dog walking past, too.

Follow the "Leave it" exercise with a "Watch me" (which means "pay attention to me") so your puppy learns to look to you for instructions on what to do. Have a treat in your pocket to help her look at your face and then praise and reward her when she does.

When you see another dog on your walk and your Yorkie turns and looks at you on her own, throw her a party! Praise her, give her a handful of treats, jump around, and be silly with her. Acknowledge her self-control and her understanding of what you want from her.

No Rudeness Allowed

Far too many owners of tiny dogs let their dog be rude to other dogs. Lunging toward another dog and barking, or even barking at other dogs from the safety of your arms, is rude. Although it might seem harmless—after all, what harm does barking do?—it isn't.

When your Yorkie barks at other dogs with no repercussions, she learns she can do it and get away with it. Because she gets an endorphin high from this behavior, she'll continue to do it in the future as long as she's allowed to do it.

Unfortunately, she may bark at a dog who thinks she's rude, and if he can reach her, he could grab her, shake her, and maybe even kill her. This has happened far too many times.

> **HAPPY PUPPY**
>
> A dog who often (or always) barks at other dogs is not a happy dog; she's a fearful dog. A happy, well-adjusted dog has no need to bark constantly at other dogs. If your Yorkie is barking a lot, call a trainer or behaviorist for some help.

It's up to you to both protect your puppy—from other dogs and from her own bad behavior—and let her know what's allowed and what isn't. When she begins to bark at other dogs, interrupt her, "That's enough." And then tell her what to do instead, "Watch me. Good!" With consistency, she will stop barking or at least allow herself to be distracted by your training.

The Joys of the Daily Walk

Several studies have shown that dog ownership is good for people in many ways. Petting and touching a dog is known to lower blood pressure, and the companionship of a dog alleviates loneliness. Walking a dog provides exercise and decreases social isolation for both the dog and the owner.

By walking your Yorkie every day, the two of you will get some exercise and also see other people and dogs. You get to spend some time outside, in good weather and in bad, and see the birds flying past, the butterflies in the summer, and the neighborhood kids' snowmen in the winter.

Making the time to walk your dog every day takes some scheduling effort on your part. But the payoff is huge.

Avoiding Isolation

During early puppyhood, you knew about the importance of socialization and made a point to take your Yorkie to a variety of places. You made sure she walked on different surfaces, heard a variety of sounds, and met all kinds of people. Socialization at that age was very important for your Yorkie's mental health and development.

What many owners don't understand, though, is that Yorkies should never be isolated from the world around them. A Yorkie who spends too much time alone, at home, without social interactions, will become bored, depressed, and very fearful. She'll lose her socialization skills when she's isolated and has no one to practice them with.

It's vitally important that you continue taking your Yorkie out of the house and yard. Let her go out front with you when you visit with neighbors. Take her for walks in different places. Let her go camping with you or go for walks in the local forest. Just make a point not to isolate her from the world.

Behavior

Yorkshire Terriers are bright, alert, active little dogs. They love to play, they pay attention to everything, and they're watchful of both their people and their home. Yorkies like to snuggle with their owners, but they aren't couch potatoes. Your Yorkie would much rather be doing something—anything—with you than simply snoozing.

Working Through Another Fearful Stage

Although your puppy is working her way through adolescence and is rapidly approaching adulthood, she may go through another fearful stage. Many Yorkies have one at about 13 or 14 months old, and some have one last fearful stage at about 2 years old.

As with the fearful stages earlier in your Yorkie's life, these usually appear as changes in normal behavior. Your Yorkie may react fearfully to something she's not been afraid of previously. Perhaps she's worried about a lawn chair in the backyard, the vacuum cleaner, or the delivery person bringing a package.

When you see behavior such as this, don't coddle her. Instead, be silly. "What is that? Silly puppy, come see!" By acting silly, you can show her that there's nothing to be afraid of.

The fearful stages at this point in life are usually short-lived—they might only last a few days to a week. Don't add to her fears by agreeing with her. Instead, be silly and help her through it.

Dealing with Dog Aggression

You may notice that your friendly Yorkie puppy is growing up to be an adolescent who isn't nearly as happy about other dogs. This isn't unusual. Your Yorkie's ancestors were independent hunters who caught mice and rats around the home, business, or farm. They weren't designed to be social with other dogs like some other breeds were. Beagles, for example, are pack hunting dogs and are very social with other dogs. Yorkies, however, were bred to be independent hunters.

If you want two Yorkies, if the first was well socialized, you may be able to have a neutered male and a spayed female who can get along. Two neutered males can often get along, too. Two females will often squabble.

> **TIPS AND TAILS**
>
> When you decide to add another Yorkie to your family, contact a local trainer or behaviorist for some help introducing the two dogs. Don't simply bring home the new Yorkie and set her down in the living room. That's a recipe for disaster.

As your Yorkie gets older and you find that she always seems to be in the middle of a fuss when she's around other dogs, don't stop taking her places. She still needs to get out for walks. But you can stop allowing her to play with other dogs. After all, it's unfair for the other dogs and owners if your dog is always causing trouble, and one day a larger dog might try to put a stop to her antics, and she could pay for it.

Coping with a Challenging Puppy

Although the worst of your puppy's adolescence may be behind you, she'll still have times when she challenges you. She may be asleep on the sofa and when you try to sit down, she may growl at you. Or she may growl when you go to pick up her food bowl. You may ask her to sit and stay at the open door, and she'll instead dash out anyway. The challenging aspect is, unfortunately, a part of adolescence.

The best way to work through this stage is to continue your training:

Basic obedience training: Review the basic obedience training you've previously done, and continue to practice it. If your puppy is trying to convince you she's never heard these commands before, reteach them to her.

Positive but firm: Keep the training positive. Use rewards your dog likes, such as high-value treats, verbal praise, and petting. But at the same time, don't let your Yorkie ignore you. Positive training is important, but she also needs a leader.

Be a leader: Adolescents—human and canine—need a parent who cares and will be a leader. Show your puppy what to do, help her do it, and interrupt bad behaviors.

Cooperation, not confrontation: Work on having your dog cooperate with you rather than make everything a confrontation. Use your training skills to help her do what you ask her to do.

Punishment doesn't work: Punishing your dog for something she previously did—such as raiding the trash can—doesn't work. In addition, your Yorkie will think you're unreliable and not to be trusted.

Here are some commonly seen human behaviors you shouldn't do:

Don't hit: No matter how frustrated you are, never ever hit, slap, spank, or otherwise strike your Yorkie. It's not an effective training technique, it will scare your puppy, and it will teach her you are untrustworthy.

Don't scruff shake: Grabbing your Yorkie by the loose skin around her neck and then shaking her is not effective. This is especially true in a tiny dog who could be seriously injured.

> ### TIPS AND TAILS
>
> The only time using the scruff of the neck as a handle is necessary is when your Yorkie is throwing a temper tantrum and is trying to bite you. Use one hand to grab the scruff of her neck while you try to restrain her with your other hand. But even then, don't shake her, and don't pick her up by the scruff.

No alpha rolls: Don't throw your Yorkie to the floor, forcefully roll her over on her back, or use any other type of action that pins her on her back. Again, this is not effective training and will only teach her you aren't trustworthy.

Too much love: One of the most common problems behaviorists see with Yorkies is that they have been loved so much the little dogs feel the world revolves around them. Even though you love your little dog, the world should not revolve around her. Don't pet her constantly, don't pet her every time she asks for it, and certainly don't give her a treat every time she begs. Be a good parent and leader.

If your Yorkie is exhibiting behavioral problems related to her adolescence, call a trainer or behaviorist for help. Just remember that this stage, like others before it, will pass. You both may need help to get through it, but it *will* pass. Your Yorkie is a nice puppy, and with your help, she'll grow up to be a nice dog.

Reading Her Body Language

Spending time with your puppy, learning everything you can about her and how she reacts to things, is the first step in learning how to think like she does. Watching her will teach you a lot, too. Look where she looks, and try to figure out what she's seeing and hearing. There's no way to understand what she smells—we can't even imagine it—but you can look for visual cues as to what she might be seeing and sniffing.

Learning to read her body language is a great way to help understand your Yorkie's thoughts:

Relaxed: A relaxed Yorkie stands with her head up, ears standing upright, and the ears swiveling to catch any sounds. Her mouth will be open and her tongue may be showing. If she's warm, she'll be panting slightly. Her tail will be slightly wagging.

Friendly and excited: When your Yorkie is friendly and excited, her head will be up in a normal position, but may be more forward than normal. She will be looking directly at the person, dog, or thing that has her excited. Her mouth may be closed so she can sniff. Her legs will be braced under her so she can dash forward.

Worried: If your Yorkie is worried about something, her head will be low and her mouth closed, although the tip of her tongue may appear to lick her nose. Her ears will move back and forth—forward to focus on what bothers her and then back against her head. Her tail will be low and, if she's really worried, it will be clamped to her hips. Her back will be arched and her hips tucked.

Ready to fight: If your Yorkie is ready to fight, she will be leaning forward and all of her body will be emphasizing this. Her ears will be erect and aimed forward, her mouth will be open and her teeth will be showing, her tail will be so upright it may even be leaning forward over her back. Everything is expressing the action to come.

Watching dogs communicate with their body language is fascinating. Although most dogs share similar language, and each breed has certain tendencies, every dog has his or her own personal body-language quirks. It's fun to find those in your own puppy.

Enjoying That Yorkie Sense of Humor

Yorkie puppies love to play, and they carry that attitude with them into adulthood. Retrieving games are a favorite, as are scenting games, hide and seek, and of course, chasing critters. Trying to catch the water spraying out of the hose or the sprinkler is also great fun.

You also might find that your adolescent has a great sense of humor. If she catches a lizard in the backyard, she may be pleased to bring you the dead lizard—or better yet, the live lizard she'll then release in the house.

If you pick up her dog toys and put them away, she may act like someone is coming to the door. As soon as you walk away from the dog toys in the toy box, she'll double back and grab a toy out of the box. She distracted you so she could get a toy, and she'll be so pleased with her cleverness.

> **HAPPY PUPPY**
>
> Laughter is not limited to humans. Primates laugh and enjoy humor, and even rats chirp when they're having fun. Dogs have a specific laughing-type pant with their mouth open and their lips pulled back that appears to be the canine version of a laugh.

Many animals enjoy humor, but it takes an intelligent dog to come up with some of the tricks Yorkies routinely use. Just be sure the practical jokes your adolescent comes up with are safe. If they're not, put a stop to them.

Training

Training is more than just teaching your Yorkie what to do when you ask. Training also helps teach housetraining skills, household rules, and social manners. Training can keep your Yorkie's mind busy so she doesn't get into trouble. Trick training, for example, is great fun, and you can make it as complicated as you want by choosing the tricks you teach your puppy. Simple tricks are easy to teach and do, while more complicated tricks may take more time.

You and your Yorkie can participate in dog sports together. These, too, range from simple to more complicated. No matter what you decide to do with your Yorkie, just keep training, challenging her mind, and choosing activities both of you enjoy.

Yorkies are great at trick training because they're so bright and love to have fun. They learn quickly that when they do a trick, people are thrilled. More important for you, trick training is still training. Your Yorkie is cooperating with you, she's working with you, and the two of you are perfecting your training skills while having fun.

Teaching the Leg Weave

The leg weave—when your Yorkie weaves through your legs in a figure-eight pattern—looks awesome when done well.

To begin, you need a pocketful of high-value treats and one in each hand. Don't put her on leash for this one:

🐾 Have your Yorkie in front of you, facing you. Stand with your legs shoulder width apart. Let your adolescent smell the treats.

🐾 Don't give her any commands yet, but with your right hand, reach behind your right leg and lure your dog from front to back between your legs.

🐾 Continue leading her by the nose, and bring her back to the front of you by making a circle around your right leg. Praise her and give her a treat.

🐾 Do this several times until she's comfortable with it.

🐾 At your next training session, do the same thing except with your left hand and your left leg, and circle her to the left.

🐾 Again repeat several times and take a break.

Practice these two exercises several times over several training sessions until your dog is comfortable circling both legs.

To put it all together, again have a treat in each hand:

🐾 Tell your dog, "Sweetie, weave," and have her circle your right leg.

🐾 When she comes back to the front of you, immediately draw her back between your legs to circle your left leg.

🐾 When she comes to the front again, praise her, pop the treat in her mouth, and tell her how wonderful she is.

Over time, you can decrease your hand motions and emphasize the verbal command. Eventually, you'll be able to simply stand with your legs apart and ask her to weave.

Teaching the Step Weave

Here's a trick to teach your Yorkie when you really want to show off. Once she knows the leg weave trick, you can teach her to weave between your legs as you walk. Well, you really aren't going to be able to walk, but you can slow-motion step.

🐾 Once you have her weave a figure eight around your legs, take one exaggerated step forward and have her weave around that leg.

🐾 Then take another exaggerated step and ask her to keep weaving.

When you've both mastered this trick, you'll be able to walk with slow, exaggerated, large steps while your Yorkie weaves through your legs. Your dog is going to look awesome, and you're going to look like a great dog trainer.

Teaching "Find It"

When you teach your Yorkie the concept of finding an item you name, you really can put your adolescent to work. Lost your keys? Ask your Yorkie to find them. She can also find your wallet, your purse, the family cat, or even your spouse. All you need to do is teach her what "Find it" means and then the names of a variety of different items.

To teach her the name of an item, you need that item, starting with a toy she likes—let's use a ball as an example—and some really good treats:

- ☙ Have your adolescent on leash and ask her to sit in front of you. Have the ball in one hand and some treats in the other.
- ☙ Let her sniff the treats in your hand. Hold out the ball, and hold a treat behind the ball so she has to touch the ball to get the treat.
- ☙ Move both hands toward her nose as you tell her, "Sweetie, ball."
- ☙ She doesn't know what you're saying yet, but she's going to want the treats and will nose the ball. When she noses the ball, praise her, saying, "Good! Ball!" and give her the treat.
- ☙ Repeat this four or five times, take a break, and play with her with the ball. Then repeat the exercise.

Over several days, as she's moving her head toward the ball, draw back your hand so she has to reach to touch the ball. Then keep the hand with the treats close to your body and have her reach only toward the ball. Continue to reward her with praise and treats.

After a few more training sessions, move your hand with the ball toward the right, then left, and finally set the ball on the floor.

When you think she understands the ball's name is "ball," you can move on to teaching "*Find it.*" You'll start teaching this with treats, but as soon as she understands, you'll switch to the ball.

> **DOG TALK**

"**Find it**" is the command that means "search for the [named item]."

Here's how to teach "Find it":

- Have some really high-value treats, such as Swiss cheese or pieces of beef, in your hand.

- Ask your adolescent to sit. Praise her, and let her sniff one of the treats in your hand.

- Tell her to stay, and walk away from her. Hide one of the treats about 6 feet in front of her. Just tuck it slightly behind something. If you're in the house, this could be behind a chair or hassock, with the treat showing a tiny bit.

- Go back to your puppy, praise her for staying, and release her as you tell her, "Sweetie, find it!"

- Move forward with her, point to the treat, and tell her, "Sweetie, find it!"

- When she finds the treat and eats it, praise her, "Good to find it!"

- Do this a few times, hiding the treat in several easy-to-find places, and take a break. Play with your puppy and then come back and repeat the exercise.

Over the next several training sessions, do this exercise in different places—other rooms in the house, out in the backyard, and in the front yard—but keep the hiding spots nearby and easy for your Yorkie to find.

After a week or two of training, when your puppy is eager to go find the treats, make the process a little more difficult. But do so very gradually so she doesn't get discouraged. Hide the treat completely rather than barely hidden. Instead of 6 feet away, hide it 12 feet away and then 20 feet away.

When she's doing this very well, turn her away as you hide the treat. Don't let her see where you hide it so she really has to use her scenting abilities to find it.

> **HAPPY PUPPY**

When she can't see you hide the treat, she's going to use her scenting abilities to find it. If she's smart, she's going to follow your tracks as well as the smell of the treat.

When you've made the find-it game more challenging and she's succeeding in finding her treats, it's time to bring back her ball. Play the find-it game with the ball rather than the treats. Start with the beginning training steps, hiding the ball close and barely hidden, but then make it more difficult as soon as you see she understands the new game.

Later, you can follow these same steps to teach her the names of various items and to find those items. You can also teach her to identify people in the household by name and then find them by name. That's a lot of fun.

Performance Sports

You and your Yorkie can participate in many different performance sports, either competitively or just for fun. Most of these provide exercise for you and your dog, a chance to increase your training skills, and a mental challenge for your bright dog.

You can begin training in these sports now, or if you prefer, wait until your dog is a little more mentally mature. Just keep in mind, you can always begin training now and wait to compete until your puppy is more grown up. The choice is yours.

Excelling in Agility

Many Yorkies have been quite successful in agility. This sport is like a combination of an obstacle course and an equine jumping competition. You and your Yorkie have to follow a set course, and you guide your Yorkie from obstacle to obstacle while she climbs, jumps, or goes through the various obstacles.

The obstacles vary somewhat depending on the organization holding the competition. The jump heights are set according to your Yorkie's height. Some of the obstacles can include the following:

Weave poles: When photos of agility are published in magazines or online, one of the most common is of a dog going through the weave poles. A dog weaving through the upright poles is quite amazing. The poles are spaced from 20 to 24 inches apart, and the dog needs to flex her body as she goes between the poles in a weaving fashion. Yorkies don't need to flex as much as larger dogs, obviously.

Tunnels: These are generally about 2 feet in diameter, which is like a four-lane highway for your Yorkie. Where other dogs need to duck to get through, your Yorkie has plenty of room. Some of the tunnels have a flap of fabric she'll have to push through, while others are just a long tube.

Jumps: There are many different types of jumps. Some are simple bar jumps, some are solid that the dog can't see through, and others, called broad jumps, are flat and wide. There can be a window-type jump that looks like your dog is actually jumping through a house window. The height of the jump depends on the dog's height.

Teeter or seesaw: Much like a child's teeter-totter, this is a plank balanced on a center support. Your Yorkie must walk up the plank and then walk down the other side when it lowers.

Dog walk: Similar to a balance beam in gymnastics, this is an elevated obstacle that requires the dog to maintain her balance. The dog doesn't have to perform acrobatics but instead walks up the ramp on one end, walks across the level plank at the top, and then walks down the ramp on the far side.

A-frame: In this pyramid-type obstacle, two solid wooden boards meet at the top, forming an A-frame. The dog must climb up one side and then descend the other side without jumping off in mid-climb or descent. It looks like a huge obstacle for your pup, but Yorkies are great climbers, so it's not a problem.

These are just a few of the more common obstacles you might find in agility. If you're interested in this sport or just want to look into it more, many dog trainers and dog training clubs offer agility training. Call around to trainers in your area, and ask about classes. Several organizations, including the American Kennel Club (AKC), offer competitions where your Yorkie can earn titles.

Competing in Conformation

If your breeder sold you your Yorkie puppy as a show puppy, she may be able to compete in conformation dog shows. The best-known of these is the televised annual Westminster Dog Show held in Madison Square Garden in New York City every February.

We talked about the Yorkie breed standard in Month 9, but unless you've had experience visualizing what those words mean, it's tough to evaluate your own dog against the Standard. Ask your breeder for an opinion as to whether your dog should compete.

Go watch a few dog shows in your area. Watch what happens on the sidelines before the dogs go in the ring—especially the grooming. Also watch the competition and talk to people outside the ring. Leave your dog at home when you go watch, though, because dogs aren't allowed on the dog-show grounds unless they're entered in the competition.

Before entering and competing in a conformation dog show, take a handling class. This class teaches you how to show your dog, how to move her around the ring, and how to stack (or display) her. There's an art to doing this right, and it takes practice.

Having Fun with Freestyle

Canine freestyle, or musical freestyle, is basically dancing with your dog. You and your Yorkie perform obedience skills, tricks, and other movements choreographed to music.

This is a fun sport that requires a great deal of precision. Yorkies aren't always patient enough to perform the same exercise over and over again to create the precision this competition requires. But it's a great sport to have fun with, even if you never compete.

Go to Ground

Go to ground, or earthdog, competitions mimic the abilities of dog breeds bred for hunting rats and mice. A caged rat is placed at the end of a tunnel, and the dog must go into the tunnel, maneuver through it, and show a willingness to take on the rat at the end. (The rats are not harmed.)

Yorkies are considered toy-breed dogs rather than terriers and are not allowed to compete in earthdog competitions through the AKC. However, if a club is having a competition that's not through the AKC, many allow Yorkies to participate. Do it at least once if you can because it's a wonderful demonstration of the breed's original occupation.

Competing in Obedience

Several organizations offer obedience competition for titles, including the AKC. There are various levels, from the basic, called Novice, through the advanced, called Utility. Many Yorkies have been spectacular obedience competitors.

In Novice competition, your Yorkie is required to heel with you both on leash and off leash following a pattern called out by the judge. The pattern will include left and right turns, an about-turn, and both slow and fast paces as well as the normal walking pace. You and your dog will also have to heel in a figure-eight pattern around two people. Your dog will also have to come when called, sit in front of you, and then, on the judge's command, move back to the heel position on your left side. She will also have to do a sit stay and a down stay as well as a stand stay while the judge touches her.

In Open, the middle level of competition, your dog will have to heel off leash, come when called, and then, during the come, drop in place on your signal. She has to retrieve a thrown dumbbell and retrieve the dumbbell over a jump. She has to do a broad jump and do both sit and down stays while you leave the ring and go out of her sight.

Utility is even more difficult. Your dog must heel with you off leash and perform a number of commands via hand signals—no verbal commands allowed. She must also find and retrieve a metal and a leather article you have touched from among several identical objects that don't have your scent. She also has to run away from you on command, turn, and sit. You will then direct her to a jump on your right or on your left, and she has to turn and jump the correct one.

> **HAPPY PUPPY**

Although advanced training can be tough, especially for the first dog you train to this level, it's immensely rewarding. You and your dog will have a lot of fun, and it's quite an accomplishment when you win your first ribbon or trophy for a job well done.

After Utility, there's still more you can do, including Utility Dog Excellent and Obedience Trail Champion, just to name two more titles. If you think this might be something you'd like to try, find a dog-training club in your area that offers competition training.

Participating in Rally

Rally is an obedience sport in which your Yorkie can compete and earn titles. A judge arranges a number of different exercises in any way he or she pleases. Each time you compete, the course will be different—that keeps it fun and interesting.

The exercises can include heeling, making a left turn, making a right turn, making an about-turn, weaving through traffic cones, staying, jumping, and more. Additional exercises can be walking in a 360-degree circle to the right or left, doing a stay while you walk around your dog, doing a side step while heeling, and having your dog back up.

Many dog trainers teach rally classes, so talk to your trainer. Dog-training clubs also offer classes.

Therapy-Dog Volunteer Work

This is one of the most rewarding volunteer activities you can be involved in, especially because you and your dog do this together. Therapy dogs visit people in nursing homes, retirement complexes, assisted-living facilities, hospitals, and more.

Many libraries like reading programs with dogs because a child can read to the dog rather than a person. The dog is patient, doesn't critique, and lets the child read at his own pace.

Therapy dogs provide warmth, affection, touch, and something to talk about to other people. The owner is very much a part of this, too, by presenting the dog and initiating conversation.

Therapy dogs must be well socialized to people and have a good foundation of obedience training. Many dog trainers offer therapy-dog classes, so talk to your local trainer if this is something you're interested in. The trainer will also help you decide what type of therapy-dog work you and your Yorkie should do. If you and your Yorkie both like children and your dog is gentle with them, you might want to participate in reading programs or visit special-education classrooms. Or you may prefer to visit the elderly. Sometimes it's best to visit a couple of different kinds of facilities or situations before making up your mind. But talk to your trainer about this, too. (See Appendix E for a list of therapy-dog organizations.)

Putting Her Nose to Work: Tracking

Yorkies may be tiny, and their scenting abilities may not be up to par with Bloodhounds or Basset Hounds, but they can still be awesome tracking dogs. Tracking has several applications. Tracking-and-scenting games, often called nose work, are a lot of fun. You and your dog can compete for tracking titles through several organizations, including the AKC.

Dogs can earn several tracking titles through the AKC. Each has requirements for the types of tracks the dog must follow.

Tracking Dog: Your Yorkie must follow a 440- to 500-yard track with 3 to 5 turns that's 30 minutes to 2 hours old.

Tracking Dog Excellent: This track is 800 to 1,000 yards long, with 5 to 7 turns, and 3 to 5 hours old. The track crosses a variety of terrains, including plowed land, streams, bridges, lightly traveled roads, and brush and trees.

Variable Surface Tracker: This track is 600 to 800 yards long, 3 to 5 hours old, and covers a variety of surfaces. The goal is to provide a track laid over surfaces normally found when tracking in a real-life situation, such as when looking for a lost person. It can be on vegetation, bared soil, concrete, asphalt, or even through a building.

A dog who earns all three tracking titles is awarded the Champion Tracker title.

Many dog trainers offer tracking-and-scenting classes. Call your local trainer and ask for a referral if he doesn't offer them.

You and Your Puppy

Your adolescent Yorkie puppy is on the verge of growing up, and although she looks quite adult, she's still a puppy. It's important to remember that fact because she's going to continue to make decisions that might surprise you. Perhaps one day she'll grab something out of the kitchen trash can even though she hasn't done anything like that in a long time. Occasional misbehaviors like this are just reminders that she's not yet grown up.

Even though she's still a puppy, she's in the process of growing up, and in the months that follow this one, she'll continue to mature, both mentally and physically. Some of the changes will be gradual—so gradual you won't even notice them until you look back one day on the way things used to be. The relationship you have with your dog is going to change, too, but again, that change should be gradual and happen over time.

Standing by Your Rules

At this time, don't slack off on the household and social rules you established for your puppy months ago. Because your puppy—your teenager—isn't yet grown up and isn't always making good decisions, it's important to remind her that those rules are still in effect.

In fact, because she's still an adolescent and continuing to challenge those rules, it's even more important to enforce those rules so she doesn't slack off and start up with bad behaviors. She could challenge you even more than she already has, and you don't want that.

If your adolescent's behavior does change—if she gets in the trash, chews up some shoes, or begins chasing the family cat again—consider that a wake-up call. Obviously, your teenager isn't taking you seriously at the moment.

Take a look at the household and social rules you established several months ago. Now that you've had some experience raising this puppy, what's important to you? What do you want your Yorkie to do or not do in the coming years? Then talk to everyone in the household and reinforce the importance of presenting a united front. Everyone needs to enforce these rules just as they did when your teenager was a young puppy.

> **HAPPY PUPPY**

Enforcing your rules doesn't mean your household has to be a military boot camp. Everyone in the household can still have a good time, including your Yorkie, but with that good time come a few rules.

Continue to praise your Yorkie and reward her good behaviors. Always acknowledge when she picks up her toy and not your shoe. Praise her when she walks past the overflowing kitchen trash can. Behaviors that you acknowledge and reward will continue to happen again.

Your Changing Relationship

You'll also notice that your relationship with your dog is changing. An adult, well-behaved, cooperative, and compliant dog is a wonderful friend. And by this age, she has become a friend rather than a puppy or a teenager.

There's no human friendship quite like the friendship you have with a dog like a Yorkie. Your Yorkie cares about herself and satisfying her needs, but she cares about you and yours, too. Enjoy her and treasure her. She's your dog and your best friend.

Appendix A Glossary

activated sleep   Sleep that consists of kicking, twitching, stretching, and other movements. This is normal for newborn pups and helps them develop muscle tone.

adolescent   A dog who is past puberty but not yet an adult; he's immature.

alternative medicine   Any technique that falls outside the realm of conventional medicine for people or veterinary medicine for animals.

anorexia   A lack of appetite or inability to eat.

antibody   A substance made out of protein and produced by the immune system to protect the body against disease.

behavior rehearsal   The act of practicing a new behavior, with guidance, so it can be learned and then performed as a normal behavior.

behavioral consultant   A behavioral specialist, often also a dog trainer, who is not a veterinarian.

behaviorist   *See* veterinary behaviorist.

bite inhibition   A lesson a puppy learns from his mother and littermates that teaches him how to control his bite and to bite hard enough to communicate but not so hard as to injure.

breed standard   The written description of the perfect dog of a specific breed. This includes the physical conformation, temperament, and movement.

colostrum   The first milk a mother produces. It contains vitamins, minerals, protein, antibodies, and other immune substances a growing puppy needs.

"Come"   The command that means "Look for me, and proceed directly to me without stopping."

coming into season   The common term for a female dog being receptive to breeding.

conformation dog show   A competition where the dogs are compared to the breed standard as well as other dogs competing in that particular show.

congenital health defect   A defect that exists at birth. It can be genetic or acquired before or during birth.

cryptorchidism   A condition wherein only one testicle has descended.

"Down"   The command that means "Lie down." It shouldn't be used to ask a puppy not to jump on you or to get off the furniture.

environmental enrichment   The process of creating a more interesting living area, as a more interesting life, for animals who have limited space.

fear period   A stage of the puppy's life when she becomes worried or afraid for no apparent reason other than her age.

"Find it"   The command that means "search for [the named item]."

food-elimination diet   A diet that usually consists of feeding one protein and one carbohydrate source and then gradually increasing ingredients one at a time to identify the problem ingredient(s).

free feeding   The practice of allowing the dog to eat at her leisure all day long.

"Heel"   The command that means "Walk by my left side."

holistic   A term that means the entire pet—all of the aspects of the pet's life—are taken into consideration, including physical, mental, and emotional life as well as the relationship with the owner.

home remedy   Treatments made from plants found locally or foods from the home. The techniques are usually passed from one generation to the next.

human-grade food   Food in which every ingredient is suitable for consumption by people. The processing plant and procedures used there are also of the highest quality.

hypoglycemia   A sudden drop in blood sugar (glucose) that can occur in a Yorkie puppy after exercise, during stress, or when the puppy doesn't eat.

intact   The term that refers to male or female dogs who haven't been neutered or spayed.

integrative care   Care that combines modern veterinary medicine with alternative techniques and takes into consideration the dog's environment, relationship with the owner, exercise, diet, and activities.

leader   A human or canine who guides or commands; a guiding force as part of a team. A leader is one who is looked up to.

marking   When a male dog urinates on an object to claim ownership.

mastitis   An infection or abscess of one or more of the mother dog's mammary glands.

matt   A tangle of hair that has turned into a knot. As the knot moves, it gets tighter and eventually pulls on the dog's skin.

melamine   A compound used to make many items, including furniture and floor tiles. In the past, it was added to dog-food ingredients made in China to boost protein levels in laboratory analysis.

neonatal period   The first 2 weeks of a puppy's life.

oppositional reflex   The reflex that causes a dog to push against force.

organic   A term that means the food or product was grown or produced using environmentally sound techniques, with no synthetic pesticides, chemicals, or fertilizers.

pica   The practice of eating nonfood items.

play bow   A body posture where the head and front end are lower while the hips remain high. It's an invitation to play.

prey drive   An instinctive desire to chase something that moves and is related to the behavior of predators to chase and hunt prey animals.

"Release"   The command that means the end of an exercise for the moment.

resource guarding   A natural behavior that causes the dog to guard things she likes, including her owner, food, toys, and other items important to her. It's an unsafe behavior because a guarding dog might bite to defend that item.

separation anxiety   A behavioral problem characterized by extreme fear or anxiety when left alone.

service dog   A dog who works for his owner performing trained tasks.

singleton   The term for a single puppy in a litter or the only one who survived.

"Sit"   The command that means "Lower your hips, keep your front end elevated, with front legs straight, and hold still until I release you."

socialization   The process of introducing your puppy to the world around her, including sights, sounds, smells, and surfaces, as well as other people and animals.

"Stay"   The command that means "Hold still in this position until I release you."

therapy dog   A privately owned dog who, with his owner, goes to visit people to share affection and a break in the daily routine.

titer   A test that measures the amount of antibodies to a particular disease your dog is carrying in his body.

vaccinosis   A chronic illness that results from vaccinations.

veterinary behaviorist   A veterinarian who specializes in behavior.

"Watch me"   The command that means "Ignore all distractions and look at my face," preferably making eye contact.

weaning The process of changing a puppy from nursing on her mother to eating food.

whelping box A low-sided enclosure for the mother dog and her puppies. It's made to contain the inquisitive puppies when they are old enough to go exploring. Plus, it's also warm enough for newborn puppies.

Appendix B

Body Condition Assessment

Obesity is a fast-growing concern with veterinarians because as many as 40 percent of all dogs in the United States today are overweight or obese. Because obesity can cause as many health problems in dogs as it can in people, this is a devastating health concern.

Obesity can be caused by some health problems, but the primary reasons dogs are too heavy are overeating and a lack of exercise. Although obesity is rare in Yorkshire Terrier puppies (it's more common in adults), it is important to monitor your puppy's weight. An overweight puppy is more likely to become an overweight adult.

This body condition assessment is easy to do at home. By doing this examination, you can evaluate your Yorkie's weight and see whether he's too heavy or too thin.

This evaluation is good for puppies older than 6 months; if he's less than 6 months, his shape is still too young. If your puppy is less than 6 months and you're concerned about his weight, talk to your veterinarian.

To evaluate your Yorkshire Terrier's body condition, place him on a table and help him stand still. Look down at his back from above. Does he have a little bit of an hourglass shape—wider at the shoulders and hips with a slight indentation at the waist? If you don't see an hourglass shape or your puppy is wider in the middle, he may be too heavy. At the same time, though, the hourglass shape shouldn't be too pronounced. If it's too extreme, your Yorkie may be too thin.

With your fingertips, feel your puppy's ribs. Can you feel them? You should be able to easily feel his ribs through a normal layer of fat between the ribs and skin. If his ribs are prominent, your puppy may be too thin. If you can't feel his ribs, he's too fat.

Keeping one hand on your puppy so he doesn't jump off the table, duck down a little so you can look at him from the side. He should have a waist; his belly should tuck up between the end of his ribs and his back legs. If you don't see a tuckup or if his belly is lower than his ribs, your Yorkie is too heavy. The tuckup shouldn't be extreme, either. If it's too much—the belly goes up sharply at the last rib—he is too thin.

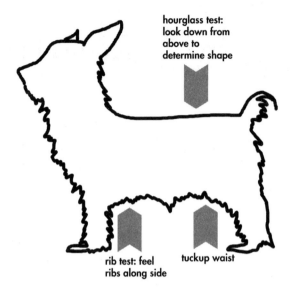

Use this illustration to help determine if your puppy is ideal, too heavy, or too thin.

If your puppy is growing out his adult coat and you can't see his belly from the side, feel for it. Place a couple fingers under his rib cage as he's standing, and run them along the underside of his ribs to his belly toward his back legs. You should be able to feel his waist.

If you feel your puppy is a good weight—not too heavy or too thin—that's awesome. However, if the results of this body assessment have you concerned, and you feel he might be too heavy or too thin, make an appointment with your veterinarian. Share your concerns, and ask your vet for her recommendations.

Appendix C   Poisonous Plants

Many common landscaping, decorative, and houseplants are potentially hazardous to your dog. Some may cause a contact allergy, such as poison sumac or ivy; others can be potentially fatal. When ingested, castor bean, English ivy, and hemlock, for example, can kill a dog.

If you have any of these plants in your house or yard, either remove them or be sure your dog doesn't have access to them. If you aren't sure of the identity of a specific plant, take a close-up photo of it and ask at your local garden center or nursery.

Flowering Plants

These plants could be in a flower bed or used as potted plants. In some regions, some are also used as houseplants.

- Anemone
- Azalea
- Bird of paradise
- Buttercup
- Christmas cactus
- Crocus
- Cyclamen
- Foxglove
- Impatiens
- Jasmine
- Larkspur
- Lilies (including Asian, Day, Easter, Glory, Japanese Snow, and Tiger)
- Lily of the valley
- Morning glory
- Snapdragon
- Sweet pea
- Verbena

Bulbs, Tubers, and Fungi

For many of these plants, the tuber or bulb contains the toxins, not the flower or green parts of the plant. Unfortunately, many times the bulb or tuber is what dogs are attracted to, especially when the bulb or tuber is planted with mulch or bone or blood meal to nourish the growing plant.

- 🐾 Amaryllis
- 🐾 Calla lily
- 🐾 Daffodil
- 🐾 Gladiola
- 🐾 Hyacinth
- 🐾 Iris
- 🐾 Jonquil
- 🐾 Lantana
- 🐾 Mushrooms and toadstools (many varieties)
- 🐾 Tulip

Trees, Decorative Plants, and Shrubs

Some of these plants are used frequently as landscape plants because they're attractive and easy to grow in many regions. Others are more commonly found as potted houseplants.

- 🐾 Asparagus fern
- 🐾 Bottlebrush
- 🐾 Boxwood
- 🐾 Caladium
- 🐾 Cocoa bark
- 🐾 Creeping Charlie
- 🐾 Croton
- 🐾 Dieffenbachia (all varieties)
- 🐾 Dogwood
- 🐾 Dracaena (most varieties)
- 🐾 Elephant ear (all varieties)
- 🐾 Emerald feather fern

🐾 English ivy

🐾 Heavenly bamboo

🐾 Hemlock

🐾 Holly

🐾 Horse chestnut

🐾 Hydrangea

🐾 Ivy (including Boston, Glacier, and others)

🐾 Kalanchoe

🐾 Mistletoe

🐾 Nightshade

🐾 Oleander

🐾 Pennyroyal

🐾 Philodendron (all varieties)

🐾 Privet

🐾 Rhododendron

🐾 Sago palm

🐾 Wisteria

🐾 Yew

Vegetables, Fruits, and Nuts

This list contains a variety of plants that have different parts dangerous to dogs. If one specific part is dangerous, that's noted. If nothing is noted, the entire plant should be avoided.

🐾 Avocado (leaves, stems, and pit)

🐾 Eggplant

🐾 Grapes (the fruit)

🐾 Macadamia nut (the nut)

🐾 Peach (and other stone fruit seeds/pits)

🐾 Potato (foliage)

🐾 Rhubarb

🐾 Tomato (foliage)

Herbs, Weeds, and Miscellaneous Plants

This category is also a mixed one, with common herbs, noxious weeds, and a variety of other plants. Many, such as jimson weed and locoweed, are also toxic to many animals, including dogs.

- 🐾 Belladonna
- 🐾 Castor bean
- 🐾 Jimson weed
- 🐾 Locoweed
- 🐾 Marijuana
- 🐾 Milkweed
- 🐾 Poison ivy
- 🐾 Poison oak
- 🐾 Poison sumac
- 🐾 Pokeweed
- 🐾 Sage

Appendix D | Household and Yard Hazards

Puppies, like young children, have no concept of what's good to eat (or play with) and what's dangerous. Never assume your puppy won't touch something. If it's different, out of the ordinary, has a smell, or is within reach, he probably will investigate it.

Problem Foods

A number of foods we normally consume can be a problem for our dogs. Some may cause mild gastrointestinal upset while others are poisonous and potentially toxic. If your puppy consumes any of these foods, call your veterinarian or emergency veterinary clinic right away.

- Alcoholic drinks (of any kind)
- Caffeine
- Chocolate (milk chocolate is the least toxic; dark and baker's chocolate are the most toxic)
- Coffee
- Grapes and raisins
- Macadamia nuts
- Onions and onion powder
- Xylitol (including baked goods, gums, or candies that contain it)
- Yeast dough

As a general rule, don't allow your puppy to eat any spicy foods, fatty foods, leftover grease, or spoiled or moldy foods. They may not be toxic, but they're likely to cause gastrointestinal upset.

In the House

A wide variety of potentially hazardous materials may be around your house—many of which you might not have realized could be a danger.

- Cigarettes, cigars, pipes, and tobaccos
- Cleaners and cleansers (including floor, kitchen, bathroom, shower, countertop, and toilet cleaners)

❧ Craft supplies (including small parts that might be swallowed, such as beads, and many paints and glues)

❧ Holiday decorations (all holidays, including Christmas trees and Halloween decorations, electrical cords, ribbons, tinsel, batteries, and plants)

❧ Laundry products (including detergents, bleach, and fabric-softener sheets)

❧ Makeup, hair-care products, and nail polish (as well as hair coloring and nail-polish remover)

❧ Mothballs

❧ Plant-care products for houseplants (including fertilizers and insecticides)

Medicines

Almost all medications, if ingested in quantity, can have a detrimental effect on your puppy. If you believe your puppy has ingested a medication, call your veterinarian or emergency veterinary clinic immediately. Do not wait for a reaction to begin.

Keep all medications out of your pet's reach but especially these medications:

❧ Cold remedies (including those with alcohol)

❧ Pain medications

❧ Prescription medications (of any kind but especially antidepressants and anticancer drugs)

❧ Vitamins

In the Garage and Yard

To keep up our homes and yards, many of us use a number of potentially dangerous substances. We know what they are, and out of habit, we use them with care. But with a puppy in the household, we must be even more cautious.

❧ Automobile care and maintenance products (gas, oil, antifreeze, cleaning products, waxes, and more)

❧ Home-maintenance supplies (including paints, paint removers, and supplies)

- 🐾 Rodent killers (including traps of all kinds as well as poisons)
- 🐾 Snail and slug poisons
- 🐾 Yard-care supplies (fertilizers, insecticides, herbicides, and fungicides)

Weather-Related Hazards

Some potential problems are only seen during certain seasons. This doesn't make them less of a hazard; in fact, because these products or hazards are only seen occasionally, they can be more attractive to a curious puppy.

- 🐾 Antifreeze
- 🐾 Blue-green algae in ponds (especially during hot weather)
- 🐾 Candles (lit or unlit)
- 🐾 Cocoa mulch (sold commercially as a garden mulch)
- 🐾 Compost piles (with decaying matter)
- 🐾 Frogs and toads
- 🐾 Ice-melting products
- 🐾 Insects (ants, spiders, scorpions, and others)
- 🐾 Potpourri (especially those used over a candle or in a heated container)
- 🐾 Snakes
- 🐾 Swimming-pool supplies

Resources

For more information on Yorkshire Terriers or anything else discussed in this book, here are a number of different resources you can check out.

Clubs

American Kennel Club (AKC)
akc.org

Canadian Kennel Club (CKC)
ckc.ca

Canadian Yorkshire Terrier Association
cyta.ca

United Kennel Club (UKC)
ukcdogs.com

Yorkshire Terrier Club of America
ytca.org

Yorkshire Terrier National Rescue, Inc.
yorkierescue.com

Performance Sports

Earthdog
akc.org/events/earthdog

North American Dog Agility Council (NADAC)
nadac.com

North American Flyball Association (NAFA)
flyball.org

United States Dog Agility Association (USDAA)
usdaa.com

World Canine Freestyle Organization (WCFO)
worldcaninefreestyle.org

Health and Health Insurance

ASPCA Pet Health Insurance
aspcapetinsurance.com

Pets Best Insurance
petsbest.com

VPI Insurance
petinsurance.com

YTCA Foundation
yorkiefoundation.org

Pet Sitters

Love on a Leash
loveonaleash.org

National Association of Professional Pet Sitters (NAPPS)
petsitters.org

Pet Sitters International (PSI)
petsit.com

Therapy-Dog Training and Certification

Pet Partners (formerly Delta Society)
deltasociety.org

Therapy Dogs Inc.
therapydogs.com

Therapy Dogs International (TDI)
tdi-dog.org

Training

Association of Pet Dog Trainers (APDT)
apdt.com

International Association of Animal Behavior Consultants (IAABC)
iaabc.org

National Association of Dog Obedience Instructors (NADOI)
nadoi.org

Veterinary

American Animal Hospital Association (AAHA)
aahanet.org

American College of Veterinary Opthamologists (ACVO)
acvo.org

American Holistic Veterinary Medical Association
ahvma.org

American Veterinary Medical Association (AVMA)
avma.org

ASPCA Poison Control Center
aspca.org/pet-care/poison-control
1-888-426-4435 (North America; fees apply)

Canine Eye Registration Foundation (CERF)
vmdb.org/cerf.html

Healthy Pet
healthypet.com

Orthopedic Foundation for Animals (OFA)
offa.org

PennHIP
research.vet.upenn.edu/pennhip

Pet Poison Helpline
1-800-858-6680 (United States and Canada; fees apply)

Miscellaneous

International Association of Canine Professionals (IACP)
canineprofessionals.com

Index

O

oatmeal shampoo, 183
obedience competitions, 302-303
obedience training, 143-144, 237-238
obesity, avoiding, 180-181
OFA (Orthopedic Foundation for Animals), 24, 130
off-leash training, 241-242
oil, cleaning, 211-212
one-on-one training, 144
oppositional reflex, 238-239
organic products, 177
Orthopedic Foundation for Animals (OFA), 24, 130
Ottosson, Nina, 236

P

pain, recognizing, 201
paint, removing, 212
panting, 261
parainfluenza vaccine, 32
parasites, 226
    internal, 33-34
parvovirus vaccine, 31
patellar luxation, 129, 130, 281
paten ductus arteriosis, 281
paws
    evaluating, 256
    grooming, 67-68
performance sports, 300-304
permissions, granting, 191-192
personality traits, 75
pet first-aid classes, 127
pet first-aid kits, assembling, 128
pet health-care insurance, 249-251
pet medical information, 252
pet sitters, 23
phosphorus, 63
physical development, 53, 96, 121, 197, 228, 247-248
    adolescence, 154-155, 175-176
    adults, 273-274
    breed standard, 197-200
    coordination, 55
    docking tails, 96-97
    ears, 124
    eyes, 124
    female sexual maturity, 121-122
    improved bowel and bladder control, 228-229
    life expectancy, 248
    male sexual maturity, 122-123
    noses, 123

puppies, 27-28
    sexual behaviors, 229-230
    teething, 53-55, 96
pica, 63-64
pills, administering, 203
pin brushes, 66
plastic bags, 19
play
    indoor games, 222-223
    retrieving games, 171
    scenting games, 172-173
    scheduling, 195-196
    sessions, 171
    tug-of-war games, 116-117
play-biting, 146
play bow, 108
playful body language, 108
porcupine quills, removing, 213
porphyromonas vaccine, 33
portosystemic shunt, 282
potty pads, 45
practice, training, 168-169, 190-191
PRA (progressive retinal atrophy), 282
preventative medicine, 249
preventatives, heartworms, 99-100
prey drive, 109-111
private training, 144
progressive retinal atrophy (PRA), 282
protecting puppies, 118-119
protein consumption, 133
proteins, 61
protein-losing enteropathy, 282
public misbehavior, 234
pumpkin, 162

Q–R

rabies vaccine, 32, 276
rallies, obedience, 303
rattlesnake venom, 33
rat-tail combs, 66
raw food diet, 104-105
recalls, dog food, 254-255
regression, adolescent, 235-236
relaxed body language, 108, 295
"Release" command, 82
resource guarding, 207-208
retrieving games, 171
rolling, 262
"Roll over" command, 145-146
round-tipped scissors, 67
roundworms, 33
rules, enforcing, 305-306

U–V

W–X–Y–Z